INVISIBLE FIRE

FIRE

Traditional Themes in
Western Mysticism and
Sethian Gnosticism

ABOUT THE AUTHOR

Mgr. Nicholaj de Mattos Frisvold Esq. is a consecrated Bishop in Gnostic, Catholic, Old Catholic, and Orthodox lineages. He is a Commander Reaux Croix of the Ordre des Chevaliers Maçons Élus Coëns de l'Univers, a Grand Initiator of the Martinist order (I::L::/Initiateur Libre/S.I.IV), a Doctor of Ordre Kabbalistique de la Rose-Croix, and a Hierophant of the rite of Memphis-Misraïm. He graduated with a degree in psychology, anthropology/science of religion, and cinema studies at the University of Oslo and NTNU, Trondheim, Norway. He is the owner of the Sacred Alchemy occult shop as well as the Monastery of St. Uriel the Archangel retreat center.

Besides a long academic career, he has also traveled extensively in pursuit of wisdom and knowledge, which led to a wide array of initiations in several African and Afro-derived cults and forms of spirituality. He has been living in Brazil since 2003 where he has dedicated much of his time studying, both as a practitioner and as an ethnographer, the varieties of Brazilian spirituality and sorcery.

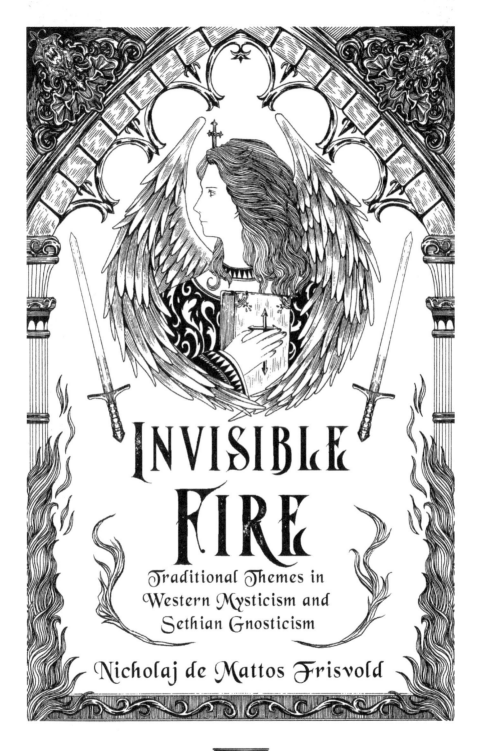

INVISIBLE FIRE

Traditional Themes in
Western Mysticism and
Sethian Gnosticism

Nicholaj de Mattos Frisvold

Paperback ISBN: 978-1-959883-60-9
Hardcover ISBN: 978-1-959883-85-2
Library of Congress Control Number on file.

Cover design by Cho-Hyun.
Edited by Becca Fleming.
Typesetting by Gianna Rini.

Many thanks to William Kiesel at Ouroboros Press for granting Crossed Crow Books permission to reproduce select quoted material herein.

Published by:
Crossed Crow Books, LLC
6934 N Glenwood Ave, Suite C
Chicago, IL 60626
www.crossedcrowbooks.com

Printed in the United States of America.

OTHER BOOKS BY THE AUTHOR

Seven Crossroads of Night (Hadean Press, 2023)
The Canticles of Lilith (Troy Books, 2021)
Trollrun (Hadean Press, 2021)
Ifá: A Forest of Mystery (Scarlet Imprint, 2016)
Obeah: A Sorcerous Ossuary (Hadean Press, 2013)
Exu (Scarlet Imprint, 2012)
Pomba Gira (Scarlet Imprint, 2011)
Palo Mayombe (Scarlet Imprint, 2010)

CONTENTS

PART I
GNOSIS

PART II
PRAXIS

PREFACE

Invisible Fire is a work that presents the traditional themes in Western Mysticism as it pertains to the Celestial Way or Stellar Magic. When we speak of Western Mysticism, it is important to understand that this refers to a cultural conglomerate of shared cosmologies and epistemologies. This means that Sufi schools, schools of Kabbalah, Christian Mystics, Gnostics, and even Eastern traditions are bound by similar cosmologies through shared ideas and a common focus on divine revelation. For instance, the word *Kabbalah* means "to receive" in a prophetic way, and for the Sufi schools, the essence of practice is to facilitate a connection with Allah, the sacred centre of divine revelation.

Several monastic orders have a strong emphasis on the prophetic through spiritual revelation and epiphany, like the Carmelites, of which Saint John of the Cross and his teacher Teresa of Ávila are well known for their prophetic capacities. Elijah, Isaiah, Ezekiel, Jeremiah, Daniel, and Saint John the Baptist all represent the idea of the "upright one," a person that is connected to the divine realm and cosmic centre, revealing divine mysteries to the world. We find the same activity among Hindu sadhus and Tantrikas, Kabbalists like Abulafia and Luria, and Sufi saints like Ibn al-Arabi, Suhrawardi, and Rumi.

A distinct non-dual cosmology is found at the heart of Western Mysticism, along with the importance of divine revelation. These are paths of prophetic activity that focus on how we can connect to the

Empyrean realm in such a way that we become subject to this revelatory fire that gives luminescence to stars and angels.

In the *Sefer Yetzirah* 3:4, it is written that *"Heaven was created from fire"* from the Hebrew mother-letter *shin*, and later in 4:4, this mystical text speaks of how the Holy Palace was placed exactly in the centre of the Empyrean realm with the purpose of supporting the building blocks of creation.[1] Fire is also the central element in alchemy, the "secret fire" that Vulcan used to forge the thunderbolt and the fire that Prometheus stole and gave to humankind. The alchemist Pernety considered the secret fire to be composed of "thought," an intellectual fire of the mind that makes itself known through word and imagination revealed from the Holy Palace at the centre of the Empyrean realm. After commenting that the central fire represents the effect of the will of God on matter in relation to the Divine Mind, he emphasises that the celestial fire is related to thought as One:

> *"The Celestial Fire passes into the nature of the Central Fire; it becomes internal, engendering in matter. Though the Central Fire [within matter] is pure in itself, it is mixed and tempered. It engenders and enlightens sometimes without burning, and burns sometimes without giving any light. It is invisible and therefore known only by its qualities. The Central Fire is lodged in the center of matter; it is tenacious and innate in matter; it is digesting, maturing, neither warm nor burning to the touch."*[2]

In the second *Ennead*, Plotinus writes: "No doubt Aristotle is right in speaking of flame as a turmoil, fire insolently rioting; but the celestial fire is equable, placid, docile to the purposes of the stars."[3]

And what about heaven itself? What is its substance and being? Perhaps Meister Eckhart perceived it with more clarity than any other in his Sixty-Ninth Sermon:

> *"Heaven is untouched by time and place. Corporeal things have no place there, and whoever is able to read the scriptures aright is well aware that heaven contains no place. Nor is it in time: its revolution is incredibly swift. The masters say its revolution is timeless, but from its revolution, time arises."*[4]

---

1   Aryeh Kaplan, *Sefer Yetzirah* (Weiser Books, 1990) 145, 163.

2   Antoine-Joseph Pernety, *An Alchemical Treatise on The Great Art* (Samuel Weiser, 1973) 164.

3   Plotinus, *The Six Enneads* (William Benton Publisher, 1952) 38.

4   Don Jumsai, *Mystical Works of Meister Eckhart* (Crossroad Publishing, 2009) 354.

This is the basic principle of what underlies the Primordial Tradition. The Primordial Tradition is also known as timeless because it is a tradition that expounds a celestial mystery where heaven is "untouched by time." In his poetry, Rumi describes the Primordial Tradition as "traceless," likened to the thought and breath of Divine Love, "which like the wind left no trace." [5]

The Primordial Tradition is explained in great detail through the works of metaphysically inclined philosophers like René Guénon (1886–1951), Titus Burckhardt (1908–1984), and Ananda Coomaraswamy (1877–1947), who, in various ways, gave great attention to the threshold between time and timelessness, or "no-time." This threshold is marked by the Empyrean realm (no-time) and the individual experience in the formal or material world (time). In the traditional perception, the formal world is experienced as fragmented in which the human being is disconnected from the Empyrean realm, the world of Platonic ideas. God is seen as the luminous centre and container of all things in the worlds, visible and invisible. Hence, all appearances and phenomena reflect the Divine Light. The experience of something divine, something celestial, is only possible if humans go beyond their materialistic confinements and realise that the corporeal world mirrors a higher, more perfect order that we can realise through the starry firmament that reflects this higher Divine Order in a way that is tangible yet perfect, quite similar to how a noetic idea and its form reveals degrees of perfection and difference. As Titus Burckhardt writes:

> "The traditional vision of things is above 'static' and 'vertical.' It is static because it refers to constant and universal qualities and it is vertical in the sense that it attaches the lower to the higher, the ephemeral to the imperishable. The modern vision, on the contrary, is fundamentally 'dynamic' and 'horizontal'; it is not the symbolism of things that interests it, but their material and historical connections." [6]

When we speak of Gnosticism in this context, it is with the particular figure of Seth that represents the Primordial Tradition more than any other. Seth was the third son of Adam and Eve, the "replacement" of Abel. Due to his perfected state, Seth enters the world as a perfected one, the upright one, and, as such, becomes the symbol

---

5   Nigel Jackson, *Guide to the Rumi Tarot* (Lewellyn, 2009).
6   Titus Burckhardt. *Mirror of the Intellect* (Quinta Essentia, 1987) 25.

of redemption, prophecy, and tradition. In his *Of the Antiquities of the Jews*, Book 1, Chapter 3, the First Century historian Flavius Josephus tells us that Seth erected two pillars, one of brick and the other of stone, and inscribed upon them their astrological and celestial revelations and observations. Here we read:

> *"Now Adam, who was the first man, and made out of the earth... after Abel was slain, and Cain fled away...He had indeed many other children: but Seth in particular...became a virtuous man: and as he was himself of an excellent character, so did he leave children behind him who imitated his virtues...They also were the inventors of that peculiar sort of wisdom, which is concerned with the heavenly bodies, and their order. And that their inventions might not be lost before they were sufficiently known, upon Adam's prediction that the world was to be destroyed at one time by the force of fire, and at another time by the violence and quantity of water, they made two pillars: the one of brick, the other of stone: they inscribed their discoveries on them both."* [7]

Invisible Fire is about this legacy left by Seth and is explored through examining the Primordial Tradition and the Sethian themes found in Western Mysticism. This theme is concerned with the various spiritual modalities that make it possible for humans to maintain a true connection with the Empyrean realm.

In *The Prescription Against Heretics*, Tertullian (155–220) writes that Abel and Cain were created by angels, while Seth was created directly by Sophia, who is Wisdom personified, the cosmic mother that also became the world-soul when she descended into matter. Tertullian further states that Sethians saw Seth as the Christ—or rather a Christ, the first Christ, in the sense of being anointed by light in the form of the oil of perfection and restoration. Hence, Seth became a symbol for what the Kabbalistic sage Isaac Luria called *tikkun olam*, meaning "the restoration of a broken world." This concept had a great bearing on Western Mysticism and, in particular, the French Gnostic Tradition through the text *Treatise Concerning the Reintegration of Beings* by

---

7   Flavius Josephus and William Whiston, *The Genuine Works of Flavius Josephus, the Jewish Historian* (S. W. Bowyer and J. Whiston, 1737).

Martinez de Pasqually (1710–1774). This text was circulated among the members of his order *L'Ordre des Chevaliers Maçons Élus Coëns de l'Univers,* or "The Order of the Masonic Knights and Elect Priests of the Universe." The reference to "elect priests" is about Melchizedek and the work of restoration and reintegration of the corrupt and fallen humankind into its original perfect state.

A similar approach is also found in the theology and Gnosticism of the *Église Gnostique,* or the "Gnostic Church," founded in 1890 by Jules Doinel (1842–1903). The Gnostic Church was born through divine revelation in 1888 when Doinel was ordained through vision and epiphany by the *aeon* Jesû and two Bogomil bishops in order to spread the gospel of Sophia—where her gospel is largely about the restoration and reintegration of fallen humanity into its original perfection. The Gnostic Church went through several patriarchs and Doinel's successor, Léonce Fabre des Essarts (1848–1917), who led the Church in the years 1895 to 1908. These leaders took measures to incorporate elements from Sufism and Vedanta into the Gnostic Church. After being obfuscated by the Christian rivalries between Lutheranism and the Catholic Church in the sixteenth to eighteenth centuries, Sufism, Vedanta, and Hinduism started to resurface in Europe in the nineteenth century, catching the attention of academics and intellectuals.

In Doinel's Church, the restoration was done through ritual and the Eucharist, and it was especially the *consolamentum,* the baptism by fire, which he saw as vital for this aim. The fire baptism was inspired by the baptism and initiation of the Cathars, who believed that this ritual, through which they were anointed by celestial fire, would free them from the blemish of sin and restore the original perfect state, making them *perfecti.* A form of this ritual is found in the praxis section of this work.

In Orthodox Judaism, this restoration is done through acts of *tzedakah,* which take on a quality of charity and giving. For a mystical-inclined rabbi like Isaac Luria, it was about developing saintly qualities and the effect of mystical prayer that sought the unification of all things that are in a state of fragmentation. Tzedakah is of interest for this work, as the root *tzedek,* meaning "righteousness," is found in the name *Melchizedek,* "the righteous king." In Genesis 14, it is this righteous king who anoints Abraham and blesses him through the sharing of bread and wine. In the Epistles of the Hebrews, Jesus Christ is identified as a priest in the lineage of Melchizedek. In the Sethian Tradition, Seth is also in the lineage of the righteous king as (Slavic) *Enoch* 2 states: "Therefore honor him (Melchizedek) together with your servants and great priests, with Seth." [8]

This means that every saint, prophet, and "holy person" who aids in the restoration, the *tikkun olam* of a broken world, could be considered a priest and a saint in the manner of Melchizedek, of Seth. Through this idea of restoration of the world, we must naturally touch upon cosmology, cosmogony, soteriology, eschatology, and Christology. In addition, we must consider other themes from theology, philosophy, and metaphysics, which explain the intricate dimensions of this presentation of the epistemology and cosmology that are the foundation of the Celestial Way, the path of Seth.

"All possibility is in the Father, likeness in the Son, and non-duality is in the Holy Spirit." [9]

8 B. Pearson, "The Figure of Seth in Gnostic Literature," In *The Rediscovery of Gnosticism Volume II* (Leiden University Press, 1981) 498.

9 Wolfgang Smith. *Christian Gnosis* (Angelico Press, 2008) 190.

PART I

GNOSIS

ONE

THE TIMELESS PRIMORDIAL TRADITION

"Nature, alike in everything, is the same in everyplace."

—PYTHAGORAS

For the French metaphysician René Guénon (1886–1951), the idea of tradition refers to a doctrine of spiritual authority that underlies theology, spiritual philosophy, and theurgy. Hence, we are not speaking of beliefs and customs being passed on through generations but about the ideas and forms that make possible temporal manifestations of the ideas resting in the ideal world of forms. Guénon states in *The Reign of Quantity and the Signs of the Times* that the "traditionalist" is merely a "seeker" for the eternal principles governing being and non-being in their ambition towards a restoration of the "primordial" tradition.[10] Guénon uses the words *integral* and *perennial* to define the nature of tradition, always seeking to include the eternal, essential, and timeless elements as vital requisites for what he at large calls the "Primordial Tradition." The Primordial Tradition is characterised by its focus on the Empyrean or celestial dimensions, the realm of Platonic pure ideas where we find the common unity of all religious and spiritual symbols and concepts.

Primordial Tradition will form this focus on the aspect of the revelation of these celestial or divine ideas through forms of prophetic

---

10   René Guénon, *The Reign of Quantity and the Signs of the Times* (Gallimard, 1945).

activity, whether they are exercised in religious or mystical ways. Since the Primordial Tradition is occupied with the celestial or stellar, it is also here that we find the epistemological explanations for celestial magic. This stance will, in turn, concern itself with a cosmology that will seek to understand how the eternal or divine takes shapes and forms that are visible and tangible and how these symbols appearing in different spiritual ambiances speak of a common truth. Analysing Christian cosmology against Greek, Muslim, and Jewish cosmologies, we see that there are great similarities to be found. This is obviously due to the frequent exchange between these cultures across time and geography for several decades. Yet, as Guénon remarks, this is beside the point because the family resemblance of all traditional cosmologies speaks of an intuitive knowledge present in these cultures, a knowledge that is "vivified by a sacred science, the written and oral repository of a divine revelation."[11]

There is a great simplicity at the root of Guénon's cosmology, consisting of the point, the circle, and the two axes on the cross, representing the centre of the world. Guénon uses several ideas that all refer to this simplicity, such as *omphalos*, which, in Greek, signifies quite precisely the "umbilical" but also the hub of a wheel. The point can also be represented by a mountain, signified by the Tibetan and Hindu *Meru,* the Greek *Olympus,* or the Arabic *Qaf,* all mountains that are said to be found at the centre of the world. Guénon gives these mountains the attribute "polar mountains" in reference to how the pole star serves as the celestial centre. The pole star, by assuming this central position, is then the point we use as a reference in how we navigate in both the material and the transcendent worlds. Guénon writes that this relationship between the pole star and the heavens is similar to how the hub of a wheel ensures the movement of the circle, which is similar to how a sacred mountain becomes the focal point for spiritual radiance and circumference. The point, often assumed by mountains, can also be represented by trees, the *axis mundi*, like the Nordic Yggdrasil or the Tree of Life in the Garden of Eden that marked the centre of a limited paradisal circumference.

What we find then is that from a given spiritual centre, when it becomes manifest, a set of doctrinal rays will spread out and generate a circumference, the form of a given mystery. This is quite similar to how we can understand the relationship between *chakra* and *loka* in Vedanta. *Chakra* represents a unique spiritual centre that gives access

---

11   Titus Burckhardt, *Mirror of the Intellect* (Quinta Essentia, 1987) 19.

to a particular *loka*, or world, in the sense of a mystery representing the doctrine stemming from a particular spiritual centre. This idea of the sacred centre placed within a greater cosmogony is then found with names like Adocynt, Hurqalaya, Agarttha, Atlantis, and perhaps more than any other, Hyperborea. Hyperborea represents the idea of tradition being situated in a place beyond time and space, but at the same time, it is the North Star, Polaris, that serves as a focal point for the Empyrean abodes where spiritual authority is found, just like the station of Polaris defines an empty centre due to the slow but constant movement of the stars that take turns inhabiting the location of Polaris. It is in this way that tradition is viewed as timeless and traceless, an invisible Empyrean or stellar fire that blazes out from the centre of the world like a sun.

When the timeless or eternal becomes manifest, it is also given to the laws of matter, and entropy is immediately set in motion. Here, Guénon uses the terms *vertical* and *horizontal* in a wide range of situations. The horizontal axis represents the Empyrean or timeless influence, whilst the vertical axis represents the temporary and material, what unfolds on the line of time. However, at the precise moment when these two axes meet in the perpetuation of tradition, they do join at the cosmic centre and establish scripture, dogma, and religious forms as a manifestation of a given timeless idea. Timeless ideas that are bound within the spiritual authority of tradition will find themselves manifested in variations of themselves, guided by time, geography, and other material factors, whilst at heart still being the same core idea. Timeless tradition will always exist—it is outside time and space, yet it is found everywhere. As Guénon comments in *The Lord of the World*:

> *"It would appear that the Meru assumes a different position for each manifestation by a dwipa,[12] but in fact the centre Meru remains immovable, and it is the orientation of the terrestrial world dependent on it which changes from one period to the next."* [13]

---

12 A *dwipa* in Sanskrit and Hindi means "continent" or "island," but it also means "planets." The text *Sri Chaitanya-charitamrita, Madhya-lila* states that "Outer space is like an ocean of air. Just as there are islands in the watery ocean, these planets in the ocean of space are called dvīpas, or islands in outer space." This simultaneously terrestrial and celestial meaning attached to the word *dwipa* would be used to describe the eternal as well as the temporal.

13 (Coombe Springs Press, 1983) 42.

Entropy is of great importance in traditional thought, as everything that is material is given to the same laws of decay and death. This is also true for time itself, as in the Masonic allegory of "squaring the circle," which, on its deeper level, does refer to this process of making the eternal more attainable for a moment, making the timeless being subject to time and a temporary form. For Guénon, this entropy in terms of time is seen in the doctrine of Yugas or Ages in the Vedas that replicates a similar idea as we find in the far North, namely Scandinavia, about the end of the world. In the ancient poem "Völuspá" from the *Prose Edda*, we learn that the World Tree is rotten, that the powers of fate are doing their work on the tree, and that a great oceanic dragon is gnawing at its roots, leading to a fall of the world into darkness and deluge. To be reborn through the presence of another symbol of the centre of the world, namely the Sun, which in this situation is also represented by the son of Odin and Frigg, Baldur; the shining one, the beautiful one, the son of the Sun.

For Guénon, when a traditional theme becomes "solidified" in the sense of being turned into scripture, rituals, customs, and dogmas, the heart of the traditional theme will be forgotten, and the figuratively horizontal axis that supports the sacred centre will disintegrate. In a similar vein, the biblical deluge that submerged the world would be a symbol of the loss of tradition, how the world again becomes overcome by chaos and wisdom of no form. Even in a condition like this, the Ark of Noah found its way to the mountain Ararat, which served as the centre of the world and gave way for land and a variety of forms; from darkness, a new world took shape around the mountain.

After being disconnected from the sacred centre, when the two axes—horizontal and vertical—break, the circumference also starts to shatter. Guénon views this process as fissures being generated in the wall that protects the traditional mystery, making it possible for the forces of Chaos to seep in. Hence the darkness of Kali Yuga and the Nordic *fimbulvinter*, the winter of eternal cold and darkness, heralding the end of the world, makes us ready for the restoration of the sacred centre.

This means that when we speak of the timeless tradition or integral tradition, we are speaking of the traditional themes that make Western theurgy and magic possible. We are speaking of a non-dualism, similar to what the eighth-century Indian philosopher Shankara called "Advaita Vedanta." A similar non-dualism is also found in the philosophy of Plotinus (240–270) and the sixth-century philosopher Parmenides as in the Kabbalah of Abraham ben Samuel Abulafia (1240–1291) and

Reuchlin (1455–1522). Quite simply, non-dualism will insist that the perception of division and difference is born from illusion caused by the transient nature of all things manifest. Shankara defined the true reality behind the ever-changing appearances of forms in the world as consciousness. What Plotinus called *nous* and what the founder of prophetic and mystical Kabbalah Abulafia called *Ain Soph*.

If we look at thinkers like Jacob Boehme (1575–1624), we see that things manifest from God, such as pure consciousness, due to love. God wanted to be known, and hence, the world of formation or illusion came into being. In the Upanishads, the basic texts expounding Advaita Vedanta, we find the idea of *lila* or "love-play" being the act that generates worlds and appearances. We also find the same ideas in the visionary revelations of William Blake (1757–1827), who saw the spiritual world, or "the New Jerusalem," being formed through an act of selfless love, a form of cosmic eroticism.[14] This love might be similar to the allegorical image of the bond between the invisible and visible described in the medieval Kabbalistic treatise *Sefer Yetzirah* 1:7 as bound *"like a flame in a burning coal."*[15]

TRADITIONAL THEMES AND CONCEPTS

Tradition, in its perennial understanding, takes place in the realm of the mystic and unfolds in the divine imagination of the cosmic consciousness. This cosmic consciousness remains the same idea no matter if it is called God or is referred to as *Hen*, the One, as in the case of Plotinus. We are speaking of what is hidden yet influences the cosmos and our world. It is in terms of its influence that we must understand why Guénon viewed tradition as spiritual authority, as it assembled the cosmic themes in a similar fashion as the world of pure ideas or divine archetypes in Plato's philosophy. When these ideas manifest, they can take specific shapes and forms—in organic phenomena like animals and plants, for instance—but these ideas can also generate religions and ideologies. It is in this field we encounter what Guénon calls "solidification," when an idea is shaped by matter and takes on a unique life along the vertical axis of time that will

---

14 For in-depth analyses of these motives, please confer the study of John Higgs, *William Blake vs the World* (W&N, 2021).

15 Aryeh Kaplam, *Sefer Yetzirah* (Weiser Books, 1990) 57.

always hold some form of entropy. The Swiss metaphysician Titus Burckhardt (1908–1985) comments in this regard how modern psychology, in its use of archetypes, demonstrates the difference between a material form and its original Empyrean idea. He writes: "According to the Platonic and hallowed meaning of the term, the archetypes are the source of being and knowledge and not, as Jung conceives them, unconscious dispositions to act and imagine."[16]

This process is of fundamental importance for tradition as we are here speaking of a misunderstanding or re-interpretation of traditional symbols that no longer teach us in a metaphysical way but in a material, rational, and limited way. In continuation of this, let's remember the use of the idea of love to define how God or the cosmic consciousness wanted to be known; hence, the variety of forms appeared as a consequence of this love. Even more subject for different interpretations is the erotic love play or *lila*, which will be the subject of a different understanding in a mundane situation rather than in an Empyrean. It is of great importance to discern between cosmic truth and personal truth, and perhaps the best avenue toward a conscientious attitude is the path of the mystic.

Mysticism is what we can describe as realizations made from being "upright" in the sense of being connected to the Empyrean realm. This is what is also what Guénon understood to be a horizontal connection to all things, where mind and heart are aligned in such a way that we are touching both the ancestors beneath our feet and the Empyrean realm of pure ideas, igniting the invisible fire of inspiration and insight. It is a state that brings clarity and a certain peace within as the horizon of our perception extends far beyond the perimeters of our corporeal and mundane existence. It is about being anchored in the *axis mundi,* and in this, we are able to see how the landscape flows forth from this sacred centre.

Today, with the solidification of the world and with both the material and vertical perception of quantity being dominant, it is easy to confuse the empyreal, inner, and infernal planes, but it is also, with a lack of discernment, that profane dogma and rudimentary experience can be mistaken for Empyrean inspiration and contact, due to the obsessive focus on the self and self-worth. The persona, as the perceiver of its sensorial data, becomes a vertical prophet for its inner dimensions and not those outside the person.

---

16   *Mirror of the Intellect* (Quinta Essentia, 1987) 60.

The field between the Empyrean and the material finds an analogy in the oneiric realm, as Burckhardt comments, that upon waking from a dream, the images we retain upon awakening are mere shadows of the forms experienced in the dream state.[17] On passing to the waking state, a certain level of vaporization of these forms occurs, which leaves a field open for obscuration, impressions, and interpretations. These interpretations are made in reference to oneself as the centre of the experience with disregard for the traditional meaning of the symbols appearing in dreams. For Guénon and Burckhardt, this is typical of the spirit of modernity and, as such, can be understood to represent certain "anti-traditional" impulses. In this regard, it is important to remember that no one makes a tradition as such; rather, tradition makes itself through the revelation of eternal wisdom and perennial truths through traditional symbols and cosmology.

The World Tree or *axis mundi* is, along with the circle, a simple design signifying the presence of tradition. The tree connects the Empyrean with the infernal, or terrestrial, and generates the world between the poles. The circle represents the world as a space, a field, an enclosure, a garden, and the like. When we encounter the occurrence of squares in relation to the *axis mundi,* we encounter the solidification and materialization of the circle, often revealed in dogma, something extemporal given temporal form and function. The circle is commonly secured by a snake or a dragon, which is yet another frequent symbol where tradition is concerned, symbolizing the never-ending cycle of wisdom embedded in decay and regeneration, the constant skin shedding of worlds upon worlds, and the stability of change in the divine entropy.

This entropy is frequently referenced to be ages, phases, and cycles that move from perfection toward imperfection, often typified by what Guénon saw as a "solidification of the eternal" and "celebration of matter over mind."[18] This is symbolised by the *axis mundi* turning in such a way that its crown goes to the matter and its roots to heaven, an "inversion of the natural poles." This means that all things celestial become a part of the Age of Dissolution and spiritual darkness. We find ourselves in a world where all has been inverted, and the sensorial egomaniacal soul reigns supreme over the ethereal winds of the cosmic intellect so vital for the Primordial Tradition. These are some of the

---

17 *Mirror of the Intellect* (Quinta Essentia, 1987) 121.
18 *The Reign of Quantity and the Signs of the Times* (Sophia Perennis, 2001).

negative tendencies of modernity in relation to traditional cosmologies; it often generates the idea of a world fragmented by a myriad of forms and illusions that are no longer naturally connected with the world of ideas, the One. Modernity is signified by syncretism and eclecticism that encourages a mixture, if not a confusion, of planes, ideas, symbols, and expressions. These are assembled in a private universe dislocated from their original cosmology and symbolic meaning and given new, subjective interpretations. The Primordial Tradition is occupied with not confusing the microcosm with the macrocosm and avoids accepting the illusion of duality as a cosmological and ontological truth.

THE CULT OF DEAD LETTERS
AND THE REVELATION OF WISDOM

The concept of ages or cycles is central to Guénon. According to Vedanta, the ages are known as *Satya Yuga, Treta Yuga, Dwapara Yuga,* and *Kali Yuga.* These four ages form a cycle that corresponds roughly to Hesiod's presentation of the five ages of men in his epic poem "Works and Days," written somewhere between 750 and 650 BC. In this poem, he writes about how the First Age of Man was the Golden Age created by the Titan Cronus or Saturn. The poet describes a people who lived in a perpetual spring of constant bliss and satisfaction and that men were like gods. Upon death, they became *daimones* who would inhabit the world.[19]

The Silver Age introduces the reign of Zeus and the Olympians, and he created men inferior to the gods. Humans had to work and labour, suffer and die under the harshness of the changing seasons and the linear progression of time. People didn't honour the gods as Zeus expected men to do, so he destroyed them. The humans destroyed in the Silver Age became denizens of the underworld, and subsequently, Zeus created a new form of humans made from ash wood. These creatures were hard and warlike and forged weapons from bronze, hence the name the "Age of Bronze." This violent race of men was destroyed in a flood, similar to the

---

19   In relation to *daimon* and how they would inhabit the world, it is of interest to recall Giordano Bruno and how in his *De Umbris Idearum* (1582), he sees *daimon* as similar to *numen*. In Roman Antiquity, *numen* was considered to be the guardian spirit of an emperor. Over time, the word came to signify the spirit of a place as well as the presence of spirit in general, whether it was connected to a person or a place.

Deluge in Genesis, that wiped out the offspring of angels with human women, the Nephilim.

After the Age of Bronze and before the Age of Iron, a smaller period unfolded, which Hesiod called the "Age of Heroes." These were strong, brave, and upright people. Upon death, many went to a blessed island like Hyperborea. The last age, the Age of Iron, was dominated by the astrological ruler of iron, Ares or Mars, and is described as an age where humankind, burdened with weariness and sorrow, become selfish, evil, and hateful of all things virtuous and good. The Yugas of Vedanta follow a similar cyclical decay, in which humans disintegrate from their primordial blissful divine state into a being overcome by the wickedness and darkness present in the Kali Yuga. This cyclical transformation is what Guénon refers to as "the inversion of the poles" throughout his oeuvre.

Guénon sees this inversion as represented by the "spirit of modernity." In his view, modernity was signified by a "spiritual and intellectual myopia" where the progress of a material order, dominated by the exaltation of quantity over quality, led to a natural decline, a degradation of all things spiritual. As a consequence of this inversion, typified by the world exercised in the Iron Age, the Kali Yuga, we find ourselves living in a spiritual darkness. Hesiod, in his poem *Theogony,* composed around 700 BC, comments that Zeus will destroy the humankind of the Iron Age, but due to the hardiness of iron, it is a slow grind to bring it to its dissolution.

In his critique of modernity, in *The Reign of Quantity and the Sign of the Times,* Guénon also writes about how the condition of the Age of Iron, this Kali Yuga, leads to the appearance of pseudo-tradition and counter-tradition. These phenomena appear in the modern world due to a confusion of the *psychic* and the *spiritual,* the acceptance of a Cartesian dualism that merges "soul" and "spirit" into a category of sameness, the spiritual being categorically different from the body and all things material. It is in this realm that Guénon directs his most severe criticism of spirituality and the world through what he describes as "'counterfeit spirituality."[20]

In simple terms, this is the convergence of the psychic (psychological) with the spiritual wherein the psychic is mistaken for the spiritual, meaning that which is in contact with the world of the ideal—or as in Guénon's

---

20   *The Reign of Quantity and the Sign of the Times* (Sophia Perennis, 1945/2001) 240.

vocabulary, the sacred centre. He sees this as an anti-traditional activity, not necessarily done on purpose, but a natural phenomenon unfolding in the Modern Era that generates an Age of Darkness, inversion, and spiritual decay. In particular, Guénon is interested in how this affects traditional initiation through processes that he terms "pseudo-initiation" and "counter-initiation," through which their purpose is to oppose the primordial, timeless tradition. Like an inverted shadow, they usurp the role of the timeless tradition with the aim of undermining it, replacing the spiritual with the material.

Pseudo-tradition is typified by its neo-spirituality, and here, Guénon goes hard on Theosophy and Spiritism as examples. His critique is aimed at, in the case of Theosophy, the uncritical appropriation of symbols that are grouped together without any real understanding of what they truly represent in the context of the various traditions from which they have been taken. This runs the risk of generating confusion between what is from one's inner world and what is from the spiritual world. In the case of Spiritism, his critique is aimed at the practice of trafficking among the souls of the dead, portraying it as something shifty and dangerous. It is somewhat hard to agree with Guénon when he enters into the trains of thought in which he elevates the invisible realms so much, the palaces of pure ideas and consciousness, that he, at times, holds disdain for matter.

In simple terms, modernity opens the creation of pseudo-tradition by allowing the composition of spirituality to be of a certain mixture of elements based on personal preferences and opinions, taken without regard for their cultural root and meaning, an eclectic blend invented for the purpose of creating one's own personal spirituality. Hence, uncritical and solipsist syncretism of sacred and traditional symbols and doctrines appears to be at the root of what Guénon refers to as "pseudo-tradition." Over time, these counterfeit traditions start to imitate the Primordial Tradition in such a way that they claim to be traditional. They use traditional sources, however, this use of traditional symbols and sources is subject to a distortion that obscures the invisible fire, the light of cosmic consciousness, by presenting an inverted shadow of tradition as the "truth."

Let's explore this further because Guénon was very specific about which forms of spirituality were traditional in the timeless and primordial sense and which were not. It was here that he discussed the role of religion and mysticism and the importance of religion maintaining its spiritual centre. This is seen in Islam maintaining a mystical core, known as *Sufism,* or more correctly, *tasawwuf.* With the work of perpetual contact with the celestial through prayer, chant, recitation, and meditation, the Sufi becomes a *pir,* an axis for the perpetual flow of the timeless tradition.

For instance, in his critique of the Catholic Church, Guénon suggests that the Church has become a cult of dead letters due to its lack of this prophetic and revelatory spirit that can be found in the interplay between Islam and Sufism.[21] Religion can become a fallacy for tradition by becoming dogmatic, stagnant—or "solidified." Since spirit is breath, movement, and the dance and the flickering flame of the invisible fire of the Godhead and its angels, bringing this spirit into a material context leads to some form of limitation on the spiritual and invisible. Doctrine becomes dogma.

Along with Sufism, Guénon saw a great variety of schools of Tantra, Vedanta, and Buddhism perpetuating the Primordial Tradition. The key to this view is found in how these schools and cults reveal metaphysical and divine truths that communicate the same perennial truth through a proper understanding of their symbols, revealing a common origin. This is exemplified through the words of the Andalusian Mystic Ibn al-Arabi (1165–1240) in his *Bezels of Wisdom:* "Praise be to God Who has sent down the revelations of Wisdom upon the hearts of the logoi (the word) in a unique and direct way from the Station of Eternity, even though the sects and communities may vary because of the variety of nations." [22]

Ibn al-Arabi was born in Moorish Murucia, but he stayed in Seville and Cordova for large parts of his life, places that were seething and boiling with the mysticism and Gnosticism of his time. It should be enough to remark that in the thirteenth and fourteenth centuries in these regions, we find the contribution to visionary Kabbalah through the work of the Kohen brothers, Abraham Abulafia and Joseph Gikatilla. The undated Kabbalistic text *Sefer Yetzirah* had a great impact on the Spanish Kabbalistic revival, and it was also from this melting pot that we see the Kabbalistic mystical work of the Zohar take form. But it was not only Jewish mysticism that took shape in this place

---

21   See Guénon, *Symbols of Sacred Science* (Sophia Perennis, 2001) 46, 47, and *Insights into Christian Esoterism* (Sophia Perennis, 2001).

22   (Paulist Press, 1980) 45.

and during these years. We also discover that Sufi schools, *silsilahs*,[23] found their centre and formed here alongside Christian Mystics and Gnostics.

For Guénon, a movement like this would represent a temporal manifestation of traditional doctrine through a divinely inspired intellectuality and adherence to spiritual authority. It would have been perceived as a moment when the heavenly revealed itself upon Earth, the invisible making itself visible, the City of God opening its gates with the purpose of restoring and perpetuating a tradition that is timeless, rooted in an eternally burning invisible fire.

It is important to understand that Sufism was in itself a conglomerate, or perhaps more correctly, a tradition that managed to reflect itself in other mystical wisdom traditions to such extent that the tenth-century Arabic astrologer al-Biruni understood that the word *sufiyyah* was derived from the Greek word *Sophia*, meaning "wisdom."[24]

Also, for Sufism, the ecstatic and the prophetic revelation of God was intrinsic. Saint John the Baptist, Moses, and Jesus were like Muhammad, seen as vehicles, as pillars for the reception of divine doctrine. Through their periodic isolation, whether in the wilderness, desert, mountaintop, or cave, they managed to connect with God. In the visions of al-Arabi, Suhrawardi, Rumi, and others, Sufism was the Way of the Mystic Lover, the goal of union with God through acts of purification, which made the heart and soul inclined to God. This Path of Love was paved with the colour emerald green and seen by all of these philosophers as the Celestial Way.[25]

To be an upright person in this sense represented the *axis mundi* itself. This upright person, the perfected human, was represented by a state of mind and spirit that took the form of the Green Saint of Sufism known as *al-Khidir*, also called *Khezr*. As author Nigel Jackson observes, Khezr is seen as the spirit guide of Hermes Trismegistus, the prophet Elias, and Saint George.[26] Hence, Khezer represents the embodiment of the Primordial Tradition as both its prophet, Elias, and its guardian, Saint George.

The colour of Sufism is emerald green, belonging to Venus, the planet that gives Sufism its esoteric radiance. Venus, the owner of

---

23 Referring to the chain of transmission conferred during initiation.
24 Nigel Jackson, *Guide to the Rumi Tarot* (Llewellyn Worldwide, 2009) 12.
25 Ibid. 19.
26 Ibid. 20.

love, is also the inspiration for Western Mysticism. This colour, together with gold, is also attributed to the biblical Seth, who is a symbol for the upright one, the patron of the *via perfecti*.[27] Henri Corbin, commenting on the ideas of the Persian philosopher and Platonist Suhrawardi (1154–1191), states that the paradisal Earth of Light is an emerald dome, a globe, identical to *Hurqalya*, the summit of the Earth, its centre.[28] This Earth of Light was perceived to come from the celestial north, a midnight sun bursting into flames as the spiritual centre took shape in the form of an invisible fire. This realm or state is also known as the *mundus imaginalis*. In order to see into this world and create a bond, a vinculum, with the spiritual centre, it is crucial that the mirror of our soul be properly polished so that we reflect what is from the *mundus imaginalis* and not what comes from our own personal fantasy and subconscious domain.

At the heart of this matter, we find a theological and philosophical concept of great importance to the Primordial Tradition. Revelation comes from the wisdom that stems from "Stations of Eternity," according to Ibn al-Arabi in *Bezels of Wisdom*,[29] and the wisdom flowing from this station touches the heart and becomes the Word in the sense of *logoi*, a Word that refers to an eternal principle that comes from something higher, the Eternity of al-Arabi, the central axis that connects the seeker to the sacred centre of the timeless tradition.

This can easily be transposed into a philosophical query in terms of the relationship between epistemology and ontology by asking the question, is it *knowing* that begets *being*, or is it *being* that leads to *knowing*? This is an intense philosophical investigation, the question of whether creation came from nothing or something, yet taking a stance on this question will not impact the ideas set forth in this work. A non-dual interpretation, referencing Advaita, assumes the significance of a spark, a seed, a sound, or something of the sort that mirrors what is written about in John 1:1, where we read: "In the beginning was the Word, and the Word was with God, and the Word was God."[30] This verse suggests that *knowing* (Word) came before *being* (God), not excluding prior chains of formation, a sort of pre-beginning to

---

27   G.A.G. Stroumsa, *Another Seed: Studies in Gnostic Mythology* (Leiden University Press, 1997).
28   Henry Corbin. *The Man of Light* (Omega Publications, 1978) 44.
29   (Paulist Press, 1980) 101.
30   John 1:1 (KJV).

the beginning of the *logoi*. Nevertheless, it is this relationship between *being* and *knowing* that should be taken note of.

In making a bridge amongst the sects and communities of a variety of nations, let's turn to the German theologian and mystic Meister Eckhart (c.1260–1328). The philosopher Arthur Schopenhauer already pointed out the similarities between Shankara and Eckhart in the nineteenth century.[31] This thread was followed up by contemporary thinkers like Rudolf Otto, Aldous Huxley, Thomas Merton, and Wolfgang Smith. Meister Eckhart is considered the father of German Mysticism and was a theologian, always suspicious of Christian orthodoxy due to how orthodoxy tended to close itself off from the esoteric, which, theologically speaking, is always related to the concept of revelation in favour of the exoteric.

For Eckhart, the Word is related to the intellect because how else could the Word be understood? Also of interest to our subject is that Eckhart's God was a fertile God that held an abundance of love. It was this love, flowing over in the same way as the "ebullience" of God for Plotinus, that gave birth to the Son. This concept is also found in Kabbalah, both the school of Issac Luria and Abulafia's Kabbalah, where God is said to be manifest or made known through a similar overflowing of "light" or "consciousness." This overflowing is what generates the illusion of division through the *Sephirot* becoming manifest as the various faces of the Godhead. For Eckhart, this reveals itself in the relationship between the Unmanifest[32] and the Full or Absolute Manifestation. Eckhart states throughout his writings and sermons an Advaita posture here that follows from the simple logic in John 1:1. The Word came from the Unmanifest that became known through the Word, and the Word was God.

Eckhart perceived the duality existent in the exoteric and esoteric, of what plays itself out in the relationship between *same* and *other*, questioning whether there was really any essential difference at the core between *same* and *other*. He questioned whether this perceived difference was due to the distance from the divine and, thus, an illusion.

---

31   Angela Moorjani, *Beckett and Buddhism* (Cambridge University Press, 2021).

32   Or what Jacob Böhme called *Ungrund*, signifying something unfathomable, an atopical negation, something hidden from direct perception, a nothingness, perhaps not far from A.O. Spare's concept of "neither-neither" if it was given a cosmic dimension.

In this regard, his Sixty-Ninth Sermon is of interest. We are drawn to it not only because of its Advaita theme but also because of how it replicates esoteric symbols frequently used by al-Arabi and other Sufi saints after him, namely the relationship between the eye, the soul, and the mirror.

In the Sixty-Ninth Sermon, Eckhart speaks about the power of imagination in terms of getting close to the City of God. Midway through the sermon, we read: "That is because my eye is more like the sky than my foot is. For my soul to see God, she must be of heavenly nature."[33] In this sermon, Eckhart equates the soul with the Moon and, with this, the capacity to reflect God. Hence, for Eckhart, this connection is of great importance, as he writes: "The eye and the soul are such a mirror" that can reflect God.[34] He sees this as a process where we, bit by bit, get rid of imperfections, which leads us to become closer to God, and as we see more clearly and through this, the quality of our *knowing* will also improve. As he writes onward in his sermon:

"Nothing hinders the soul so much from knowing God as time and place. Time and place are fractions, and God is one. Therefore, if the soul is to know God, she must know him above time and place: for God is neither this nor that as these manifold things are: God is one. If the soul is to know God, she must not regard anything in time, for as long as the soul is regarding time and place or any such idea, she can never know God. Before the eye can see color, it must be rid of all color." [35]

For Eckhart, God is pure intellect or episteme, knowing, an inspired intellect that goes beyond conceptual thinking. When we polish the mirror of our soul and reflect this knowing, we realise that we are indeed divine beings. The clearer the mirror of the soul is, the better it reflects God. The eye perceives the Eternal or God, and what is perceived by the eye is also so by the soul, and she reflects back what is perceived upon the perceived, leading to a realisation of unity.

---

33   Don Jumsai, *Mystical Works of Meister Eckhart* (Crossroad Publishing, 2009) 353.
34   Ibid. 234.
35   Ibid. 354.

It is quite interesting to observe a passage from al-Arabi in this regard, as the symbols and the understanding of them are remarkably similar to what Eckhart wrote in his sermon:

"As for the shining of the full moon that God set up as an image in the cosmos for His self-disclosure through His ruling property within it, that is the divine vicegerent, who becomes manifest within the cosmos through the names and properties of God...in the same way, the sun becomes manifest in the essence of the moon and gives light to the whole of it. Then it is called a full moon. Hence the sun sees itself in the mirror of the full moon's essence, for it drapes it in a light through which it is called a full moon." [36]

MODERNITY AND THE PRIMORDIAL TRADITION

When we read Guénon and other traditionalist writers, we see a disdain for modernity that, in Guénon's case, borders on contempt for the world. It is important to keep in mind that Guénon lived in quite turbulent times during both World Wars and the Depression, along with the fruition of the Industrial Revolution. For him, these were all signs of the times that the age of dissolution and ignorance was truly at play in the world. What was disconcerting for him was the spirit of modernity and its effect on theology. George Tyrrell (1861–1909), a Catholic priest who joined the Society of Jesus in 1880, was a man who, with his science-friendly and modernist agenda and theology, represented the spirit of modernity with full force. Tyrrell's modernist theology took a great hold in the most significant of the papal-friendly monastic orders, the Jesuits, which led to several papal decrees announcing the errors of modernity and the legacy of Tyrrell, ending in his excommunication by Pope Pius X in 1908. However, the papal stance led the pope's order, the Society of Jesus, to distance themselves from the papacy because of how its constitution and the role of the church could be understood. This caused strife between the papal view that saw the church as "God's church" and the theologians who were friendly toward the spirit of modernity and wanted to see the church as "the people's church."

---

36   William C. Chittick. *The Self-Disclosure of God* (State University of New York Press, 1988) 213.

From this, a theology that was wholly directed toward the worldly was presented, a church that should adapt itself to modernity, to the will of the people. For Guénon, this represented a shift from inspired intellectuality to sentimentalism caused by the development of modern civilization in a purely material direction, leading to a situation in which: "they confuse religion with a vague religiosity, reducing it to morality; the place of doctrine, which is however what is essential, is diminished as much as possible, despite it is from doctrine that all the rest should logically derive."[37]

The spirit of modernity and the spirit of the Primordial Tradition stand in conflict with one another because of how symbols are understood. Primordial Tradition gives supreme importance to an intellect that is informed by the Gnostic *pneuma,* the divine breath that makes divine revelation possible. This is the "heart of the world," the centre that represents the Divine Principle, and is viewed as the central focus of the unfolding of creation. The Primordial Tradition speaks of the underlying conditions of the celestial arte and magic, how these stellar influences can be brought to the Earth, and their effect on the natural world. On the other hand, modernity locates its centre on the social actor as its own axis, severing the celestial realm from modern life and becoming, as Max Weber observed, "disenchanted."[38]

Yet another tendency of modernity concerned Guénon: the infernalisation of sacred symbols into a wholly new and egocentric context. Guénon held a vehement disdain for modern psychology because of how the primordial archetypes were removed from their ideal sphere and, instead, placed into the labyrinths of the personal human psyche, altogether disregarding the celestial source, the Empyrean realm. Insofar as the Primordial Tradition speaks of the stellar path, the celestial way, and its mysteries, it would logically follow from Guénon's discourse that if the great cosmic cross that brings heaven to Earth is broken and sacrificed in the name of materialism, there can be no true access to the Empyrean, the starry realms. This is because modernity effectively closes down access to the suprapersonal *mundus imaginalis* in favour of personal, inner psychological dimensions, what Guénon called "sentimentalism" as opposed to an inspired intellectuality.

---

37 *Symbols of Sacred Science* (Sophia Perennis, 2001) 3.
38 This concept was one of the sociologist Max Weber's (1864–1920) key phrases in how he described the devaluation of religion in the modern society.

In *The Symbolism of the Cross*, Guénon expounds on the importance of divine revelation, elucidating its essential role in metaphysics, theology, spirituality, and religion.[39] Without the divine revelation, a religion becomes static—at best, a philosophy, limited in its explanations of the religion in question, and at worst, a pastiche of the metaphysical ideas the religion claims to propose. The divine revelation comes from the source of all phenomena, and as such, this revelatory connection is necessary in order to explain cosmology, theodicy, soteriology, and the purpose and function of the human condition. Religion, void of its mystical core, becomes uninspired, rigid, dogmatic, and moralistic, snuffing its invisible fire.

Without the vertical axis of Empyrean wisdom that brings the influx of timeless knowledge of eternal being and inspired religion, it unfolds along a horizontal axis of linear time and material becoming. Religion is rooted in divine revelation and not human imagination. A religion lacking this divine component will not preserve the essence of the timeless tradition. In this regard, Brian Cotnoir, in his *Alchemy: The Poetry of Matter*, makes a great point. He writes:

"By my definition the irrational is the opposite of reason and sur-reason. The irrational is more a question of awareness than a mode of knowing and being. It is blind, ignorant of its own source and effect. Unaware, it often leads to superstition. That is, we project our own noise (fears, anxieties and desires) onto empty phenomenon, then objectify, reify and energize it, in a system of symbiotic relationships and interactions (i.e. superstitions, neurosis etc.). This morass leads to nowhere except the satisfaction of its own self-created needs. By contrast, reason and sur-reason can lead to wisdom." [40]

Guénon's solution to this dilemma of modernity vs. tradition is to generously cut away everything false, profane, and material and convert to a traditional school of thought and spirituality. By doing this, you will constantly aim to place yourself under the influence of the divine and thus contribute to the fortification and presence of tradition. However, this might not be feasible or attractive for many of us. Not everyone is ready to renounce the world, yet many are the saints who

---

39   Sophia Perennis, 2001.
40   (Khepri Press, 2017) 43.

walked the earth with the pleasure of being alive. It is here the many Sufi prophets, saints, and sadhus give us clear examples that can be followed. Al-Arabi was denounced for spending time with unworthy people, Rumi was disapproved of for taking too much pleasure and interest in material life, Jesus Christ was criticised for loving Mary Magdalene more than his students, and al-Khidir was critiqued for several incidents of meaningless cruelty.

Buddhist communities, the *sangha,* give supreme significance to retreat, as Sufi *silsilha* give great weight to meditation and prayer, and Christian Gnosis and Mysticism focus on the importance of seclusion, prayer, and meditation to ensure that the connection with God is maintained. However, this all comes down to the cultivation of awareness, and we shall return to this matter at the end of this work as we close this chapter with yet another part of Meister Eckhart's Sixty-Ninth sermon:

> *"A man may go out into the fields and say his prayers and know God, or he may go to church and know God: but if he is more aware of God because he is in a quiet place, as is usual, that comes from his imperfection and not from God: for God is equally in all things and all places, and is equally ready to give Himself as far as in Him lies: and he knows God rightly who knows God equally in all things."* [41]

---

41   Don Jumsai, *Mystical Works of Meister Eckhart* (Crossroad Publishing, 2009) 353.

TWO

THE THREAT OF TRADITION

*"Without initiation, there can be no liberation…
And there can be no initiation without the preceptor of a lineage."*

—KULARNAVA TANTRA 14:3

In the context of this work, the meaning of the word *tradition* should by now be established, and it should also be easy to see how some actors in the modern world see tradition as a threat to their temporarily created ego that often is mistaken for authentic selfhood. In order to represent tradition, the presence of a double initiatic lineage of sorts must be present as typified by the cross that binds the vertical and horizontal into the carrier of tradition as a cosmic point true to its own centre.

In modern times, often both of vertical and horizontal natures, tradition tends to provoke the sense of freedom that modern humankind holds. In a world where people search for freedom by turning inward to free something within the Wastelands of ensouled passions and self-exalting games of the mind, this is quite understandable. Today, the very idea of self is understood completely on "infernal premises,"[42] which is the spirit of modernity. This infernal perspective tends to turn

---

42   I mean this in exactly the same way as the French metaphysician René Guénon. The infernal here represents a glorification of active matter, strength, and individualism as contrary to the contemplative and collective nature of the celestial perspective.

the axis of the world in such a way that matter crowns the immaterial. Together with this great focus on the individual and their strength, will, and autonomy comes the idea of progress being equal to qualitative improvement and a sense of linearity concerning time that moves our being away from the traditional perspective.

Modern-day psychology—in particular, psychoanalysis—expresses this infernal aspiration greatly with its intense focus on the layers of the soul that are denied for the consciousness, the sub-consciousness. This idea relays to us that there is something more real under the layers of consciousness; it is here, underneath it, where our true self rests. This term is often confused with what is "un-consciousness." When the British poet S. T. Coleridge introduced this term into English, the faculty he had in mind related to dreams, vision, and insight[43]—closely tied to the prophetic potency that rests at the core of tradition proper. With infernal modern psychoanalysis, this became solely a category within the mind-body continuum of a person. If you pay attention to the way most of us speak about "archetypes," "the un-conscience," personae, anima, and several other terms derived from psychoanalysis, we will notice how language has adapted to a certain meaning, meanings we do not reflect over.

This terminology reveals the adoption of a Cartesian worldview, which expresses that the mind and body are separate and that we live in a dualist universe of competing essences. It means that we accept that the conditions for the world are based on the existence of two contrary, creative, substantial principles. It means that we accept that "good" and "evil" are two equal qualities that are in constant fight, unrelated and in eternal enmity. A dualist worldview often generates a focus on matter as superior to what is not yet manifest, what is yet a possibility. It is a perspective that naturally drifts away from the idea of unity and embraces the abyss opening up, thus generating a differentiation between sameness and otherness: me and you. It is the cornerstone of a profane perspective upon the world as the distance from the celestial makes men spiritually dull and materially self-centred.

A traditional worldview sees dualism as an illusion brought about by this distance. It sees manifestations as circles within a circle or emanations along a golden chain—as reflections in mirrors and ponds. The idea is that everything is connected, that separation is an illusion that

---

43   Loren Eiseley, *Darwin, Coleridge, and the Theory of Unconscious Creation* (Daedalus, 1965).

turns our perspective "downward" to matter. This perception provokes humankind to embrace separation and fragmentation as its reality, and total trust is given unto material facts, like the facts that speak for themselves. A traditional perspective will see the individualization of humankind using matter as its guide and orientation, leading to imperfection and dislocation from truth.

Matter is the subject of a greater mixture and represents an inferior manifestation from its archetypical principle, the celestial idea that originated its manifestation. A traditional worldview will insist on the importance of looking upward in search of perfection, and perfection is governed by what is beautiful and true in a Platonic, realist sense. So, when tradition tells us that matter, strength, and social ambition are inferior to contemplation and the work of ascent to the celestial spheres where true happiness, truth, and beauty rest, it challenges the idea of meaning and the worth and value of matter.

When seeing the modern world from this perspective, it is no mystery that tradition presents a threat to modern humanity. We might understand tradition as telling us to "know yourself by transcendence," which is the opposite of the modern tendency where humankind is advised to turn its gaze inward to the forbidden avenues of a suffering psyche to find selfhood. It is a gulf between the traditional perspective of humankind and the modern view. Take yet another modern idea from the field of psychology that has been embraced by many seekers. Jung saw humanity as complete when they had accomplished a merging with their shadow, as this would release humankind from tension and frustration and enable humanity to actualise the potential of self to its fullest.[44]

This process speaks of the modern condition that modern humankind is now in a state of fragmentation so severe that our celestial origin seems confused, dense, and unreachable. Instead, we seek within and down rather than within and up. In this way, Jung presented a diagnosis of the modern condition and provided humankind with some tools to solve this fragmented condition, with suggestions for ways to liberate from the shackles of the diseases of modern society. The divergence between his mystically oriented psychology and traditional psychology is the focus.

---

44   For an in-depth analysis of Jung and the shadow, see, for instance, Carl G. Jung, *Aion: Researches into the Phenomenology of the Self* (Routledge, 1991).

When we seek personal strength by exalting our social personality, we are constantly seeking affirmation by aspiring to lower levels of existence, and herein, we find the fallacy of modern psychoanalysis. By reorganizing the subtle order into material categories, an inversion appears, which leads to a materialistic attitude, relocating the archetypical ideas solely within the corporeal mind of humankind.

The sense of individuality and freedom modern humankind experiences when challenging intolerance, prejudices, and moralist demands of thought and action gives the feeling of liberating oneself; however, it is not authentic. This process liberates you from the stillness and solidity of matter, yet to be the master of your own terrestrial life is solely an awakening. It can be the beginning of a new perspective. Instead of seeing this liberation as a way of clearing the ground for perspectives to be turned upward, it is often seen as a goal in itself.

The illusion of victory often makes the victorious develop a posture of self-assertive arrogance, where the focus is repeatedly on their capacity for generating "their own systems" and accepting truths in accordance with what feels good and right in conformity with this illusory self that has been uncovered. When such a person enters groups of a traditional nature and is asked to submit to the natural order and the idea of a timeless truth that exists in spite of personal opinion, they see it as another act of enslavement, so rebellion and arrogance enter the field. For people with profane perspectives, it is more important to find one's own way and create something new, tailored to their material being.

Tradition threatens this infernal and profane perspective upon the self, sacredness, truth, and being. It threatens modern humankind's feeling of individuality by seeing matter as inferior and by seeing solidification as inauspicious. This contrast can, at times, invite rebellion, seeing in the natural order of tradition yet another form of enslavement in submitting to truth and wisdom. The rebellion rests on a silent acceptance of a Cartesian world, where the "I" seeks to define its unique nature in relation to "the other." From this arises the illusion of opposing substances, and a process of further fragmentation and alienation begins.

At the end of this process, an acceptance of opposing bi-polarities will be accepted, and from this, a complete rupture between truth and its multiple emanations will be established. From this arises an extreme on both sides of the island of illusion. On one side, we find the world-renouncing pilgrim who ceases seeing the flesh as a limit and instead imbues it with demonic and filthy qualities, rejecting that divine materialization can be a thing of beauty. At the other extreme, we find those who say they embrace a "left-hand path" and glorify rebellion, murder, and strength, venerating everything chthonic and sinister, turning hateful toward what they see as merciful and kind.

On both sides of this extreme, the word *tradition* is divided and often used to legitimise its existence and not relay its adherence to traditional doctrine. It follows that the word *tradition* is often used to give credentials to something not traditional, referring to a wholly material idea of some lore being subject to some form of "transmission" without verifying if the transmission in question is of a traditional character. Consequently, reconstructive activity, flights of fantasy, and the sheer force of will to make some form of mystery to replicate a unique tradition are generated.

Today, claims of traditional provenance are often used to induce some form of legitimacy to one's claims. In a strict sense, where one adheres to the metaphysical doctrine that informs a tradition properly, it is, in fact, rare to find living traditions in the modern Western world. The watermark of tradition rests in a genuine prophetic vinculum with the source. It is a connection with the fountainhead of creation that ensures support and understanding of the inherited unity of the worlds.

Tradition must then reflect a traditional worldview and its sacred technology must be of an order that generates recognition across boundaries of time and location. We can find tradition alive today in *tasawwuf* or Sufi lineages, amongst *Tantric kaulas,* amidst certain Gnostic lineages and sodalities. To claim to be traditional is not limited to a lineal transmission; it must also reflect a cosmology where creation is seen as an emanation from the One as well as a connection to the origin of all things. It sees a supra-natural connection between the celestial and infernal; it sees humankind as divine beings having a human experience, and liberation is intimately linked to redemption and reintegration of being into its original state.

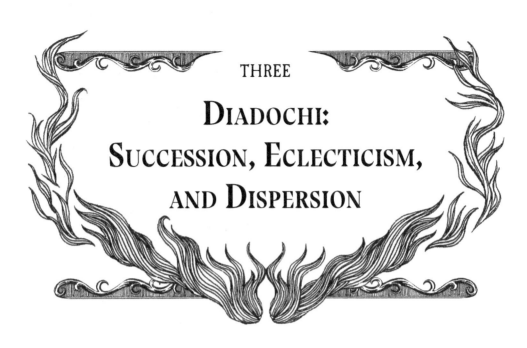

THREE

DIADOCHI:
SUCCESSION, ECLECTICISM,
AND DISPERSION

*"I came into the unknown and stayed there unknowing rising
beyond all science. I did not know the door but when I found the
way, unknowing where I was, I learned enormous things, but
what I felt I cannot say, for I remained unknowing,
rising beyond all science."*

—SAINT JOHN OF THE CROSS

The spirit of modernity is, to a large extent, signified by the extreme importance given to individualization and the taxonomy rooted in opposition and dualism that mediates the understanding of the modern self. It is a spirit that operates on principles of exclusion where sameness and otherness through money and worldly popularity generate the idea of self. In other words, we define ourselves often in relation to what we feel we are *not* and of a sameness that is played out on a social level. It is in this field that we shape ideas of truth, religion, and spirituality. We make our own truths as self-referencing subjects, and in this, we elect social roles in conformity with ambition as we choose spirituality in conformity with personal and social needs and desires.

The modern self, its identity, is relentlessly understood in reference to the material and social—and thus, we end up defining the social construct of our identity as it were our selfhood. The identity of self-born from social structures will naturally be mediated by the forces that uphold and shape these social structures. In the case of modernity, these are rooted in democracy as a political ideal and the post-Cartesian idea of the mind, which easily calls upon psychoanalysis and Heidegger (1889–1976). In the latter, we find an ambiguity of the self at the core, and it is about discovering the self by generating distance and perspective. Post-Cartesian psychoanalysis invites us to succumb to the acceptance of a certain degree of social neurosis as something built into the structure of the self.

Heidegger's *Selbstheit* (selfhood) was understood by him as a quality prior to the establishment of "I" and "we"—*Selbstheit* was something we became aware of as we developed a sense of belongingness. For modern humankind, it is this sense of belongingness that has become the axis of selfhood and not the mediating powers to become aware of that category prior to the concept of "I." If we invite our favoured political model, democracy, into this, we find another factor entering the game: the issue of equality. There are naturally many issues that could be discussed concerning democratic equality, but at the root, it is extremely simple—so simple that even the simplest participant in a society can understand it. It is about counting heads in the population. The equality rests in the fact that each subject has a voice and a vote. As the vote and voice are given, a simple count is made, and the majority decides on the action under the premise that the decision of the majority is the best course of action for the many.

The rift between modernism and traditionalism gives way to the possibility of modern eclectic magic. It is a possibility born from the refusal to acknowledge hierarchy, a possibility born from compromise and freedom of choice. Eclecticism is an activity where we choose from whichever dogma, faith, paradigm, and avenue of wisdom that we feel will help us on a personal and social level. It is an activity that places the one who elects in a supreme position, ascribing a complete self-knowledge to the one who elects.

There is no succession of philosophical wisdom in this, no reverence for authority, nor any value given to those who mastered the mystery of life and found happiness. Rather, it is an insistence on aping a God one disbelieves in where one calls upon, in the name of freedom and equality, to repeat history and mistakes of the past. Magic becomes something the modern mage engages in because they seek to empower the subject and give it powers to manipulate the world in conformity with a material will that ultimately is motivated by ambition. And so it follows that as we choose who we want to be using social structures as references to molding this identity born from desire, we do the same with spirituality and magic.

Magical capacity and potential, as well as the ability to heal, rest within the spirit and soul of humankind, but if it is worked solely within material confinement, it will not expound and express itself in such greatness as it could if the ideal and celestial origin were taken into account as a living reality. Surely, magic reveals itself in attitude, and magic can cultivate the raw potential for power in reference to the subject alone, working the magic of soul and spirit.

Magic is something we do because we seek improvement in our lives, and for some, this improvement is about domination, power, and control. For others, it is about developing a power to understand and accept and, by these potencies, turn misfortune into fortune. Magic is an art of balance, empathy, and sympathy. It is the knowledge of how to use the occult currents in the world to one's benefit. I believe that for the traditional mage, "the use of occult science to one's benefit" will not stop there but will be rooted in the acknowledgment that "if my life gets better, then your life gets better." There is a deep sentiment of love found at the root of any manipulation of natural, yet occult, currents from a mage rooted in traditional and eternal wisdom because they will recognise that we are all connected through the dust of stars and not the temporal social constructs we make from it.

Here, I find a contrast and challenge to the modern eclectic ways where tools and affinities are chosen based on a selfish protocol in how the traditional mage is mediated by care, love, and understanding of creation in their election of tools and idols. This contrast ultimately rests in diverging worldviews.

The traditional worldview is rooted in the idea of belongingness and asks, like Heidegger, how to realise this through one's being. As a premise, the traditional worldview holds that God—the Divine Source, or whatever you call the beginning of possibility—is a unity of "oppositions." There is no dualism at play unless you see this as the two hands of the body embracing itself. This material world is seen as movements in the divine mirror, a reflection that encourages ascent. The hands of God make shapes and forms in the waters of possibility. It is about primordial unity, a belief that home is with the Source and that this world of matter is a place of joyous experience and possibilities.

The modern worldview can cause an application of similar strategies and convictions as we find in traditional doctrine, but all too often, it becomes nefarious and infernal in its focus on the worldly. Battles in the name of spiritual freedom are declared as one announces the right to worship whatever god one feels drawn to worship or use. The reference is always to one's self, and in this, there is often a rejection of legacy, lineage, and ancestry that is sacrificed in the name of self-reverence.

An example might be useful to explain the difference. Let us take Satan as an example. The idea or spiritual concept of "Satan" can be understood in many ways. Academic knowledge will tell us that Satan was the name of a juridical office in Mesopotamia, the *hâ-satân*, which played the role of the prosecutor in trials. The "Satan" could be a man or a spirit. Christian theology will tell us that "Satan" is the enemy of humankind, a force that wants to see us fail and slip. A philosopher of the more phenomenological bent will see that it is a category of challenge; a Sufi will perhaps see this force as a limit of divine unfolding, while a Satanist will see this concept as the antithesis of God and the subject of veneration.

We can't really say that any of these stances are wrong or right; they are just different perspectives on a cosmic phenomenon. The problem occurs when one stance is taken as truth because any perspective assumed as truth will exalt the temporal into a dislocated state that impairs the interaction with the eternal.

I believe that a respectful acceptance of our current station and the legacy of the hermetic philosophers hold the potential to direct us to the subtle nature of truth as a state of being that reveals itself in ideal resonance with beauty. I speak here about *diadochi*, about succession and lineage.

The hermetic philosophers, or *prisci theologi*, considered *diadochi* fundamental in how they expounded upon their philosophy. It was *diadochi*, succession, which gave power to their words and thoughts. For Marsilio Ficino (1433–1499), *diadochi* was considered to be a lineage of wisdom that was being transmitted intact through the hand of its many portents that ensured a unique transmission. Ficino used this term often, and I am sure it was with intention because, in his time, the word *diadochi* was connected to the feud between Alexander the Great's six Macedonian generals. These generals instigated a sixty-year-long war for dominion, defining which one of them was the rightful heir to Alexander's legacy, a war that led to division.

Ficino most certainly had this in mind as he expounded upon his own Platonic idea of succession as a transmission of timeless wisdom that could be brought into corruption and also further succession by dispute, argument, and dialogue. For Ficino and the *prisci theologi,* the crucial matter concerned the timeless truth that was passed on, and this succession invited a creative element. It was creative because the timeless wisdom was ultimately rooted in the *mundus imaginalis,* the world of ideas, and not in fantasies rising from the self-referring subject.

Here, we find another crossroad: the one where imagination and fantasy meet and part. There is a difference here. The faculty of fantasy invites us to imagine, yes, but the realm of fantasy sees no distinction between phantasmagorias, desires, wishes, imposed will, and the forms and images of an eternal essence. The realm of fantasy is where ghosts and wishes dance with the eternal and temporal. It is difficult to discern the gold from the dross.

If we return to Heidegger, he saw modern selfhood as a consequence of the Cartesian *cogito,* which made the individual human reason the sole source of certainty. This focus also led to subjectivity being the only way to become certain about anything, whereas other subjective existences became objectified or at least subordinated to the "certainty of the individual." Later on, we find the French physician La Mettrie in 1748, launching the concept of "man as machine" as a continuation of the materialistic drift ascribed to Descartes.[45]

It is possible to insist on this supreme importance of the individual, in the end, originating from Plato and his ideas as they were understood by Leibniz in his *Monadology* (1714). After all, he held that each monad was self-sufficient in itself. But we should also keep in mind that for Leibniz, as for Plato, the monads and ideas executed their nature within the world of a preordained harmony. There is more to subjectivity than the subject. However, with the rise of the Enlightenment era and up to modernity, the self became disengaged from this cosmic harmony and is no longer using the world at large as a mirror or attractor. Modern humankind seems to be confronted with two choices. Either they can lose themselves in a material and objective universe—or they can empower their individuality and subjectivity as their axis and anchor.

---

45   La Mettrie, *Machine Man and Other Writings* (Cambridge University Press, 1991).

The effect this has on spirituality is dramatic, as the self steps in and takes the place of God.

For instance, the most important concept of truth or *veritas,* which Plato saw as a veiled virgin, had more in common with Heidegger's ideas of "being," ontologically paired with "truth" rather than affirmations of facts and measures of sameness and contrast. For Plato, these affirmations were signposts of the presence of truth. In the end, truth led to the awareness of a deep knowledge, guided by a sense of love, joy, and connectedness with what felt good and was revealed as beauty. The *diadochi* originated with the illumination from the realm of ideas. It was a torch of truth that was passed on that lit up humankind as a microcosm, a wonderful mirror of the greater cosmos, and it was God who contemplated himself in humankind as we contemplated God in humankind.

Modern eclectic spirituality can use the same techniques, but the reference is always one's subjectivity and individuality. In the words of René Guénon, in *The Reign of Quantity and the Sign of the Times,* "modern man creates an infernal spirituality," meaning that instead of seeking transcendence, modern seekers sought self-knowledge and deification mediated by a material society.[46] This often struck down and inward instead of up, bridging an understanding of how we are connected in the cosmic web. Instead of looking out and seeing how we are connected, modern humanity looks inward and uses its subjectivity as the secure pole that gives certainty. Modern humankind has consequently made themselves into a terrestrial God, informed by material and social vectors, and it is upon these infernal facets much of modern spirituality and theosophy is then erected as castles for kings and queens living in the absence of the true crown, in halls emptied for any real and true spiritual afflatus.

---

46   (Sophia Perennis 1945/2001) 228.

FOUR

SETH AND THE TRACELESS PATH

*"Once man divorces himself from the divinity, he corrupts himself
and everything he touches. His actions are misguided
and end only in destruction."*

—JOSEPH DE MAISTRE

The mysteries of Seth are found on the Traceless Path of the upright and straight. It is the path of the prophetic light guided by the winds of inspiration. The path of Seth leaves no trace because it is the mystery of the subtle order, the mystery that enabled the fallen humanity to restore themselves within the sacred centre. It is the mystery of deliverance under angelic contemplation and guidance. Seth perfects the hermetic dichotomy that "the wise one dominates the stars."

This path of ascent along the unbroken chain of light is enabled at the heart of the fallen estate of humankind. It is a soft breach of Empyrean heat, barely noticeable for material-oriented people. It is the rays of air stemming from the Emerald City of Hermes, also known as *Terra Lucida* and *Hurqalya*.[47] These rays empower the inferior and earthly sanctuaries and become like an image caught in matter, reflecting its celestial perfection, almost like a moment of the heavenly virtues frozen in time and grievance. The process of solidification that took place through the

---

47   Henry Corbin, *The Man of Light in Iranian Sufism* (Omega Publications, 1971) 23.

separation instigated with the fall brought to affect a particular mystery replicated in the tripartite hypostasis of the One.

This mystery unfolds from the teachings given to Adam by the angel Raziel, which are the secrets of sacrifice and passion. Raziel, the angel of secrets, showed up in the same sequence as Uriel. He gave his Book of Secrets to Adam. However, the book was lost due to angelic envy and was thrown into the sea and given to the marine dragon Rahab. Rahab was ordered by God to give back the book that was then given to Enoch, then Noah, and finally, to the descendants of Seth. The mystery reveals itself as the soul finds itself limited and restrained in matter. Suhrawardi, in his treatise *The Shape of Light: Hayakal al-Nur*,[48] describes the soul, which he understands to be the cosmic reason itself, as a light that does not occupy space or place; it is eternal and free from contradiction.

When the soul meets the material body, the yearning and indifference they have toward each other births a unique relationship. This relationship paves the way for a certain mystery that unfolds between the two pillars of Seth. These pillars were inscribed with the secrets Adam was given by the angel Raziel, and these mysteries gave the necessary support and knowledge needed to maintain a spiritual awareness while humankind was caught in the state of matter. These pillars were crucial for the restitution of God's house, or presence upon Earth, as when Solomon erected the temple.

The temple itself had to be raised on the summit of the mountain, signifying the centre of the world. At the centre of the world, transfiguration is possible, and so the heavenly Jerusalem was transformed into a sanctuary for divine presence upon Earth. Here, at the centre of the world, the cosmic pulse is found: it is a one-pointed state of mind supported by the mysteries of sacrifice and destruction. The mystery of the pillars as preserved in Masonry deepens this arcanum by relating the pillars to Jachin and Boaz. The Masonic mystery speaks of the architectural principle that enables and supports the divine presence on earth and makes reintegration possible.

Jach-in and *Bo-az*, along with their Hebrew letters *yud* and *beith*, are significant. *Jach* means "he will establish," and *bo* means "confusion." From the destruction of the temple, the confusion was established, and humanity was given an opportunity for deliverance.

---

48   (Fons Vitae, 1998).

Humankind was also hurled toward the terrestrial sphere, where demonic intellects attempted to pervert it. As such, the temple was erected as a throne over the house (*beith*) of confusion (*bo*). Interestingly, Martinez de Pasqually[49] (1727–1774) says, "The number of confusion of the second column is designated by the binary rank held by the first letter of the word Boaz."[50]

Ultimately, the pillar of confusion carries the secrets of Cain's legacy as the pillar of Jachin reveals the mystery of Seth, which Cain made possible. Pasqually says about the contrast between the pillars that "... confusion derives from two powers in opposition, to sustain on the one hand, and to liberate on the other."[51] This comment also carries the mystery of the left hand and the right hand to protect and liberate.

Here, we are presented with what seems to lie at the heart of the mystery of the first sacrifice. When Cain murdered Abel, this was caused by fire, but not necessarily the fire of rage. For instance, the rune *naudhiz* also expresses the principle of fire, but rather the need-fire, and carries the burden of duty coming with opening the hand of Fate. What takes place is a deeper mystery that releases the divinely animated soul from matter. When Cain takes the blade to his brother and kills his flesh, he enables the possibility of transfiguration and celestial return.

In a later motive of the same drama, we see the heavy-hearted betrayal of Jesus ben Yusuf by Judas ben Iskariotes. The same theme appears to replicate itself between Set Sutekh and Osiris and between Loki (through the blind act of Höne) and Balder as it did between Cain and his blind descendant, Lamech. In all instances, the murder has a redemptive function; it serves the aim of salvation. It is the redemption of the soul from its material state that is enabled through the betrayer and the betrayed, the murderer and the murdered, dissolving the dyadic illusion and becoming one.

I believe it is here we find the hidden law that makes the trinity so central in all traditional faiths, be it by colours, caste, theogony, or

---

49   He was born around 1727 and founded *L'Ordre des Chevaliers Maçons Élus Coëns de l'Univers,* whose doctrine was oriented toward theurgic operations for restoration of humankind's original state, what he called "the reintegration of being."

50   As recounted by René Guénon in *Studies in Freemasonry and the Compagnonnage* (Sophia Perennis, 1964/2004) 179.

51   Ibid.

cosmology. This eternal truth is from the rabbinical Kabbalah seen as a tripartite unity of *mem*, water and the Moon; *shin*, fire and the Sun; and the mediating principle of *aleph/yud*, represented by the air (whereas *yud*, strictly speaking, represents the *ir*, or divine eye-opening for the release of the *nous*, or the divine mind as it relates to the potency of air).

On Earth, we see this replicated by an affinity between the lower and higher—what we might define as a private and active love, echoing Thomas Vaughan. Active love would be perceived as taking on the form of attraction between certain mixes of matter and spirit that met in the secret waters of the Moon, in the winds of the planets, and the fire of the Sun as it took shape in earthly domains. The Moon and the Sun will always be the king and queen of these sanctified encounters. "It is by the conversion of water that silver and gold are produced," Pico della Mirandola (1463–1494) says in his *Libri tres de auro* and calls our attention to the mercurial serpent, the double-twined one that flanks Hermes' caduceus.

A common alchemical reference in the seventeenth century was to perceive the mercurial serpent as the "creeping water," but this solely revealed its movement. Its core was still of fire, but the fire of the heavens, invisible and celestial. It is due to the "creeping water" that the Earth is full of "philosophical medicine." The Earth, spirited by the divine relation made possible by the mercurial serpent, brings forth the *anima mundi* or *terra adama*, also known as the "world soul." The secrets given to Adam by Raziel detailed the consequences of this marriage between the world soul and the celestial abodes by the "creeping water." The three principles above mirror the three principles below in such a way that humanity could realise heaven on Earth at all times.

This mystery rose in response to the need taking effect when Adam was ejected from the divine presence and became corruptible. This was the divine secret given to Adam in order to restore and rescue the divine sparks that had fallen into matter. These stellar rays, their rescue, and restoration suggest that the secret of Raziel was of a stellar nature, focused on retaining the vinculum between the worlds. One who knows their star will know themself, and from this, an ability of discernment that recognises the divine mirror upon the Earth will be born. We can say that in this process, the inferior bears witness to the superior and receives the divine light in the form of terrestrial signatures. The one walking the traceless path will, by inclination to this mystery, possess the wisdom needed to recognise these signatures.

The angelic wisdom handed down to Adam became an angelic legacy with Seth. Seth became the first to possess the double key of gold and silver and thus held power, celestial and terrestrial, by the solar and lunar keys. This motive is found in temporal time in the figures of Melchizedek and Elias Artista, immaterial and immortal prophetic presences that constantly restored the sacred doctrine in the form of pacts with elected people. These themes are relentlessly linked to the spiritual wine flowing from the Golden Age that restitutes the divine presence on Earth and upholds the sacred centre. The essence of this mystery, no one can fathom or understand, unless an angelic guide is assigned to the wayfarer. In this way, true wisdom is always secured, despite its degradation and corruption, as the world gets more and more solidified in matter.

The angelic guidance also reveals the "other law," the new law. We might understand the divine law as having a shell and a kernel. The shell of the law is revealed in commandments, morals, and ethics of behaviour. These are commandments and advice given to those veiled in *hyle* so they can support the divine truth by action alone. This law, the manifested law, provides a way for reintegration by meeting the negative condition of existence with negation and restriction. But at the heart of the law lies the eternal truth, accessible through love and prophetic vision that reveals the breath of God, and veiled within the breath lies the mystery of deliverance.

Johannes Trithemius (1462–1516), one of Agrippa's tutors, said in a commentary upon the fall and the Tree of Knowledge that "the knowledge of evil is not evil, but the practice of it."[52] What this means is that the person who walks the traceless path will possess the ability of discernment—and will choose what is good. One who has realised the possibilities gifted to humankind by Adam's secrets passed on to Abel and transformed by Cain will call upon their star and angel and gain the wisdom of the stars. This can, at times, reveal itself in a world-rejecting attitude, but in reality, it is a call to realise that the Earth captures virtues from above and to see the world as a field of stars. At all times, matter must be turned upward to the stars, where the secret of wisdom is found.

In terms of human types, Adam and Abel represent the nomads and shepherds who are always striving toward open landscapes where they

---

52   In Noel L. Brann, *The Abbot Trithemius* (Brill, 1981).

can breathe the silence of divine quietude. In the nomadic nature of the shepherd, we find a rejection of social limits; rather, the shepherd favours the freedom of the wanderer to be embraced by earth, night, and stars. It represents a desire to be unfettered by matter and civilization, a call for the freedom that ruled the Golden Age. This yearning toward the original state is effectuated by Cain, who then releases the potency for salvation in the form of Seth.

The Cainite disposition, as it manifests in contemporary humans, is one of restriction and heroism. Cain went out to build cities, and as such, Cain himself represents bondage and conformity to manifest law. The manifest law gives us not only heroic dispositions and antinomianism but also the illusion that matter is superior to mind and spirit. This is evident in the Western development during the Age of Enlightenment, when truth was restricted to experimental testing of perception to verify truth through observable facts. "There is no vanity like the vanity of science," Thomas Vaughan (1621–1666) says in his treatise *On the Magic of Adam* to remind us that forces that do not seek release will only contribute to solidification. Solidification raises walls between the celestial and material and hinders its fluidity and interaction. This is the Adamic secret, given by Raziel, and transmitted through saints unbound by time and land, and herein lies the legacy of Seth, which can be summed up in an Egyptian variation of the famous Hermetic axiom:

> *Heaven above, heaven beneath*
> *Stars above, stars beneath*
> *All that is above is also below.*
>
> —BARACHILAS ABENESI

FIVE

BEULAH AND MUNDUS IMAGINALIS

"Thou shalt no more be termed Forsaken; neither shall thy land
any more be termed Desolate: but thou shalt be called Hephzibah,
and thy land Beulah: for the LORD delighteth in thee,
and thy land shall be married."

—ISAIAH 62:4

When speaking about the "imaginary world," we are referring to the Empyrean realm, the *Ohr Ein Sof,* the ideal world of platonic forms. The "imaginary world" is also known as the *mundus imaginalis.* This concept is important to understand, as it is here, in the Empyrean realm, the *mundus imaginalis,* that we find the invisible fire of timeless tradition and its gnosis whispering and hissing. This realm, strictly speaking, is not tangible in itself, which is why some sort of creative vinculum is needed to make the Empyrean reveal itself. In classical Lurianic Kabbalah, this unveiling of the limitless light is called *tzimtzum* or constriction and refers to how the limitless light, through pressure and squeezing, is made tangible or possible to know.

Beulah is a realm where it is possible to know the limitless light, and for William Blake, as it was for Isaac Luria, it was only possible for humans to know the limitless light. This is because the *Ein Sof* generated the talismanic and supra stellar form of Adam Kadmon to use as its vehicle for being known. Blake, in his poem "Milton," describes

Beulah as a "place where all contraries are equally true" and that it is "created around Eternity." He says further that the daughters of Beulah "follow sleepers in all their Dreams."[53]

For William Blake, Beulah was the oneiric paradise accessible through vision, dream, and creative avenues, aiming toward giving form to the limitless light. In this way, he saw himself as Hephzibah, the Hebrew Queen who was married to Hezekiah of Judah. *Hephzibah* means "she is my delight" in the sense of being a receptacle for the Empyrean outpouring that generates legacy in some form. This allegory is also present in mystical Christianity in the relationship between the bride and the bridegroom and the mysteries of the bridal chamber. Further, Blake saw this place accessible through dreams and vision as a place temporal and subject to entropy; hence, it was a tangible realm that mirrored the formless light into temporary forms, a oneiric Garden of Eden seething with joy, happiness, sensualism, and art, a place of poetic inspiration. As Henry Corbin wrote:

"The existence of this intermediate world, mundus imaginalis, thus appears metaphysically necessary; the cognitive function of the Imagination is ordered to it; it is a world whose ontological level is above the world of the senses and below the pure intelligible world; it is more immaterial than the former and less immaterial than the latter."[54]

The *mundus imaginalis* is the realm generated from the Empyrean realm, from the invisible central fire or "the heart-altar of the cosmos," as Corbin so beautifully defined it.[55] It is a world born from the watchtower of Zeus, known as *Hurqalya*. The path of imagination is the realm of pure ideas or, quite simply, "source." It is here the rhythm of light can be broken down into telesmatic forms or celestial images. The *vis imaginativa*, the path of imagination, is very different from the *vis phantasia*, the path of fantasy. Fantasy is not only etymologically related to phantasm, a spectre or ghostly apparition, but it is also a word tied to the world of flesh in its daydreaming activity and its carnal and erotic dimensions.

---

53 Shambhala, 1978.

54 Henry Corbin, *Mundus Imaginalis or the Imaginary and the Imaginal* (University of Michigan, 1964).

55 Ibid.

Both *vis imaginativa* and *vis phantasia* partake in the oneiric realm, but the vinculums generated are very different.

For William Blake, imagination was what made human perception possible. It was the realm and eternal world, whilst our material universe was merely a shadow of the imaginary world. Blake received his visions, and he wrote and painted what he saw with his second sight. These visions came to him; it was not he who assembled a vision from material impressions and passing ideas. It came to him like the poem "Kubla Khan" came to Coleridge. This masterful poem came to him in an opium-induced dream that he started writing down upon awakening. He was, however, disturbed in this process by a visitor and was unable to conclude the poem because it was not from him. It was from the daughters of Beulah, who had followed him in his dream. The Swedish poet Esaias Tegnér writes something to the same effect in his poem "Svea"; "A deity seizes me. A god dwells in the Song." There is clearly a state of *unio mystica* at play reminiscent of the rapture of prophets, saints, artists, and visionaries. If it is John of Patmos being paralysed in fear by his visions or Michelangelo being overcome by a vision that sees the form hidden in the stone that he will chisel out is lodged in the same realm, the *mundus imaginalis*.

The *vis imaginative*—the path of imagination—is the realm of pure ideas, a vinculum where we find ourselves connected with source. The movement and locomotion associated with this field of being, between source and its stirring of the waters of the divine mind in the realm of ideas, is the spark of creativity. The oneiric path is clearly a powerful vinculum of imagination. In fact, everything that is was first a dream in the divine mind—but a meaningful dream, one given by spirit and angel, as the dreams of prophecy and illumination are very different from dreams that help us process the mundane life or give wings to our fantasies of carnal desire and rage. When we work with imagination, we will see results, we will dream solutions and realities, and we will see the ideal taking shape in the material order. Wishes will come through, and most importantly, this connection will fill us with a soft fire that we recognise as excitement and hopefully benevolence, a feeling of humble greatness and gratitude.

We can also see the creative imagination influencing our psyche or soul on a different, more psychological level, where imagination blends with fantasy. Fantasy can be deceptive, as we see in the word *phantasm*, which means "a ghostly appearance" that may or may not have an ideal existence. Daydreams and forms of escapism using this vinculum might belong to the realm of fantasy. So, even if it is a faculty brought on by the creative imagination, its sphere of work can be as deceptive as it is illuminating. Even Arthur Schopenhauer, in his *Counsels and Maxims,* remarks in § 18: "A man should avoid being led on by the phantoms of his imagination. This is not the same thing as to submit to the guidance of ideas clearly thought out: and yet these are rules of life which most people pervert."

When we touch the realm of fantasy, we are working within a sphere of material and social constructs where wishful thinking and self-ful-filling prophecies appear in a drama of illusion and self-dilution. It is here in the field of psychology that we mistake our behaviour for our thoughts. For instance, in the case of self-fulfilling prophecies, we decide upon something to be truthful and will strive toward affirming this truth we settled for as we disregard whatever in our landscape that questions the predefined truth. In the same way, if we pass judgment upon a person or a situation, the tendency is to act and talk in ways that affirm our judgment as we narrow down our horizons. We find the power of will and determination, and certainly, this gathering of personal power can influence the world, but it is not necessarily a state directly connected to the *vis imaginativa.*

When we are creatively connected with the realm of imagination, we will, in our contemplation and expression, be filled with meaning and understanding. Our landscape widens, and our creativity gets richer as horizon upon horizon reveals itself. When we work with the realm of fantasy, the tendency is to be filled with a sense of accomplishment that provides a form of satisfaction with our achievements. Thus, it gives access to work upon our own souls and the opportunity to forge a bridge between fantasy and imagination. It is never good to mix the planes, and therefore, I find it useful for our compass to differentiate when we work within the realm of fantasy and when we are truly con-nected to the imagination as the source of creativity.

In terms of what can stimulate our creativity and imagination, there is a vast universe out there of poetry, art, music, and beauty of all forms that can be contemplated and appreciated for the stimulation it causes. For me, the tavern can be as much a source of inspiration as good conver-sation and solitary walks in the woods at night. I think the key, perhaps, is to keep a sense of wonder and awe of being alive, to truly realise that we are spiritual beings on a human journey. Be always curious and never afraid to choose paths unknown that intrigue. Be always the hero and adventurer in your own life. This is a creative approach to life and living.

When we look up to the stars and in this see our home, when we look to humankind and see fellow journeyers, when we see in trees and plants the ancestors and the elders, and when we see companions both bad and good in all beasts, we will have the sensation of being connected. By being connected, we will gradually realise our placement in time and space, and a vision of purpose will spread out as we approach the world with interest and an attempt to make sense of everything. For instance, writing hymns and poetry in honour of one's ancestors is one way of generating a closer connection with source by the use of imagination and creativity—and in this work, purpose will gradually be revealed.

Likewise, to spend time in contemplation in nature that appeals to you is likely to forge a natural dynamic between you, the angel, and the *genius loci* of the place and inspire by the virtue of beauty how life can be experienced in greater fullness. By doing this, we will not be summoning images from our psyche but rather from the realm of ideas—and these immutable powers will inspire our psyche and soul so we can live well in the shadow of ideas.

Schema huius præmissæ diuisionis Sphærarum.

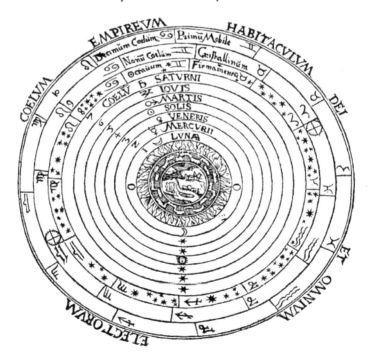

In Henry Corbin's vision of *mundus imaginalis*, this realm constitutes a world between our cosmos and the limitless formless light, what he also called the "suprasensible realm of the World Soul," the *vis imaginativa*, a realm inhabited by angels as in the Ptolemaic representation of the cosmos here reproduced.[56]

This would be in harmony with Giordano Bruno's ideas as well, as he posed that in order to make a talisman that actually was endowed with virtue, it had to be engraved by celestial forms from this very realm, the world of true and celestial images that would cast its shadow upon the world and affect it.[57] The "imaginal world" is what, for René Guénon, was the sacred centre echoing the words of the twelfth-century Sufi poet Farīd-ud-dīn Attār, author of the marvellous work *The Conference of Birds:* "Come, wandering atoms, come back to your centre, and become the eternal mirror which ye have seen."

This focus on the mirror as the central pit or pole is also found in Henry Corbin's analysis of the *mundus imaginalis*, where he writes the following:

> "*The active Imagination is the preeminent mirror, the epiphanic place of the Images of the archetypal world; that is why the theory of the mundus imaginalis is bound up with a theory of imaginative knowledge and imaginative function—a function truly central and mediatory, because of the median and mediatory position of the mundus imaginalis. It is a function that permits all the universes to symbolize with one another (or exist in symbolic relationship with one another).*"[58]

Corbin goes to the heart of the matter in his observation, and of particular importance is how he connects mirror and symbol as something supra-rational and excludes the nefarious idea that cosmic and traditional symbols have any origin within the human soul or the psychological substratum of the human being. The mirror, in this context, represents the mind or the intellect, the *nous*. It is the moment

---

56 Ibid.
57 See the article *Bruno's Telesmata and the Astrological Incantations of Circe* for a full discussion on these principles.
58 Henry Corbin, *Swedenborg and Esoteric Islam* (Swedenborg Studies, 1995) 12.

when the invisible becomes visible and finally touches the centre of the human being, the heart, just like the Sun illumines the Moon.

Furthermore, Beulah can be seen to be similar to other mystical cities, not only Hurqalya but also the mystical hyperborean city of *Na-koja-Abad* spoken of by Suhrawardi and Saadi Shirazi. These mystical worlds, like Beulah and Jerusalem of Hurqalya, due to their spiritual composure, will not be observed in the fragmentary and binary way as terrestrial perception is bound to inspire, but a unity, where all the faculties become a supra-sensory and supra-sensual to imaginative sight or perception. It is a place similar to a dream, but this oneiric realm can also be deceptive, as in a dream, the process can be interrupted and disturbed by mundane and physical factors related to the dreamer.

We know the difference between the "infernal" oneiric realms and the celestial ones in their quality and how when the visionary realms of Beulah open their panorama, we are truly in a world of paradox and contraries existing in a realm void of conflict and fragmentation. This causes an ecstasy in its own right, a prophetic clarity that can be seen in the works of Ignatius of Loyola (1491–1556), Saint John of the Cross (1542–1591), Saint Teresa of Ávila (1515–1582), Eugène Vintras (1807–1875), Abbé Boullan (1824–1893) and others that all said they were touched by some "angel" that caused the ecstatic revelry. Of great importance for these mystical visionaries was the validity of these visions. They had to be soberly anchored in "heaven," the spiritual centre, to give these dreams and visions truth and validity. Only in this way would the spiritual essence of the prophetic revelry and revelations become visions of truth.

Being touched by the angelic is what dislodges the visionary and prophet from ordinary consciousness, and this might suggest that the touch of the angel is the prophetic ecstasy, something supra-sensual and supra-spiritual that causes the *mundus imaginals* to unfold as the visionary becomes the pole in the sacred city, or at least as Saint Paul wrote in his letter to the people of Corinth: "For now we see through a glass, darkly; but then face to face; now I know in part; but then shall I know even as also I am known."[59]

---

59   I Cor. 13:12 (KJV).

SIX

TERRESTRIAL JERUSALEM AND CELESTIAL JERUSALEM

"Places don't stay where you left them. You go back there, anywhere, and even if it looks exactly how it did before, it's somewhere else."

—ALAN MOORE, *JERUSALEM*

In the previous essay on Beulah and the power of the imagination, the Empyrean and eternal dimensions were explored in relation to the pneumatic and perfect realms of the formless. Jerusalem, however, is a different place. The celestial Jerusalem is a point, represented by the heart, the pole, and the temple, which rests in the Empyrean realm but touches the primum mobile and establishes itself between dusk and dawn. The celestial Jerusalem is, therefore, subject to motion and movement and is a city radiating prevenient, or active grace, as the centre of the world. The celestial Jerusalem is mirrored in the terrestrial Jerusalem in how it also symbolises the centre of the world wherein the divine grace rests at the centre of the temple's twelve pearls of foundation and its four walls and twelve gates. The celestial Jerusalem is described in the Book of Revelations 21: 10–23 (KJV).

"And he carried me away in the spirit to a great and high mountain, and showed me that great city, the holy Jerusalem, descending out of heaven from God,

Having the glory of God: and her light was like unto a stone most precious, even like a jasper stone, clear as crystal;

And had a wall great and high, and had twelve gates, and at the gates twelve angels, and names written thereon, which are the names of the twelve tribes of the children of Israel:

On the east three gates; on the north three gates; on the south three gates; and on the west three gates.

And the wall of the city had twelve foundations, and in them the names of the twelve apostles of the Lamb.

And he that talked with me had a golden reed to measure the city, and the gates thereof, and the wall thereof.

And the city lieth foursquare, and the length is as large as the breadth: and he measured the city with the reed, twelve thousand furlongs. The length and the breadth and the height of it are equal.

And he measured the wall thereof, an hundred and forty and four cubits, according to the measure of a man, that is, of the angel.

And the building of the wall of it was of jasper: and the city was pure gold, like unto clear glass.

And the foundations of the wall of the city were garnished with all manner of precious stones. The first foundation was jasper; the second, sapphire; the third, a chalcedony; the fourth, an emerald;

The fifth, sardonyx; the sixth, sardius; the seventh, chrysolyte; the eighth, beryl; the ninth, a topaz; the tenth, a chrysoprasus; the eleventh, a jacinth; the twelfth, an amethyst.

And the twelve gates were twelve pearls: every several gate was of one pearl: and the street of the city was pure gold, as it were transparent glass.

And I saw no temple therein: for the Lord God Almighty and the Lamb are the temple of it.

And the city had no need of the sun, neither of the moon, to shine in it: for the glory of God did lighten it, and the Lamb is the light thereof."

Unlike the celestial Jerusalem, the terrestrial "centre of the world" or Holy City, will, at given moments in the history of the world, suffer destruction due to the law of material existence—because it is temporality embedded in a given cycle of unfolding that can be short or long. This is true for vegetation, organisms, and social organizations. The temporal signifies impermanence. The impermanence of decay that makes all things perish, which in the case of the terrestrial

Jerusalem, as a symbol of the centre of the world, means that when the light of the Lamb and the golden streets are overcome with the darkness of dissolution, hypocrisy, lies, and wickedness, the walls will crack asunder and the city will fall and perish until it is yet again rebuilt. William Blake writes in the opening lines of his poem "Milton," from 1810, the following:

"DAUGHTERS of Beulah! Muses who inspire the Poet's Song
For Death Eternal in the heavens of Albion, & before the Gates
Of Jerusalem his Emanation, in the heavens beneath Beulah.
When shall Jerusalem return & overspread all the Nations?
Return, return to Lambeth's Vale, O building of human souls!" [60]

Also, for Blake, Jerusalem was embodying the idea of what happens to something Empyrean and perfect in the world of matter. It will be subject to the laws of matter and slowly decay along its allotted cycle. The terrestrial Jerusalem is clearly located in a different realm than the Empyrean Beulah, yet its deeper meaning as "the centre of the world" is always intact, no matter where we might find "the City of God." Blake's Jerusalem was at one time found in the isle of Albion, and it will again make itself known in the green pastures of England—and perhaps even in London. Clearly, Jerusalem represents an ideal state and place for Blake, typical for his insistence on the material and immaterial being equally divine due to the axiom, "If I am made in God's image, God needs me to see himself," hence, "if there is no man, there is no God."

Different from the celestial Jerusalem or Beulah, terrestrial Jerusalem is a construction akin to a temple or a garden around a sacred centre. From this centre, grace, goodness, and all things divine spread across the Earth in a pantheistic dream, similar to the ideas Giordano Bruno (1548–1600) expressed in his work *On the Infinite, the Universe and the Worlds* from 1584. Blake was most likely in resonance with what René Guénon wrote about the meaning of Jerusalem as a spiritual pole in his work on the esotericism of Dante from 1925:

"...the being must above all identify the centre of its own individuality (represented by the heart in traditional symbolism) with the cosmic centre of the state of existence to which this individuality belongs, and

---

60   Shambhala, 1978.

which it takes as a base from which to raise itself to the higher states. It is in this centre that perfect equilibrium resides, an image of principal immutability in the manifested world." [61]

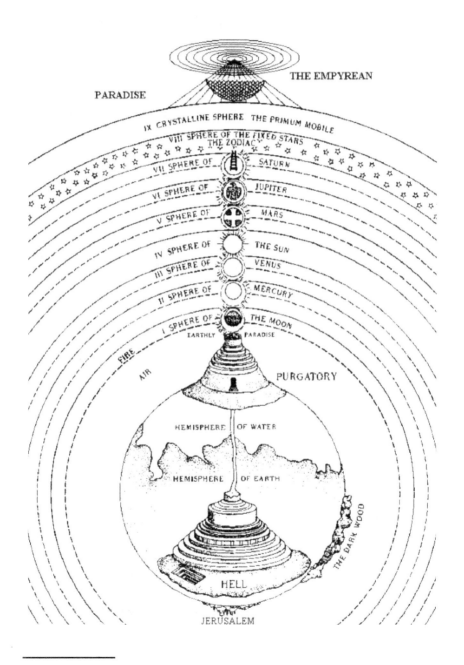

---

61   *L'Ésotérisme de Dante* (Gallimard, 1925/1957) 47.

Dante envisioned Jerusalem, as he explains in his *Cantos*, located between the Pillars of Hercules in the west and the Ganges in the east, and beneath Jerusalem, we find the gate to Hell, as written in the prelude to Dante's *Divine Comedy:*

> *"The concave of Hell had been formed by his fall, when a portion of the solid earth, through fear of him, ran back to the southern unin-habited hemisphere, and formed there, directly antipodal to Jerusalem, the mountain of Purgatory which rose from the waste of waters that covered this half of the globe."* [62]

Looking at the drawing of Dante's Hell, Purgatory, and Paradise, the structure Dante envisioned is almost identical to the blueprint of the Islamic hell, but his cosmogram also mirrors the Kabbalistic idea attributed to the *Etz Chaim*, or Tree of Life, where *Malkuth* or kingdom, the material sphere, is seen as being the materialization of the formless ideas in *Kether*, the crown or Empyrean Paradise. When the formless is given form or made manifest on some level, its eternal quality is damaged in favour of decay and temporality.

The etymology of *Jerusalem* is ambiguous. *Jeru-Salem* is most commonly translated to mean "foundation" or "city of peace." We should also keep in mind that the city of Jerusalem has a long and rich history where the earliest mentions of this place being sacred date back to the nineteenth century BC, as spoken of in Ugaritic and Mesopotamian texts.[63] These texts would reveal important factors of the foundation of the terrestrial Jerusalem as the centre of the world as again we meet the importance of dusk and dawn.

These texts impart to us that Jerusalem was named after the two Akkadian/Chaldean deities Shachar and Shalim, numina of dusk and dawn. The latter is a deity associated with grace and kindness in the form of the evening star that brings the daybreak. The root of *Shalim*, *s-l-m*, also gives us the Akkadian words for "completion (of life)" and

---

62   Dante Alighieri and Charles Eliot Norton (trans.), *The Divine Comedy, Volume 1, Hell* (Project Gutenberg, 1999).

63   For more information, a valuable resource is G. Johannes Botterweck, et al. (ed.) *Theological Dictionary of the Old Testament.* XV volumes, Erdmans verlag, 1986.

"corps" and was considered to be a numen of the netherworld, also associated with the fertility of the land. We see a reference to this when the Sun leaves its place in the world of the living to enter the netherworld and thus changes places with the Moon. This transition is always heralded by *Shachar* and *Shalim*, with Venus as the morning and evening star.

Shalim is also spoken of in another text where *Baal* asks *Anat* to pour *Shalim* into the inner parts and centre of the Earth for the sake of the Earth's well-being.[64] Besides the suggestive hypostasis of *Shalim* of Astarte or Venus, a curious detail should also be mentioned, namely how in Elephantine, the Chaldean Lachish letters,[65] we find that *Shalim* is the name used to greet the dreamer who reveals augurs and oracles, suggesting that these Venusian numina were crucial for the oneiric and visionary capacity of the imagination.

If Jerusalem does reflect being "founded by *Shalim*," it would indicate a strong Luciferian quality in a city being founded on the Evening Star and the Morning Star, the numina or sons of Asherah or Venus. Seeing that the name "King Solomon" carries the root of *Shalim, s-l-m*, it would suggest that the cult of *Shalim* and Ashera-Venus was a significant part of the worship found at the royal house of King David, passed down to Solomon.

Again, the Book of the prophet Isaiah shows itself to be most intriguing when it comes to revealing the deeper secrets of Jerusalem, especially *Shachar* and *Shalim*. In Isaiah 14:12 (KJV), we find the famous verse: "How art thou fallen from heaven, O Lucifer, son of the morning! how art thou cut down to the ground." When Jerome translated the Bible and gave us the Vulgate, Lucifer was his rendering of *Helel ben Shachar*, which would roughly mean, "Oh Shining One, son of Dusk," but all this in reference to the rising and setting of Venus, announcing daybreak and sunset. *Shachar* or alternatively *Shahar* or *Shachor*, interestingly enough, gives us the gematric value of 510, *Resh*, which means "head."

The Irish religious cantos *Saltair na Rann* (Four Lined Psalms) from 988 gives a presentation of the sacred themes of the world from

---

64 *Theological Dictionary of the Old Testament.* Vol XV., Erdmans verlag, 1986.
65 Most likely dating back to 588 BC.

creation to doomsday in the form of psalms. If we look at the earlier designs of the heavenly Jerusalem, they all appear to be first developed by the Asturian monk and cartographer Beatus of Líebana (730–785) from his eighth-century commentary on the Apocalypse of John or Book of Revelations.

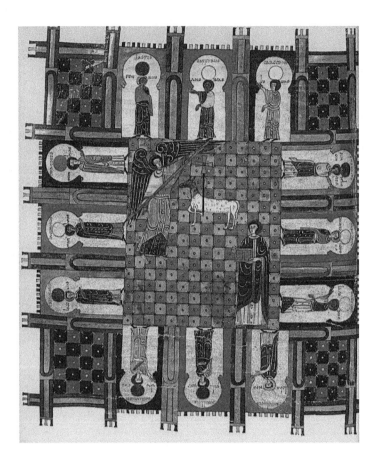

The heavenly Jerusalem is modelled on the first temple and shown to have four cardinal sides with three gates in each direction, totaling twelve "pearls," "angels," or "apostles" that "square the divine circle" and make the timeless temporary. The twelve gates represent the zodiacal stations throughout a solar year that mirrors a greater cosmic cycle. At the heart of Jerusalem, we find the Lamb and the Cross flanked by the Evangelist and the Angel of the Golden Reed. The Angel of the

Golden Reed is spoken of in the Book of Revelations 21:15 as the angel who would measure the city, its gates, and its walls.

Considering that the Golden Reed represented justice and was also the staff used to hang the scales for measurement, it is possible to see yet another Venusian tangent at play in the mystery of Jerusalem. Also, the divine presence that would make Jerusalem holy was placed in the centre of the original temple, as a "square within the square," to use Masonic jargon. If this proto-map of Jerusalem would reveal anything of the presence of God, the holiest of the Holy, we can conclude that the Lamb, the Cross, the reed of the scales, the power of vision, and angelic justice would come together with the void. Together, they would contain the holiness representing the six elements supporting the holiest of the Holy, commonly symbolised by the hexagram and the number of wings carried by the seraphim.

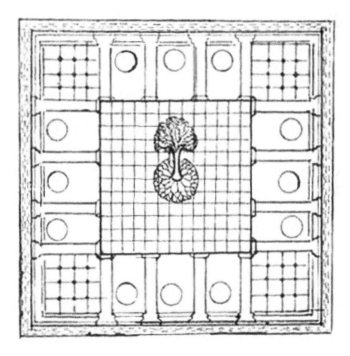

Seeing the design of the heavenly Jerusalem, it is interesting to remark on the similarities with the Kaaba, a construction that has also been "squaring the circle," as well as the *Vaikuntha* mandala discussed by Titus Burckhardt that shows the celestial dwelling of the deva

Vishnu.[66] An identical structure is found, with the difference that where the Holiest of the Holy—the covenant—is found, here at the cosmic centre, we find the World Tree.

From within Timeless Tradition, Jerusalem is viewed as a symbol of foundation, the temporary manifestation of the divine and Empyrean afflatus. But the "foundation of *Shalim,*" who was poured into the centre of the Earth for its wellbeing, might be the hierophany of Adam. The head of Adam is brought to the place between the two hills, the midnight of noonday between dusk and dawn, where the Cross of Jesus was planted in the head, begetting Golgotha. Golgotha, the final resting place of Adam, is also what opens a new form of ascent toward the stars in conformity with the cosmogram of Dante. Thus, Adam's skull becomes the *Resh* of *Shachar,* the shining one at dusk. Not only this, but it suggests that the *axis mundi,* in the form of a World Tree or the crozier, or pastoral cross, lodged into Adam's skull, does erect the sacred centre. It does this by turning Adam's memory and wisdom into the foundation for the crozier that then stretches out toward celestial Jerusalem. Adam then rests in the Venusian powers of *Shalim* that vitalise the memory of Adam and, just like copper in a cord, enable a connection with the celestial Jerusalem, pole to pole, ephemeral and temporal.

The terrestrial Jerusalem is a temporary imitation of the celestial Jerusalem. A place of affliction and turmoil as the world and history affect its stability. Temporary manifestations of the hidden Empyrean world are important, however, not only because they make visible the invisible and make the esoteric tangible. In this way, the terrestrial Jerusalem, in its successive manifestations, does uncover the hidden to some degree, but it also reveals the celestial Jerusalem through vision and its function as a "spiritual pole."

---

66   Titus Burckhardt, *Mirror of the Intellect* (Quinta Essentia, 1987) 102–109.

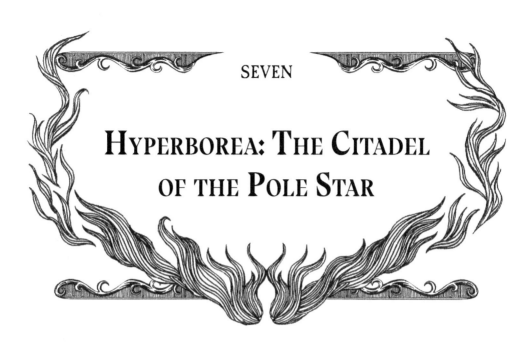

SEVEN

HYPERBOREA: THE CITADEL OF THE POLE STAR

"Her speech is not of good or evil, nor of anything that is desired or conceived or believed by the termites of earth; and the air she breathes, and the lands wherein she roams, would blast like the utter cold of sidereal space; and her eyes would blind the vision of men like suns; and her kiss, if one should ever attain it, would wither and slay like the kiss of lightning."

—CLARK ASHTON SMITH, *THE MUSE OF HYPERBOREA*

Hyperborea represents the cosmic centre, the land of Apollo, as the hidden Sun, obscured and guarded by Boreas, the north wind. It is from the city of the Pole Star that the sages and all the children of Seth came. Hyperborea is to Gan Eden as the Empyrean realm, or Beulah is to the symbolic Jerusalem caught in a moment of temporary eternity. The connection between Hyperborea and Eden is most important given how Eden was a temporary manifestation of Hyperborea. Mercator's famous map of Hyperborea and the polar regions shows a circular formation with a stone or mountain in its centre from where flows four rivers that stretch out into the world. These four rivers are mirrored in what Genesis 2:10 (KJV) says: "A river flowed out of Eden to water the garden, and there it divided and became four rivers." They were the Pishon or Nile, the Gihon, Chidekel or the Tigris, and the Euphrates.

In Rabbi Yaakov Culi's (1689–1732) *Me'am Lo'ez* or "Commentaries to the Torah," he highlights how the stream of water that flew out from Eden did so from under the Tree of Life.[67] He also suggests that the Tree of Knowledge, called so because it sharpened the intellect and made one's eyesight better (and perhaps also the second sight), was a tree growing in such a way that it surrounded and entwined the Tree of Life. Yet, the central trunk or *axis mundi* was still the Tree of Life.

Gerardus Mercator (1512–1594) was, like many cartographers of the past, such as Strabo, Pliny, Mela, Diodorus, and Procopius, not only a cartographer but also a cosmographer and geographer. Also, he was certainly inspired by the legends of Prester John, which were popular on the continent since at least the twelfth century and spoke of his land being beautiful and exotic, filled with marvels and virtue. This means that a cartographer forged in the spirit of Antiquity would give equal importance to the physical shape and liens of the land as its inhabitants and mythology. Hence, it becomes a philosophic art in its own right, where mythical lands should be given form and description. Therefore, for Mela and Pliny, Hyperborea was truly a land beyond the known world.

The Pythagorean philosopher Philolaus (c. 470–385 BC) is interesting to mention in this context as well. In the fragments we have from his treatise *On Nature,* he presents an astronomical idea of the universe that was neither geocentric nor heliocentric. Instead, at the centre of the universe, he placed a central invisible fire. The heavenly bodies are then found in ten concentric circles orbiting around this central invisible fire, the outer circle being marked by the Behenian stars that serve as the most remote tapestry to where the other planetary bodies move in relation.

The movement of the planetary bodies conforms with traditional astrology; the Moon orbits in a month, the Sun in a year, and so forth, with the fixed stars considered immovable. Of interest, in addition to the central invisible fire, is the presence of a "Counter-Earth." The Counter-Earth follows the Earth like a shadow body, always orbiting in the circle closest to the invisible fire, always as the Earth's twin. This means that in his vision of the cosmos, the cosmic centre is a central invisible fire that stems from the Empyrean realm as a mystical summit of the central fire.

---

67   Aryeh Kaplan (trans.), *The Torah Anthology* (Moznaim Publishing Corporation, 1988) 246, 247.

Hyperborea represents the point in the circle in the sense of being the centre of the world; hence, the world becomes from where the centre is to be found, Campanella's *The City of the Sun* and the Rosicrucian *Solar Citadel*. In Lucan's epic poem "Pharsalia," also known as "Bellum civile," left unfished due to being ordered by Emperor Nero to commit suicide, along with Seneca and Petronius, in AD 65, we can read: "For whether Fortune shall lead us beneath the icy Wain of the Hyperborean Bear, or where the burning region and the clime shut up in vapours permits not the nights nor yet the days, unequal, to increase, the dominion of the world will attend us, and empire as our attendant." [68]

---

68   H.T. Riley, *The Pharsalia of Lucan* (George Bell & Sons, 1909) 165.

When we speak about Hyperborea, what lies beyond the north wind, we are confronted with a series of imageries coloured both by malign and benign ideas. The north was simultaneously associated with dark and titanic forces. For instance, Lilith holds as one of her epitaphs *Tzaphoni*, the Northern One, and the north is traditionally associated with the mysteries of death and becoming. Hyperborea, on the other hand, represents a different land, a fortunate region. The geographer Hecataeus writes about how there is a region beyond the land of the vile Celts, the dark and violent north, an island beyond the North Pole. This place is described as dedicated to the Sun, or Apollo, and is largely covered by a rich and fertile forest as beautiful as a royal garden. Pindar describes Hyperborea as a place of dance, music, and joyous revelry, alien to war and strife. The Hyperboreans are a "golden" race that is not contaminated with sickness and aging but is still living in Saturn's Golden Age.

The North, both as a place of cosmic centre and a land of vile ghosts and darkness, is in harmony with how the spiritual centre has become a "lost world" to so many due to being hidden in this age of dissolution by humankind's fall into matter and *hyle,* the veritable Kali Yuga. Not only this, but we also see here the difference between a concept being considered polar and solar. This can be illustrated greatly through the zodiacal sign of Libra, which, according to René Guénon, was not always zodiacal.[69] They originated from the celestial scales that had Ursa Major on one side, Ursa Minor on the other, and the head of the constellation Draco surging between them, raising its head as a king on his throne in the primordial centre that mirrored itself in the terrestrial paradise. The importance of the dragon and the celestial scales is well known from Arthurian legends, where we learn that King Arthur was fathered by the Dragon King, Uther Pan-Dragon, representing the stellar temple or Thule of Hyperborea.

The seven stars in the bear constellations are associated in Vedic tradition with seven *rishi* or sages that guard the sacred centre represented by the pole star. These stars find their mirror in the Seven Maidens or sisters, in the constellation Pleiades, all three of these constellations being important for navigation in firmly affixing the "north," both in a real and celestial meaning. The pole star marks the polar mountain, Qaf, but the waters surrounding the sacred centre are also of importance, and

---

69 *Symbols of Sacred Science* (2001) 91.

again, this is visible in the name *Delos* or *Delphi*, the city of dolphins. Oannès or Dagon are also related to the dolphin, which brings these marine forces into the equation of Hyperborean Apollo, Oannès being related to the prophetic and visionary qualities of the pythoness in his temple. Through the waters, Hyperborea attracts other forces imbued with the gift of vision and prophecy in the form of the Woman of the Sea who, amongst the Greeks, was known as *Aphrodite Anadyomene, Rán* in Scandinavia, *Ishtar* under her epitaph as Lady of the Lotus, and the Japanese *Kwan Yin,* Goddess of the Deep Sea.

Apollo is he who guides the pythoness, i.e., the inspirer of her oracles, along with his lunar twin sister Artemis, who reflects the Moirai or three Fates through shared "maiden-ness." This is also a common Hyperborean trait, as we see from the amount of Hyperborean maidens that served at the temple in Delos. Not only this, but the fact that Artemis-Diana killed Orion as he tried to rape her maiden Opis testifies to the importance of the maidenhood as sacred and prophetic. Also, it is quite evident that the arrow is the token and sign that reveals Hyperborean identity and connotations.

In the Book of Revelations 1:16 (KJV), we read: "And he had in his right hand seven stars: and out of his mouth went a sharp twoedged sword: and his countenance was as the sun shineth in his strength." This vision, given to John of Patmos by the "the first and the last," reveals a Hyperborean and Sethian theme as he places himself as the pole star, taking the celestial bears in his hand whilst the twain sword represents the tongue and the utterance of vision and prophecy. Lastly, his countenance was like the Sun, this shine being a constant factor in the race of Seth, the upright ones, the immovable race. The first chapter of the Book of Revelations also announces another important feature of the solar citadel, namely its dissolution. When the different stars in Ursa Major, Ursa Minor, and Draco move into the place of the pole star and away from it, changing places, a rupture is felt in the world under the Sun. The Sun gets temporarily darkened, and the "north" becomes a place of darkness. The Land of the Gods becomes the Land of the Dead when the spiritual centre dissolves. The citadel crumbles in the polar absence of a stellar body being found in the celestial temple.

Kronos and Apollo Karneios are forces sharing the same realm or mystery. Karneios—Karn, or "high place," is represented by the stones marking the tumulus, which denotes the bond between the mountain summit and the dead ones in the bowels of the Earth. This illustrates quite beautifully the entire mystery of Golgotha (see *The Death of Adam*) as in the eighteenth verse of the first chapter of the KJV Book of Revelations: "I am he that liveth, and was dead; and, behold, I am alive for evermore, Amen; and have the keys of hell and of death."

The polar temple reflects through the night, is illuminated by the Moon, and enters into manifestation under the eye of the Sun, where it becomes subject to cycles, mirrored in the hours, days, decans, and months of the year. It is in this triple emanation that the idea of the north being the abode of death, ghosts, and wickedness enters the mysterious equation of Hyperborean Apollo.

The Christian Kabbalist, astronomer, and diplomat Guillaume Postel (1510–1581), in his *Cosmographicae disciplinae compendium* from 1561, is in a not-so-elegant way striving to make sense of the north as a place of evil and also perfection. He does this by referring to the constellation Draco, resting between Ursa Major and Ursa Minor, as being the actual presence of the "Dyvel"—but in line with Dante, he also comments that the Devil is chained by God at the pole; hence, the polar mountain or Qaf is a land bathed in the rays of the Sun, an Empyrean realm on Earth.

In *Lucidarium in Arte Magica*, attributed to Peter d'Abano, the spirits of the Sun and Sunday are ruled over by Varcam, and one of his attendants is Cinabas, suggestive of the spirit of the cinnabar ink, taken from the resin of the dragon's blood tree. These spirits are described as having the colour of polished gold, painted over with blood—or cinnabar. The union of fire and blood is exactly the elements of the Empyrean gift of prophecy given by the angels Uriel and Raziel. A Hyperborean element is also found in the seal of Varcam that presents us with archers, the arrow being a distinct Hyperborean presence, along with dragons, a beast of the north and the deep. The picture finds completion when we add that the wind of the Sun and Sunday spirits is Boreas, the north wind.

Saxo Grammaticus and Olaus Magnus both saw the north, this place "under the seven stars," in terms of Scandinavia, as a place of demons, satyrs, and ghosts, and even in William Blake's vision, we find a similar ambiguity when speaking of the north when addressing Urizen, who goes through a similar fall as Lucifer in Milton's *Paradise Lost*.

"Of the primeval Priests assum'd power,
When Eternals spurn'd back his religion;
And gave him a place in the north,
Obscure, shadowy, void, solitary." [70]

Naturally, in the greater mythology of Blake, this Luciferian archon, Urizen, is absolutely necessary for experiencing the world as he represents reason, language, and intellect that is controlled by law and material constructs. The same themes are found in the Hyperborean mythos, and perhaps the better of them is how the pregnant goddess Leto came to the island of the Delians and gave birth to Apollo. Leto was accompanied by a pack of wolves and her midwife Eileithyia, whom Pindar states was a cave-dwelling goddess more like a Moirai, that she sat with the Three Fates as if she was the fourth one due to the importance of childbirth. Properly enough, her Roman equivalent was Lucina, "she who brings to light."

---

70   William Blake, *The Complete Poetry and Prose of William Blake* (University of California Press, 1982), 70.

We already have the imagery of the dark north with its wolves and mysterious cave-dwelling spirit denizens, along with the equally enigmatic visionary priesthood, the *Boreads,* that were conceived of as the children of Boreas, the north wind. In spite of the gradual darkening of the north, Abaris appears to be quite representative of the typical Hyperborean, being a prophet of an upright character, possessing vision and curative powers. In Iamblichus' *Life of Pythagoras,* we find Abaris as Pythagoras' initiator, mimicking the relationship between John the Baptist and Jesus. It is fitting for Abaris, as a spiritual and magical authority, to have access to prophetic and visionary gifts through asceticism.

Also of interest is that the two bear constellations and Draco are all typified by a distinct wagon or chariot-like square shape, which, in Scandinavia, are seen as the wagons of the Aesir, in particular, Thor. This symbolism ties into the two wheels on the cosmic chariot represented by the two poles on the *axis mundi.* These two poles are represented by *Janua Coeli,* representing the solstice of the north, the door of the gods' taking place in Capricorn, and *Janua Inferni,* representing the doors of the solstices, the solstice taking place in the sign of Cancer in the south, known as the "door of men."

The etymology and origin of *Janus,* from whom the phrases *Janua Coeli* and *Janua Inferni* are derived, can be found in its earlier form, *Dianus,* which ties Janus to Diana-Artemis. The name itself connects to the word "day" and the Indo-European *dey,* "shine," which is suggestive of a solar and Hyperborean origin for Janus. Ovid, however, suggested that *Janus* is derived from the verb *ire,* "to go," in harmony with his function as the numen presiding over beginnings and ends, doors, and transitions. Of interest are also the theories of Jean Gagé[71] that point out how Boreas is depicted as a two-headed winged demon, *Boreas Bifrons* (Boreas and Anti-Boreas), similar to depictions of Janus. Hence, Janus, who was present at the beginning of the world with his key and staff, is the one who opens and closes the cosmic axis by his dominion over the two celestial doors.

---

71   For the full discussion, please see Jean Gagé, *Sur Les Origines du Culte de Janus in Revue de l'histoire des religions* Vol. 195, No. 2 (Association de la Revue de l'histoire des religions, 1979) 129–151.

Lastly, it is important to take note of how Abaris left Hyperborea in search of help from the Delians and other temples dedicated to Apollo and Artemis due to a plague that ended with Hyperborea. Disintegration and entropy are embedded in everything that becomes manifest in the sense of having motion, like a wooden waterwheel that slowly disintegrates over time and leaves behind the memory of its work and toil.

The phase of annihilation of the world signifies that the poles get reverted, that the metaphorical water in the river Jordan flows back to Qaf, the polar mountain of Hyperborea, to the central fire and spiritual centre. The inversion of the poles spells out cataclysm, apocalypse, and the end of the world, but in all ends lies a new beginning, and from this new beginning, the rivers from the polar mountain will yet again flow and generate another Eden.

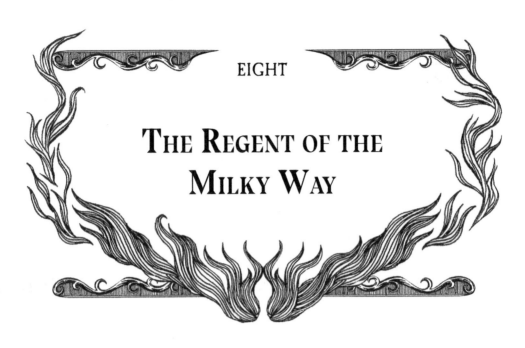

EIGHT

THE REGENT OF THE MILKY WAY

*"A broad and ample road, whose dust is gold, And pavement stars,—
as stars to thee appear Seen in the galaxy, that milky way Which
nightly as a circling zone thou seest Powder'd with stars."*

—JOHN MILTON

At the galactic centre of the Milky Way, we find the constellation of
Sagittarius shining brightly upon us. The Milky Way itself stretches from
Cassiopeia in the north to Crux in the south. This marks the division
of the two hemispheres into two equal parts, just as Ovid told in his
Metamorphoses, where he refers to the Milky Way being the road lines on
either side of the houses of the gods, the heavens, the star-paved road to
the house of Jupiter. Amongst the Scandinavians, it was the ghost road
to Valhalla. Agrippa says that Orpheus had eight deities swear to support
the hemispheres and parted them into the side of Justice and the side of
Fullness. A similar idea is found in Isaac Luria's dual division of the *Etz
Chaim* or "Tree of Life," defining the two sides as strength and mercy.

The Ogdoadic ordering is interesting as it reflects the eight spheres
associated with the Milky Way or Pleroma, a state of perfection. Here,
we find the divine ideas and Sophia, Wisdom herself. The gods Orpheus
swore to support that justice and fullness were Night, Sun, Phanes or the
Protoghenos, Fire, Water, Earth, Moon, and Heaven. The eight represents
the fullness of all and is therefore capable of transcending the fullness

and becoming one. For eight is the inheritance of the righteous; it is the number of the peacemakers of the world who, by their ways, imprisons the malefic. Eight can also be seen as related to a state above failure, what follows beyond the seven deadly sins, perfection, and immortality. The realm of the fixed stars, the crystalline firmament of angels.

This shiny river of milk that runs as liquid silver through the heavens, an ocean of stellar immortality, is the abode of Seth. It is this region that is often said to be the Pleroma because it is the level above the traditional seven planets. Here, we find the nocturnal milk of the stars. It was this angelic and perfected state that Muhammad, the prophet, chose when he was presented with the choice of being nurtured by water, wine, or milk. In choosing milk, he chose Seth, the regent of the Milky Way.

There are other interesting aspects of the Milky Way. In the Book of Job 26:13, we can read that the Milky Way is the divinely shaped "Crooked Serpent," which the Bengalis called *Nagavithi* or the "Snakeroad." In Grimm's compendium on Teutonic myths, the references to the Milky Way are mostly related to winter, Odin, birds, and Mercurial elements. The road of milk is the snake bridge to the other side, guarded by Idunn, as both contrasted to and complementary with the rainbow bridge, *Bifröst*, all forms of "creeping water." Idunn is also mentioned as one of a retinue of eight *ásynjur* in *Skáldskaparmál*, the manual of poetry written by Snorri Sturluson.

Idunn was a goddess, but like the mother of Hercules, Alcmene, she had qualities reminiscent of nymphs, which would suggest a relationship to the fairy realm. Both were reputed to be amazingly beautiful, with Alcmene's beauty being equated to Aphrodite's. Curiously, *Alcmene* is also a name used to classify species of spider belonging to the class of jumping spiders, which are hunters that do not make webs. Rather, they stalk their victims and are unique by being the only type of spiders that express curiosity for exploring their world. We find here, again, the motive of eight by the number of spiders' legs.

Likewise, its hunting skills will associate this particular spider with the nature of heroes. Since this spider does not make a web and instead stays on earth, it sets it apart from the common associations of night travels and dreams. Instead, it is a herald of the manifested perfection of wisdom in the stellar eight. This is also evidenced by this spider being diurnal rather than nocturnal, as are most other species. It is an interesting feature that the stars of Hercules, the son of Alcmene with Zeus, according to Ptolemy, are said to be of the nature of Mercury and thus being in nature similar to the creeping Milky Way. We might see the Milky Way as representing a chivalric and heroic road toward perfection. Any hero is replicating the Sun, and as such, the Milky Way is the ashen Sun, the ghost road aflame with the coals of a multitude of Suns that have turned from fire into milk.

Maybe we can see some patterns of where in the journey of the solar hero, Hercules, the hero becomes the compass on the starry road to Jupiter's court and lays down himself as the road to the dwelling of Seth. A similar motive is found in the myths of Gilgamesh, another solar hero who turns into stellar Mercury, occupying the same constellation where the Greeks saw Hercules. This constellation was also known as "the Phantom" or "Traveler on the Ghost Track." Hercules' relationship with the Milky Way was formed when Zeus tricked his wife, Hera, into suckling his illegitimate son on the milk of immortality. While Hera was asleep, he placed Hercules at her breast, and when Hera woke up and saw this, she removed him, and the milk overflowed and generated the Milky Way. Yet another legend from East Asia tells how the stellar lovers Altair and Vega met on the seventh day of the seventh month under a bridge of magpies and crows in the silver river, or the Milky Way, making it a focus for union.

If we gather the various motives here, we have the Milky Way related to the number eight, and we see that the Ogdoad is not only a number of perfection. Additionally, it reveals the eightfold divine cornerstones of creation, symbolised by the corners of the double pyramid, which marks the double hemisphere of the One. This oneness is the sanctuary of Seth, and the Milky Way is the road to his court. The stellar Mercury is guarded by nymphs and opened by heroes, and by this virtue, it possesses a different blood and harbours another seed. The mystery of the Milky Way finds its terrestrial counterpart in pilgrimage, especially the pilgrimage of *Compostela,* which means "field of stars." It is the starry field that guides the pilgrim to the sanctuary, like the celestial stars that guide humankind to their original state. We see the parallels in the pilgrim route with the "Road to San Tiago" being used interchangeably with the "Milky Way."

The eight-rayed star found in the city's coat of arms, between the crown and the shrine, reveals the identification of Compostela with Pleroma. The eight-rayed star is also what, in many representations, marks the brow of Inanna and Ishtar and suggests why the nymphs and angels of Venus guard the bridges and crossings in the realm of Seth. Their third eye, related to the energetic flow of oneness and balance, *sushumna,* flows like the milky white bridge across time and space. In this, we might even see how the Queen of Fairy, by her paleness and invisibility, has been crowned by the touch of Seth and given the dew of salvation.

The pilgrimage to Compostela was immortalised in the figure of Saint James, also syncretised with the prophet Elias. It is like the heroic icon of sanctity, the compass leading us toward the court of perfection, becoming something other as he reaches the centre of the world. Here, prophecy unfolds as the vinculum to the state of perfection is made. I believe this is the theme that plays itself out in the mysteries of Gilgamesh, Hercules, and Saint John the Baptist. With San Tiago or Saint James, a particular variation of the hero on a divine quest is revealed in the importance of the *Lwa Ogou* in Haitian Vodou. His function is to crown the journey upon the points of the *asogwe* [72] with supremacy and perfection. The aim of this particular ritual step is to bridge a transition into perfection, which automatically should, at least ideally, constitute the newborn priest and priestess into an upright defender of the mysteries. Hence, Ogou is often understood to be the King of Vodou.

The symbols of Saint James are the scallop shells and the gourd. The scallops denote his relation with water, and the straight lines of the shell ending in a point reflect the rays from the celestial centre that will guide the pilgrim to the Hyperborean Apollo—the still centre of silence within the Sun. The gourd itself is a symbol of completeness, which speaks of the heroic act of joining the two hemispheres and bringing back unity. It is also related to the secrets of the Earth and mortality—a secret that is being fulfilled with the awakening of the body of light.

We encounter milk as the preferred food of the prophet Muhammad, and it is milk that is the food of Castor and Pollux. The theme of twins is further found in the constellation of Gemini, which, together with Virgo, makes up the house of Mercury. The constellation of Gemini has been subject to several names, such as *the Peacocks* amongst Chaldeans and *Two Sprouting Plants* amongst the Egyptians. These names can provide a metaphysical link to *Shâthil*, the perfect plant that "runneth over with milk," the food of prophets and twins. This speaks of the importance of the dual poles of the axis, the celestial and infernal, that, in tandem, support the straight road, the pole. Yet other Greek myths tell how the Milky Way, envisioned as a herd of cows, finds their sojourn in the constellation

---

72 *Asogwe* is the title given to those who receive the *asson* in Haitian Vodou. The status of Houngan Asogwe will ideally make you one with Papa Loko or Ayizan and the houngan and the spirit share the ancestral memory as one.

of Gemini. This motive ultimately connects with Hermes and, through this, with Apollo, as will be discussed elsewhere in this book.

The Milky Way is also referred to in *Brihat Samhita* as the royal path of Aryaman, one of the *Adityas,* or governing principles of terrestrial order. This principle is nobleness or chivalry, and we find this in gentlemen's codes and the values held by nobles and knights throughout time. Aryaman is appointed to oversee contracts and oaths and is assigned special provenance to uphold tradition, custom, and law. The fact that he is today referred to as *Pitriraja,* or "King of Ancestors," also tells us that the royal road of Aryaman is the *Pitriyana.* It is exactly in this *yana* or path that we see the rebellion toward the sacred centre coming from.[73] It is, therefore, highly proper that the regal road of the Milky Way leads to the constellation Gemini, which challenges our choices by strength and mercy and, through this, brings unity as revealed in the legacy of Seth. Seth is the one who unites the royal and sacerdotal powers represented by the twins. We might say that this house of Mercury is where the caduceus is to be found and where the snake of mercury and the snake of sulphur are in perfect balance as supporters of the sacerdotal road.

Milk is also present in the avatar of Vishnu, Krishna, who manifests cosmic harmony in pastures where the cows and cowherdesses were the sacred verses of the Veda and Upanishads. Milk then turns into a metaphor for sacred food, the preferred food for angels. This paradise is called *Goloka,* literally "Land of Cows." In this land, the sages were the trees in the garden and were fed on milk. All this is naturally related to the churning of the ocean of milk, which produces *Mathura. Mathura* is the name of Krishna's dwelling, and it is also "the house of wisdom." The *Krishna Upanishad* tells how Krishna played in the milk released from broken milk gourds, clearly a reference to the shattering of the vessels where wisdom was spread everywhere.

Seth is the sacerdotal regent of the Milky Way; in him, the journey is at an end. He travelled to the dwelling of the twins, and here, like Hermes, he gained the two keys and was given the caduceus. By balancing the natural tendencies of the poles, he reinstalled the straight road toward the abodes of Hyperborean Apollo, the City of the Sun.

---

73 This will be discussed in depth in Chapter Twenty-Three, "Angelomachia" and Chapter Sixteen, "Perfect Solitude."

NINE

THE BODY OF LIGHT

"My place is placeless, my trace is traceless,
no body, no soul, I am from the soul of souls.
I have chased out duality, lived the
two worlds as one."

—RUMI

We begin this chapter by looking at two passages in the Bible; the first is John 1:5 (KJV), where it says: "God is light, and in him is no darkness at all," and the other is found in Saint Paul's first letter to the Corinthians, Chapter Fifteen, where he is engaged in a discourse concerning the resurrection. The great challenge here is related to the quality of the body where it is said that it (the body) is sown in dishonour; it is raised in glory, and then, in the following verse: "It is sown a natural body; it is raised a spiritual body" (Verses 43 and 44 [KJV]). It rests on reasoning in the following verse, which states how Adam was made a living soul and that the last Adam was a "quickening spirit." We shall not attend or entertain the counter discussions that generated this letter; we will just remark that the question came from the Sadducee scholars who held Stoic and Epicurean inclinations.

Likewise, they seemed to be focused on the written law and discarded any mystical inclination amongst the Phariseees, who are the predecessors of rabbinical tradition. That we see here a shift in terms of the continuation of tradition and the light of the *Tzohar*[74] would be logical to assume, given the fundamentalist image created by the Sadducee opposition, but we shall leave these speculations aside and focus on Saint Paul's argument. What is interesting in this scope is that the same argument is found in *Chandogya Upanishad*, where we read: "When the Sun of Spiritual Knowledge rises in the heavens of the heart, it dispels the darkness; it pervades all, envelopes all and illumines all."[75] This state is certainly the condition described as "Perfect Solitude" elsewhere in this work. But here, we shall concern ourselves with the transformation of the animal body into a body of light.

A transformation always reveals a death; something is left in the transformation, which lies at the heart of the alchemical principle of *solve et coagula*. The mystery of the Body of Light reveals itself in the transformation of the external faculties and a withdrawal toward the centre of silence. In this, we see how the first Adam can be symbolised by the pentagram, while the celestial man is more properly symbolised by the hexagram.

The Body of Light spoken of here is the light in Genesis 1:3 (KJV), where we find the passage: "Let there be light." It is this light from the beginning, the splendour, which Saint Paul has in mind when he argues for the nature of resurrection. This is quite obvious in light of his discourse in Corinth, where he focuses on how differences partake in an original sameness that resonates with what we find in Proclus' (412–485) *Elements of Theology* and in several of Plato's dialogues concerning the nature of the One. This is the true mystical union where the imperfect perception encoded in matter and conditioned by the spirit of dissolution in our time and age dies away. This is when we unite with what is absolutely good, true, and beautiful. This actually means that evil is nothing but a negation needed to realise all possibilities, but it is not God.

Actually, evil is hardly any ontological factor at all but more like a movement that, due to lack of understanding, is perceived as, for

---

74 Genesis tells how the Tzohar was a bright shining gem given to Noah to bring illumination. It might also signify a "window," but it clearly refers to the divine light from the beginning of time, the light of perfection, being held by Noah as a successor of Seth.

75 Swami Lokeswarananda, *Chandogya Upanishad* (Ramakrishna Mission Institute of Culture, 2017).

instance, evil. The mechanism described both in the *Upanishad* and by Saint Paul is telling. Here, the Sun is knowledge, and the heart is heaven or, more correctly, the centre or *Brahmapura*. This is the resurrection in glory, and this is the quickening spirit of the soul, the reason of *nous*, the light of the universal mind, and rising over the heart and dispelling darkness.

This is the mystery of Golgotha, the glowing skull that has shed its skin and sensuous terrestrial form and given up corruption in favour of perfection. It is a transition from the phenomena played out on the canvas of possibilities and a transcendence that indicates the dissolution of duality by attaining the *Nur al-Anwar*, the Light of Lights. It is a return to the beginning where light was made. It is the retrieval of the light that is the premise for reintegration and *tikkun*. The gift of the forbidden fruit accomplished a loss of light, and in its absence, the world seemed dark for Adam and Eve. Darkness is, as such, a consequence of creation and not from God, but rather, a natural consequence.

Golgotha, the mystery of the skull, is proper in many ways. The cranium represents the time when we lived our human experience filled with conditioned reasoning, a sort of lower mind that was shaped in relation to how our soul and emotions reacted to the bodily experience. This situation tends, under the modern atheist bonds, to create a shadow self, a mimic of our individuality or selfhood, which we can call personality. This condition leads to spiritual raptures being referred to as a sort of awakening because our mind is shaken by some influence that, in turn, shakes the soul to give attention upward to the *coelum* instead of the body and the *mundus Infernum*.

Upon bodily death, either in terms of bodily slavery and attention or a transcendent perspective, the skull is emptied for its conditioned personality, and space is made for light. We even see a similar mystery being played out on the night of All Hallows, where pumpkins are carved out, and their earthly matter is replaced with candlelight. This thread is far too complex to dwell on here, but it is worthy of mentioning in terms of the mystery of Golgotha related to the retrieval of the *Tzohar* and how its beacon shows itself for those with eyes to see as a remembrance of *pax pleroma*, like the rainbow bringing the remembrance of the sapphire.

In the symbolism of the tarot, this mystery is encoded in the interplay of the Sun and the Last Judgment, naturally following each other in sequence. In this sequence, the Sun represents the soul made perfect.

We might say that the Sun represents the condition necessary to transcend the dyadic human condition upon *manvantara,* the great *pralaya,* the great restoration. We are speaking of the culmination of initiatic insight, referred to by Apuleius as the Sun at midnight, and how its radiance dispels the darkness by *rubeata,* the process of reddening base matter into gold.

The fire hived off from the Sun will turn the body into a glowing crystalline form, the Body of Light. This is seen in several traditional tarot decks, such as Marseilles, which depicts two children, one female and one male, on the card. These children of Apollo represent the golden seed as transmitted in sacerdotal and regal transmissions. The fact that the maiden in the card can represent Circe, daughter of the Sun, is also worth mentioning. Here, especially, her reclusive nature is similar to Na'amah, which, in light of the motives of restoration and redemption, will cast a different light upon Circe.

The resurrection is, in reality, a restoration of the natural perfected state, which is why, as we have mentioned earlier, the hexagram, being formed by the terrestrial and celestial triad, is such a proper symbol for perfected man. In the hexagram, the Great Work is accomplished by its key secret *solve et coagula.* Marsilio Ficino once commented in one of his writings: "There is a continuous attraction, beginning with God, going to the world, and ending at last with God, an attraction which returns to the same place where it began as though in a kind of circle."[76] This can be seen as a good summary of the motivational force for embarking on the Great Work.

Also, in the sixth surah of al-Quran, this process is described as "drawing the living from the dead and the dead from the living" in conformity with the alchemical observance of how the dissolution of the body is the fixation of the spirit. This is also evident in the production of the alchemical salt in spagyrics, which reproduces this act by turning the body into white ash that, in the final process, releases the spirit. The whitening is also seen to be the lesser mysteries and, therefore, the mirror of the greater mysteries, namely the reddening. This is further revealed in the relationship between the celestial and terrestrial Jerusalem and how Paradise can be brought to Earth again.

Here, we again are confronted with the keys of Janus and Saint Peter that simultaneously dissolve and fixate. It is the power of the keys that

---

76   Marcilio Ficino. *Platonic Theology, Book II* (Harvard University Press, 2001).

led to the pure *sattvic* road being established into the union of sacerdotal and regal initiation. It is this condition, *sattvic* and solar, which
enables the final transition from the movement of stillness, where the
Sun rises above the heart in the red glowing sunset.

Resurrection is intimately related to judgment, and its motives are
usually accompanied by angelic choirs and sounding trumpets. In the
Penitence of Adam, a similar situation occurs when Eve is seduced to
share the fruit with Adam. She is actually challenged to not give the
fruit to Adam because if she alone eats of the fruit, she will be like
a God, and this will lead to Adam being like a beast for her. In this
moment, Gabriel sounds his trumpet and descends to the garden to
judge Adam. Here, an interesting comment is presented by Gabriel.
His concern is that Adam will be boastful and victorious in the war
the enemies are about to make with him. We can then read in *The
Penitence of Adam:*

> *"When you go out of the Garden, guard yourself from slander, from
> harlotry, from adultery, from sorcery, from the love of money, from
> avarice and from all sins. Then, you shall arise from death, (in the)
> resurrection which is going to take place. At that time, I will give you
> of the tree of life and you will be eternally undying."* [77]

We see here the first instance of the *Tzohar* being replaced with the
Torah, how the Law is entering the world as a compass to show the road
toward the *Tzohar*. The recommendation is to avoid falling into corruption. By performing *tikkun*, he will rise and again be given the angelic
food and rise in the Body of Light.

The greatest symbol for this mystery is found in the toad, the grand
symbol of resurrection. Not only is the toad contemplative and patient,
but it also enters within the earth to rise with the birth of the Sun.
Also worthy of mentioning are the various legends speaking about
the golden or reddish stone that can be made available by engaging in
certain rites that mimic the sacrifice of Abel and Iesu, the anointed. The
release of the golden seed or stone reveals the transition of the Body of
Light from the body of flesh in the form of a seed.

In the mysterious relationship between the circle and the square
or the circle and the crossroad, we find the astrological symbol of the

---

77   Michael E. Stone (trans.), *The Penitence of Adam* (In Aedibus E. Peeters, 1981) 17.

planet Venus. The astrological symbol of Venus represents the effect of the celestial dew upon Na'amah and Lilith, for instance, whose resurrection is, in form, proper to Venus, their *Malaz* or star. The association with Venus, the hexagram, and the number six as total perfection is also found in the symbol of chrism. The basic symbol of chrism or anointing is a vertical axis overlaid with a Saint Andrew's Cross. In total, it consists of three axes and six points and is, as such, like the caduceus in form and function.

The toad, like the symbol of chrism, speaks of the relationship the angel of anointments and restoration, *Heli,* has with this mystery (see Chapter Twelve, "Seth and the Golden Seed"). The anointment of the forehead with the oil of olives under the watchful eyes of *Heli* is the single act that restores and quickens the golden seed within. In this, the grace of the celestial dew unfolds. It is the act that initiates the process of resurrection into a body of light, in the ways of Abel, Iesu, or within the many ways of the toad.

TEN

THE DELIVERANCE OF ADAM

*"I am the rose of Sharon, and the lily of the valleys. As the lily
among thorns, so is my love among the daughters. As the apple tree
among the trees of the wood, so is my beloved among the sons.
I sat down under his shadow with great delight,
and his fruit was sweet to my taste."*

—SONG OF SONGS 2:1–3

In the *Book of the Penitence of Adam*,[78] we find several mysteries related to
fall and redemption expressed and explained. We also find the essence
of *tikkun olam*, "restoration of the world expressed." In this text, both
the importance of *mitzvoth* and mystical forms of *tikkun* are presented,
reveled in purification, contemplation, and prayer. The text introduces
us to the first couple immediately after being exiled, and they are clearly
confused concerning the cause of the punishment. They are in complete
distress, hungry, and ceaselessly crying. The despair grows to such pro-
portions that Eve asks Adam to kill her, to which he responds: "How,
indeed, can I do you any evil, for you are my body." [79] This comment
indicates that the notion of unity was not lost at this time.

---

78 This book has proven difficult to date, but its content would suggest it was writ-
    ten sometime between the third and seventh centuries. The book itself presents a
    complex Kabbalistic zymology on the nature of fall, redemption, and restoration.
79 Michael E. Stone (trans.), *The Penitence of Adam* (In Aedibus E. Peeters, 1981) 1.

The search goes on, and the hunger grows. The food outside the garden is alien to the couple; not only this, but the food outside the garden will turn them into beasts. As such, their hunger is caused by the avoidance of becoming beasts, and they are actively working against a further fall from their perfected Edenic state. As the hunger grows, Adam suggests that they engage in penitence or *tikkun* for forty days. For Eve, this period will be shortened by six days, as she was created on the sixth day, on the same day as the Sun was created. The practice consisted of standing silent in the middle of the running waters with the water up to the neck.

Adam went to the river Jordan for his *tikkun* and purification, while Eve left for Tigris to make penitence. The motive of the penitence was to appeal to God and be given the angelic food of light from the Garden. Adam engaged himself in prayer while he stood in the river Jordan, and as he did, "All moving things which were in the Jordan gathered to him and stood around him like a wall. And the waters of the Jordan stopped at that time and became stationary from their flow."[80] Adam knew that a motion contrary to perfection was started, and his *tikkun* aimed toward making the river flow back. We see here the true mystery of going against the flow, which is actually a turning of the flow from its natural course of cultivation, a change of the bestial nature upward toward the angelic, back to Eden.

While Adam and Eve were separated, Satan came to Eve in the form of a cherub of light and told her that the penitence was over. She left the river, and "When Eve came forth from the water, her flesh was like withered grass, for her flesh had been changed from the water, but the form of her glory remained brilliant." [81] For three days, she lay at the shores of the river with Satan and was then taken by him to Jordan, where Adam revealed to her that she had been seduced. In despair, Eve left toward the west, and there she gave birth to Cain.

Naturally, the birth of a child begotten through communion between Eve and Satan is one of pain. Adam heard "the weeping of his flesh" as Eve gave birth to Cain. At this stage, Adam had concluded his penitence, and an angel of God instructed him on how to cultivate the land. The angel Michael went with Adam to Eve, where the birth of Cain was witnessed, and the angel said: "For you are Cain, the lawless one, who will be destroyer of the good and living, you will plant adultery,

---

80 Michael E. Stone (trans.), *The Penitence of Adam* (In Aedibus E. Peeters, 1981) 2.
81 Ibid. 3.

bitterness and not sweetness."[82] Adam then took Eve and Cain to the eastern part of the land, and there, *Gap'at* or Abel was born after Adam once again engaged himself in penitence, this time of abstinence, prior to fathering Abel.

The power of abstinence is well described in the form of Shiva, which we shall return to shortly, but for now, remark on how abstinence and contemplation have the power of generating *tapas,* a creative light or flame. Ganapati represents the product of abstinence and contemplation, born from the dirt his mother washed off in the waters. Not without importance, Ganapati's mother is *Parvati,* whose name means "Lady of the Mountain." If we continue this theme according to the description in *Ganapati Upanishad,* where he is described as the living being and given the mantra *tat tvam asi,* "thou art that," in light of his beheading, then the function of Abel gains quite a different dimension in being the consciousness that must be sacrificed in order to establish the consciousness of Seth.

This might be revealed in epitaphs such as Ganapati being associated with Brihaspati, the Primordial Brahma in the Rig Veda. Likewise, he is married to Siddhi and Raddhi, or success or power and prosperity. In here lies the mystery of completing the lesser mysteries and transcending to the greater by fixating the spirit and causing the matter to fall off, like dross and dirt from the body while standing in the river of contemplation. The acts related to Adam, Abel, and then Seth mark the necessary steps that must be taken in order to turn the poles" and thus go against the flow.

There is also an angelic host overseeing the transmission of this seed of light by Michael, Raziel, and Metatron, who are the angelic guardians of the golden seed. When the first couple ate of the forbidden fruit, this caused a rupture, and the union of royal and sacerdotal power was torn apart, making Adam able to restore the union of the royal and sacerdotal function through his seed. But still, the shattering led to a gradual alienation and suppression of the sacerdotal seed as the royal seed underwent its terrestrial corruption.

In a startling passage in *The Penitence of Adam,* we see also what kind of race was born by this seductive action between Satan and Eve: "I fell asleep and I saw in a night vision that the blood of my son Abel was entering the mouth of our son Cain, his brother, and he drank his blood without mercy. Abel beseeched him to leave a little and he did not leave

---

82   Michael E. Stone (trans.), *The Penitence of Adam* (In Aedibus E. Peeters, 1981) 6.

any, and did not hearken to him, but drank his blood completely." [83] We are not only seeing the revolting origins of vampires and lycanthropy here but also how the hunger or the appetite toward the terrestrial guides the natural course of the rivers of the world away from the Garden. The flow leads away from the garden, and with distance grows confusion and the confused hunger. Cain is, as such, representing the seed corrupted by appetites and terrestrial power, the natural flow that manifests in the antinomian rebellion focusing on suppressing the sacerdotal seed.

It is this process that was instigated with Adam's death because the poles must be completely overturned in order for the restoration and unification of the shattered vessels to be accomplished. This is again made possible by another angelic descent meant to result in a pregnancy. This time by Michael, who says on behalf of God: "I shall give you Seth, who is like my first image, and he shall show all memories through me, and not only what you shall say to him." [84] What actually is taking place here is a return to the sixth day of creation where the Sun, represented by Michael, again allows the "grass to shine"; light returns to nature in the form of Eve, redeemed to be the "grass that shines with glory."

This green light is the light of Khzer and is the prophetic light of *tasawwuf*. It means that within the "Book of Nature" herself, the lost light can be retrieved. This is why the lesser mysteries focus on the terrestrial Eden, while the greater mysteries transcend the material in favour of the true metaphysical realm of being. We see here how Michael, the Sun, brings back the *Tzohar* in the shape of the golden seed that gives birth to Seth. And it is Seth who will bring the remedies that cause Adam's death to become the seeds of perfection because, as suggested by Michael upon Adam's deathbed, Seth is perfection: "Go to Adam your father, for his times will be full in three days and you have to see many wonders in heavens and upon earth and in all luminaries which are in the heavens." [85]

What is taking place here is a precise outline of the mystery that Saint Paul expresses to the Corinthians, where he speaks of that which is sown in corruption resurrecting in glory.[86] The angelic seed that impregnates is important to notice. Likewise, the Orthodox Chassidim doctrines indicate that the direction of the woman's desire can bring a particular

---

83   Michael E. Stone (trans.), *The Penitence of Adam* (In Aedibus E. Peeters, 1981) 7.
84   Ibid.
85   Ibid. 11.
86   For a more complete discussion see Chapter Nine, "The Body of Light."

angelic potency to shape within the womb. In the case of both Abel and Seth, the direction of the desire was one of mercy and contemplation, a desire directed upward to the City of the Sun. In the case of Cain, Eve was lying at the shore of the river where she was one with nature, and her body had turned into grass. The seed was undirected by Eve and sown by the instigators of discord and bitterness.

The angelic importance is also present in the conception of Mary with Iesu. Here, the angel Gabriel announced the pregnancy. Properly, Gabriel is the angle of mercy, revelation, and resurrection. In Islamic lore, he is called "Jibrail" and is the angel of truth. Mercy is the *Sephirah* opposite of Martial and rebellious *Din*, namely *Chesed*, the divine face opposing the bloodlust of the children of Cain. Iesu was the third redeemer in the line of Adam, in a way, the sum of his penitence, the fulfilment of God's promises to Adam.

Upon Adam's death, God said the following: "But I will turn their rejoicing into sorrow, and I will turn your sorrow into rejoicing. I shall make you the beginning of rejoicing and I shall set you on the throne of him who deceived you." [87] It is also in this instance that Eve, who had taken on the custom of Adam and engaged in acts of prayer, contemplation, and penitence, was greeted by angels, "and all the angels assembled before her, each according to his rank. Some of them bore censers in their hands, others bore trumpets and others bore blessings. God came to the Garden and all the plants [moved], and all the people who were with Adam fell asleep. Only Seth alone, the virtuous one, was awake, according to God's direction." [88] This naturally refers to Seth being spiritually awake and, therefore, sent to the Garden of Eden and granted access.

When Seth entered the garden, the two trees had grown together, and Michael gave him three seeds that he was to place in Adam's mouth. These seeds from the intertwined trees of Life and Knowledge were revealed at certain instances of prophetic revelry through time. From one of the seeds grew the burning bush, where Moses entered into communion with the fire. From this bush, Moses cut his wand, which, upon his death, was placed in the Ark of the Covenant. King David was said to have planted this wand or staff, and it grew into the tree that Solomon cut down to make the pillars of the temple, *Jach-in* and *Bo-az*. The tree cut down grew up again and was used to make the cross of Christ.

---

87   Michael E. Stone (trans.), *The Penitence of Adam* (In Aedibus E. Peeters, 1981) 19.
88   Ibid.

The three stages caused by the three seeds are a reference to the Great Triad of Man, Earth, and heaven and describe the stages of restoration caused by Adam's penitence that led to him becoming the possibility of deliverance. With Adam's death, what is known as the mysteries of the poles and the secret of its reversal is unfolded in mystery. The reversal of the poles that Adam's death restitutes commenced when Adam consumed the forbidden fruit. In Kabbalistic literature, this is referred to as "the shattering of the vessels," where the unity of light is shattered, and a process of reversal and restoration is simultaneously started.

Adam must first die, be veiled in the linens of light, and given to the Earth before the restoration can begin, in the same fashion that the natural flow must be completed before the reversal of the poles can be accomplished. It is from the shattering of the vessels that the mysterious *Sephirah Da'at* enters the world. This *Sephirah* has, in Western perceptions, been seen as the divine principle of knowledge, and the most dislocated and erroneous ideas have been derived from its location and function. The original meaning of *Da'at*—or, more correctly, *Leda'at*—rightly refers to knowledge, but it is manifested in the function of the mind that identifies what is perceived. It is the knowledge as it attaches itself to what it contemplates or perceives.

Da'at is, as such, the faculty that forms personality and can do so both by incorporating celestial and infernal perspectives in its creative reasoning. It is common to see *Da'at* as a bridge, a rainbow bridge, that links heart and mind; if so, it is the portal between thought and action. The quality of knowledge *Da'at* represents is the active establishment of personality; it makes the abstract material. As such, it represents an important factor in the lesser or royal initiation, represented by the royal wardens and knights, the *Kshatriyas*.

The concept of *tikkun* was established as a consequence of the *shevirat ha-kelim*, or the shattering of vessels, and is the sacerdotal activity focusing on uniting the shards of the Tzoharic light by prayer, meditation, and ritual. By the sacerdotal work of restoration, the reversal of the poles is accomplished. By *tikkun*, the distance from the *kilkul*, or damaging powers, is made greater in this reversal of states into their primordial order. *Tikkun* itself can have a variety of different interpretations, all of them interesting, and of these especially are the words *to fix* or *fixate* and *to establish*. In particular, *to fixate* is interesting, as this would reveal the alchemical work of restoration at hand.

The fixation of the spiritual will naturally lead to a putrefaction of the body, as a fixation of the body leads to an annihilation of spirit. By the coagulation of spirit, the world, *olam,* is restored as the poles turn, and we head toward the last judgment, where the living will be torn from the dead and the dead from the living. *Tikkun* is clearly a reference to Genesis 1:7 and 8, where the *olam* was established and "it was good."

Plato saw the good, the beautiful, and the true as terms designating the One—the original state of transcendent purity and unity, and we can conclude that it is the unity that was, from the beginning, the famous Golden Age that is spoken of. These three Platonic references also lead our attention to an angelic emissary of Metatron, *Yofiel,* meaning "God's beauty," who was the angel who executed the exile of the first couple. Yofiel is also known as the *Sar ha-Torah,* or the "Prince of the Law." That he is an angel associated with Jupiter also tells us that this was the exact moment when the reign of Saturn, the Golden King, ended, and the Law or Torah was established.

There is also a small section of the *Hekhalot* that is referred to as the *Sar Torah* tradition. These texts are mostly concerned with obtaining a relationship with Yofiel so that he can bestow great knowledge, magical skills, and a great capacity for memorization—and, by this, make the successful practitioner into a great rabbi. The location of these texts within the *Hekhalot* does signify a relationship both to Raziel and Metatron, as revealed by its contents, focusing on communion, divination, and forms of prophetic activity. What is important here is that these texts focus on the Torah as a gateway to the mysteries and thus suggest a contemplative and almost magical exegesis to be used in order to understand the truth being the Torah—which is, of course, the *Tzohar.*

Here, we even see a procedure of reversing the poles by creating a counter-movement within the fallen fold of selfish magical activity where the goal is to re-enter the terrestrial Paradise. This is clear by the two main practices: to memorise the Torah and then use it for contemplation, and the other is the use of wine. For instance, one of the key practices, referred to as opening the heart, instructs in the need for purification and how one then, in a state of purity, will take a cup of wine, recite a specific psalm over it seven times, and drink it. This will then open one's *leb,* or heart.

In general, the texts contain several instructions using prayers, incantations, and contemplations—often together with wine. The focus is in each and every text on how the practitioner must be wise and conduct themselves wisely in order to be worthy of the revelation of the secrets. For this is the end goal of these texts, the revelation of divine secrets, to go beyond the law and to its source, in itself a form of *tikkun*. *Tikkun* is, namely, the cornerstone in what has been referred to as the Enochian and Luciferian traditions.

The famous section in *The Book of Enoch*, where the angels under the leadership of Shemyaza seek out women and teach them the secrets of heaven, is often seen as a Promethean act. But clearly, there is nothing Promethean about this fall, rather a direct effect of the terrestrial Paradise becoming dislocated from its centre—in the same manner, this leads to the dislocation from the celestial centre by angelic forces literally falling out of order.

Some commentators have seen the fall invariably as being one of bringing forbidden secrets of heaven to humans. Yet others have highlighted the unnatural sexual encounters between the *Grigori*, or watchers, and humans. As we have mentioned, the word *Da'at* was used in Genesis 3 to refer to sexual union, and this is occurring here as well. That angelic beings' sires children is not an abomination per se, but it is the particular type of union that gets problematic. *Da'at* indicates a separation; it is a faculty entering Kabbalah in the thirteenth century and entering the world with the shattering of the vessels. *Da'at* is, as such, the acceptance of fragmented perspective, the very power that drives humankind today to exalt their personality or personae, dislocated from the City of the Sun, the Celestial North.

Enoch himself walked with God for three hundred years, and he suffered amongst his fellow people. His revelation is one of restoration. In order to understand the powers of restoration, it is important to understand the powers of corruption. Actually, his book reveals how the "mingling of casts," so typical for our time and age, reveals a predominantly disinterest in restoring the sacred sacerdotal centre. The lesser, i.e., the royal mysteries, have become the end of the entire initiatic journey. It all begins and ends with the material, with the recognition that the transcendent or metaphysical is no longer intact. The natural acceptance of thought leading to action is gone as the rebellion, from the beginning, has gradually usurped tradition and thus reversed the poles completely.

ELEVEN

THE DEATH OF ADAM AND THE MYSTERY OF GOLGOTHA

"Now I, the perfect forethought of all, transformed myself into my offspring. I existed first and went down every path. I am the abundance of light, I am the remembrance of fullness."

—*THE SECRET BOOK OF JOHN*

The Syriac apocryphal text *The Book of the Cave of Treasures* is usually ascribed to the Mesopotamian Saint Ephrem of Edessa (d. 373), even if the texts available to us appear to have been written by some other Syrian holy man in the same Nestorian school as Saint Ephrem around the year 600. *The Book of the Cave of Treasures,* together with another Syriac Text, *The Book of the Bee, The Book of Adam and Eve,* and its Greek rendition known as *The Apocalypse of Moses,* are texts that provide us with the inner mysteries of Golgotha, or Calvary, the place of Jesus' crucifixion and death. As the Gospel of John 19:17 (ISB) says: *"And he bearing his cross went forth into a place called the place of a skull [Κρανίου Τόπον], which is called in the Hebrew Golgotha [Γολγοθα]."*

The skull at the centre of the hill of Calvary is the skull of either Adam or Abel. These texts, as well as the Clementine *Kitab al-Magall,* point out how Shem and Melech Tzedek retrieved the body of Adam from the ark of Noah and were led by an angelic star to bury Adam in the place where the serpent's head had been crushed when man had fallen. This place, Golgotha, then became the new sacred centre of the

Earth after the disintegration of the Garden of Eden, naturally placed either slightly off-centre in Jerusalem or outside the city walls, proper for the dislocation of the sacred centre and its axis that happened with Adam and Eve's exile from Eden.

The Book of the Cave of Treasures (hereafter known as *BoC*) also elaborates on the building blocks of Adam. He is not only made from *adamas*, dirt, and blood, but God gathered a grain of all significant elements in the creation, such as heat, moisture, ocean, earth, air, and so forth. These materials were brought by the Angel of the East, Muriel. *Muriel* derives his name from "myrrh" and is associated with Cancer and an angel of solstice, or the gate of men. This connotation he holds with the solstice gate of June is important as it is Muriel who becomes the angel of death and solitude, Abbadon, in the apocryphal text *Enthronement of Abbaton*. After leaving this body made in the triune image of God and assembled by all these forms of cosmic dust to gestate for forty days, Adam received the divine breath, and as the *BoC* says:

> *"God formed Adam with His holy hands, in His own Image and Likeness, and when the angels saw Adam's glorious appearance they were greatly moved by the beauty thereof. For they saw the image of his face burning with glorious splendour like the orb of the sun, and the light of his eyes was like the light of the sun, and the image of his body was like unto the sparkling of crystal. And when he rose at full length and stood upright in the centre of the earth, he planted his two feet on that spot whereon was set up the Cross of our Redeemer; for Adam was created in Jerusalem."* [89]

After the fall from Grace, we find God first informing Adam that he will send his son, who will redeem him, and through the son sojourning in a Virgin and taking on flesh, he will be able to return. God then instructs Adam about how his body should be prepared upon this death, namely being embalmed with myrrh, cassia, and the mysterious resin "stacte," which might be galbanum. Adam's body should then be guarded in the cave in Mount Hermon until an event that will cause his grandchildren to be expelled from the mountain. Adam's body is then to be brought with them and will then be buried again in a place guided by stars and angels; this place is "the centre of the Earth" because it is by lodging the body in the centre of the Earth that redemption is made possible.

---

89   E.A. Wallis Budge, *The Book of the Cave of Treasures* (Cosimo Classics, 2005) 72.

So, we see that early on in the narrative, after his and Eve's expulsion from Eden, Adam is told about a second expulsion, but he is also informed that his body will be buried in the mountain he was expelled from. This means that somehow, a perfect being would again be born in order to accomplish this. It was on the slopes beneath the mountain that Eve became pregnant and gave birth to Qayin, or Cain, and his twin sister, Qelimath. Not long after that, she gave birth to another set of twins, Hâbhîl, or Abel, and Lebhûdhâ. Some accounts, such as in the *BoC,* reverse the sisters and state that Qelimath was the sister of Abel because Cain and Qelimath were also married and begot offspring; hence, the question of incest was probably questioned by the composer and commentators of these Syriac texts.

Once Abel's death by the hand of Cain was done, we find Adam and Eve mourning for Abel, leading to the hundred years of penitence in the river Jordan that led to Adam and Eve, in a moment of regaining perfection, made the birth of Seth possible.[90] The *BoC* tells us: "And then Adam knew his wife again, and she brought forth Seth, the Beautiful, a man mighty and perfect like unto Adam, and he became the father of the mighty men who lived before the Flood." [91]

And indeed, we see here that somehow Seth is tied to the Nephilim, which we shall return to shortly. Seth, who, like Adam, was glowing in splendour, was told about his father's funeral rites. Upon Adam's death, Seth, together with his children, Ânôsh, Kainân, and Mahlâlâîl, brought Adam's body to the Cave of Treasure after a period of mourning lasting 140 days. Seth and his children ascended the mountain again, and in doing this, they separated themselves from Cain and his progeny. As the *BoC* says: "Thus they lived in that mountain in all purity and holiness and in the fear of God. And they went up on the skirts of [the mountain] of Paradise, and they became praisers and glorifiers of God in the place of that host of devils who fell from heaven." [92]

When Seth died, it was his son Ânôsh who made the funerary rites for his father, but this time, it also came with an oath Seth took from his son as he was dying. The oat was that his people would never, "by the blood

90   *The Book of Jubilees,* Chapter Four, on the other hand, states that Seth married his sister, four years younger, yet we might also speculate if he was not also born with a twin sister—and wife—Azura, and that the absence of the twin sister is more to affirm the Christological motive playing itself out in the person of Seth.
91   E.A. Wallis Budge, *The Book of the Cave of Treasures* (Cosimo Classics, 2005) 35.
92   Ibid. 37.

of Abel, merge with the children of Cain."[93] His son swore this oath, and until the death of Mahlâlâîl's son, Yârêd, the immovable race did stay at Mount Hebron, where they had access to Eden. With his death, it was only Enoch who remained on the mountain, and he was, in the manner of Melek Tzedek, taken to the Empyrean realm or Jerusalem on high by the hand of God (just like the prophet Elijah would be later on).

Hence, we see here the theme of Melek Tzedek playing itself out in grace and mystery as it would suggest that from Seth, and until Elijah, we find his progeny taking the shape of the seven stars in Ursa Minor, with the seventh and most important being Polaris, the guiding star of the three Magis, the star of Seth.

In terms of the importance of the golden seed of Seth, the *BoC* states that only three patriarchs remained in the mountain. These were Methuselah, Lamech, and Noah. All the others had left the mountain to mingle with the children of Cain. Another factor of great importance is that it is most likely that the peak of Mount Hermon, Ardis, is where the Cave of Treasures was, and it was either the gateway to Eden or found central in Eden. It was on this mountain, the sacred centre of the Earth, the point that tied Earth to heaven, where the fallen host fell.

If we look at *The Book of the Bee, The BoC,* and *The Ethiopic Book of Enoch,* it appears that before marrying the daughters of Cain, the fallen host was living in communion with the children of Seth on Mount Hebron. *The Book of Enoch* and the *BoC* speak about how the sons of Seth that went down from the mountain were leaders and mention some of these leaders to be the following ones: *Semyâzâ,* the commander-in-chief, *Urâkîbarâmê'êl, Kôkabî'êl, Tâmi'êl, Râmu'êl, Dân'êl, Zakîlô, Sarâkuyâl, Asâ'êl, Armârôs, Batraal, 'Anânî, Zakêbê, Samsâwe'êl, Sarta'êl, Tur'êl, Yomyâ'êl,* and *'Azâzyâl.*

This gives quite an interesting dimension to who these fallen angels were and what an angel was considered to be. These texts would suggest that nothing corrupted the light of an angel in itself but that the division between a fallen host and a holy host was about being in its destined place, perhaps a *felix culpa,* but nevertheless, from bringing light into matter, theodicy would happen, as would the seed of entropy. If the angels were living in communion with the children of Seth, who was the perfected one, "his face burning with glorious splendour like the orb of the sun, and the light of his eyes was like the light of the sun, and the image of

---

93   E.A. Wallis Budge, *The Book of the Cave of Treasures* (Cosimo Classics, 2005) 37.

his body was like unto the sparkling of crystal,"[94] would this suggest that Seth and his progeny maintained and retained an angelic status?

What appears to be the case is that when the fallen host and the children of Seth went down from the mountain, they fathered an offspring who was called "Nephilim." *Nephilim* means "fallen ones," and rabbinical commentaries on Genesis 6:4, such as those by Aryeh Kaplan, translate *Nephilim* into "Titans."[95] These observations will impact the ideas about Titans and Olympians, about the "Elder Gods," and the "Gods of Time and Law" in interesting ways.

It might also suggest the great possibility of this mixed or fallen seed, be it angelic or Sethian, by genetic necessity and spiritual logic also fused with the seed and memory of the children of Cain. If we see the legacy of Noah's three sons, Shem, Ham, and Japheth, it might look like Shem was the one who managed to bring the seed of the immovable race through the deluge. Ham, on the other hand, became the forefather of Cush (Africans), Mizraim (Egyptians), and Canaan; Japheth became the father of infamous children (and tribes) like Magog and Tubal. In the *BoC*, the elevated position of Shem, who, together with Melchizedek, took Adam's body under cover of night, guided by an angel, to find its resting place. The full account reads as follows:

"And when they arrived at Gâghûltâ (Golgotha), which is the centre of the earth, the Angel of the Lord showed Shem the place [for the body of Adam]. And when Shem had deposited the body of our father Adam upon that place, the four quarters [of the earth] separated themselves from each other, and the earth opened itself in the form of a cross, and Shem and Melchisedek deposited the body of Adam there (i.e. in the cavity). And as soon as they had laid it therein, the four quarters [of the earth] drew quickly together, and enclosed the body of our father Adam, and the door of the created world was shut fast. And that place was called 'Karkaphtâ' (i.e. 'Skull'), because the head of all the children of men was deposited there. And it was called 'Gâghûltâ,' because it was round [like the head], and 'Resîphtâ' (i.e. a trodden-down thing), because the head of the accursed serpent, that is to say, Satan, was crushed there, and 'Gefîftâ' (Gabbatha), because all the nations were to be gathered together to it."[96]

---

94   E.A. Wallis Budge, *The Book of the Cave of Treasures* (Cosimo Classics, 2005) 52.
95   In *The Living Torah* (Moznaim Publishing Corporation, 1981) 14.
96   E.A. Wallis Budge, *The Book of the Cave of Treasures* (Cosimo Classics, 2005) 61.

It is of interest that Shem decided to bring Melchizedek, the trace-less prefiguration of Melek Tzedek, the King of Righteousness, who surfaces again in Genesis 14 as both king of Salem and priest of El Elyon.[97] Melchizedek is the one who blesses Abram through the sacrament of bread, wine, and blessing, which becomes the turning point for Abram when he becomes Abraham and the father of all "Abrahamic faiths." *The Apocalypse of Moses* states that Cainan was the father of Melchizedek, while other sources suggest that his ancestry is either a mystery or that he is a descendant of Shem. As we have seen, this would, in either case, refer to the presence of the golden seed of Seth. Also, in the case of both Shem and Melchizedek, it was the archangel Saint Michael who appeared and guided them to this very place, the centre of the Earth. Here, they laid down the aromatic body of Adam, fashioned a coffin, and prepared wine and bread as offerings along with prayers when the body was placed at the centre of the Earth.

This would suggest that the first body in every cemetery would, in mystical ways, represent Adam, and through this first burial, we will have access to everything that comes after, almost like how sacred time repeats itself differently from secular time. Just like the feast day of a saint, it recurs every year on their death. With the first one buried, the centre of the Earth is established, and this centre of the axis between the Empyrean and infernal is also resurrected. In this, through the offering of wine, bread, myrrh, galbanum, and cassia, we can gain access to the cave of treasures through the mystery of Golgotha.

---

97 *Elyon* simply means "the most high," so this "most high" might refer to the Phoe-nician Zydyk/Zedek/Tzedek, equated with the Roman Jupiter, who, together with Melchi or Malik, becomes King Jupiter.

TWELVE

SETH AND THE GOLDEN SEED

"Thou art from another race, for thou art not similar.
And thou art merciful, for thou art eternal. And thy place is over a
race, for thou hast caused all these to increase;"

—*ALLOGENES*

Seth is, in the Gnostic text *Allogenes,* referred to as a "stranger." And strange he is, along with his message, in a world suffering from the effects of the inversion of the poles, a world where base desires have been exalted and where the celestial and supra-natural are rapidly evaporating. His gospel is the gospel of a stranger, someone from outside of the familiar lands and terrains, from outside the beast consciousness of the fallen world. Seth is the seed of light that Adam managed to rescue from corruption by dedicating all his life to making penitence. He did this in order for this particular seed—the other seed, or golden seed—to be upright and perfect. It is from the perspective of Seth that the mechanisms and functions of the fall are realised on their original premises, in harmony with traditional teachings from all over the world. Here, we will give a presentation of the basic themes of the Sethian mythos as it is related to the function of Cain—and we must begin with the fall of the watchers.

The fall was instigated by Shemhazai, or Samyaza, and his active power *Asa'el,* or *Asael,* whose name means "made of God." The fall led these angels to become *hâ-satâns,* literally, "accusers." The first of the fallen consisted of two hundred attending angels who descended on Mount Hermon and instigated their hegemony over humans. The fall caused a cosmic disruption that generated a movement and dislocation of the world axis. By distorting the poles, they also caused a shattering of the vessels of light.

This is illustrated in the consumption of the forbidden fruit, an act that generated a fraction in the divine unity and threw shards of the *Tzohar*, the primordial light, into the world of matter outside the Garden of Eden. This knowledge that Adam and Eve gained upon eating the forbidden fruit was a dualist perspective. By being thrown out in the house of the Moon, they ventured into an eternal night where they became more and more like beasts, their appetites being turned toward the terrestrial.

According to the *Book of Enoch*, their original mission was reassigned to be one of cultivation and spreading of their seed. Hybrid creatures, like the Gibborim and the Nephilim, saw the light of day as corrupted seeds of men, and angels sought each other in unity. Further, in the *Book of Enoch*, it is told that the angels were stars who fell, and thus, they are both the star and prisoners of the same star. With this fall, stellar malefica entered the world. As such, if we look at *The Book of Jubilees*, chapters four through seven, the fall consisted of the watchers who were assigned to uphold uprightness, and judgment fell from their place. They fell out of order, so to speak, and became crooked and judgmental. This dislocation was made visible in the unruly nature of their children, be they Eliud's, Anaqim, Nephilim, or Gibborim, all of them forms of existence that *Yalkut Me'am Lo'ez*[98] considered to be "living abortions" in the sense of beings that were counter to the natural order.

This short recapitulation would indicate that we have two themes or two myths here that customarily are seen to be parts of the same motive. On the one hand, we have the myth concerning the seduction of Eve, and the other concerns the angelic descent in the form of the fall of the *Grigori* or watchers. What ties these two motives together is temptation and lust. It is about "knowing" the other, which, in conformity with Genesis 3, often indicates sexual relations. The fallen angels are said to have been tempted by the daughters of Cain, who walked around with "heavy makeup" and "exposing their genitals."

---

98   A commentary on the Torah by Rabbi Yaakov Culi (1689–1732).

The attraction thus consisted in beautifying the human form and carnal desire. The angelic bodies of fire were turned into matter, and this transition against the natural order generated offspring, like djinns. These bloodthirsty angelic half-breeds, whose souls were all fiery, survived the flood, but not in their corporeal and hot bodies, but in their spirits. They became the host of malefic and hostile spirits.

In the myths of the fall, we also see what happened to the primordial light, the *Tzohar*. As a consequence of the fall, the *Tzohar* was shattered and fell. It fell into matter and became, like the sensual flesh, an object of lust and temptation. As the desire became motivated by nefarious attention, light and lust became equally subject to desire, with a complete disregard for its natural hierarchy. The desire turned downward was the error, the direction of temptation toward flesh and matter, and the exaltation of bestial life was the effect of the fall. It was literally a fall from above downward, from the City of the Sun to the Palace of the Moon. Essentially, this tells us that the human condition is largely subject to these forces. The element of redemption consists of the shards of primordial light spread all over the world.

Even if these shards of light are often appraised without discrimination, given the terrestrial condition, they also serve as points of restoration. Since the shards of light were spread all over the world, the work of restoration is, in the same way, found to take place all over the world. Since the fall is largely confined to a limited perspective, the one found in the Palace of the Moon—or the perspective of humans as terrestrial beasts, the prophets of restoration will necessarily hold a different perspective. This perspective is encoded in the mystery surrounding Seth and the golden seed.

Seth was not born by carnal desire but a hunger for the restoration of the *Tzohar*. The penitence Adam performed in Jordan and that which Eve performed in Tigris enabled them to bring forth the golden seed. They made a return to the waters of life and beginning because, before anything else, there was only water. Water is *Shekinah*, the divine presence. By seclusion and emerging into the waters of life, they entered the bridal chamber of *Achamoth*, the mother of the divine seed, and made the transmission of the golden seed possible. We might say that their sight was restored, and they could clearly see their position in relation to the City of the Sun, the Garden they had left.

This was a celestial perspective, as was reinstalled with Seth, a focus on the polar centre from whence the divine law emerged, and upholding the Golden Age was restituted. The overall condition was a fall into matter and darkness, as explained in *The Hypostasis of the Archons*. This text tells how Samael, "the blind one," tried to rape Eve, but she managed to escape. Consequently, Samael begot Cain with her shadow. This is the birth of the condition restricted to the Palace of the Moon. Eve, upon her penitence, turns into nature and *Zoe*, significantly meaning "life." In similar ways, another text in the Nag Hammadi Library, *On the Origin of the World*, tells us how the rape of Eve's shadow led to the birth of seven children, who oppose the seven children of Allogenes, Seth.[99]

From this illusory opposition—illusory because it is born from the belief that the Moon is the only divine luminary—the *choikoi*, or "material ones," are born. The battle then focuses on how to seduce the *psychikoi* to turn toward matter so they will not go outside the Lunar Palace. The children of Samael engage in a great work consisting of sowing confusion in their souls. In all this, a large part of the children of Seth, the *pneumatikos*, maintain contemplation at the sacred centre, unable to feel the temptation of falling from the City of the Sun to the Palace of the Moon.

The battle is one concerning corruption. The uncorrupted seed ascends in the face of temptations. But here, we are also introduced to another crucial element, which touches upon the legacy of the children of Cain and their role in relation to Seth. It is a subtle and overlooked element concerning how the golden seed conquers corruption. This is done by resistance toward confusion and following the silent voice of the anointed seed, which paves the way toward the sacred centre, the Polar North. This is accomplished not by being satisfied with the walks of the journey and its dwellings but by questioning its station. There are many waymarks of the road toward the polar state.

We see here the actions of the celestial dew and how the golden seed is transmitted and waits in a state of rest, awaiting moments of quickening. These moments are always signified by a turning away from temptation or aggression. Even quickened, the golden seed survives uncorrupted by escaping the aggressive temptation of Samael and, in a similar manner, the seed. If we turn our attention to traditional witch deities, such as Lilith and Na'amah, a profound secret takes shape.

The uncorrupted seed was also transmitted to Norea, Seth's wife, by a rescue operation told of in *The Hypostasis of the Archons*, where Eleleth

---

99 James M. Robinson, *The Nag Hammadi Library* (Harper One, 1990).

watches over her. Interestingly, *Eleleth* is, in Aramaic, *'illith*, meaning "the tall one," an Irin or Watcher appointed to ensure the transmission of the seed to the elect. Na'amah's transition into Norea was taught to her by *'illith*, who gave her the secrets of the tetragrammaton, the word used to create. In this context, it seems that the word that was used to create also serves to restore. Again, we see the same movie as in *The Hypostasis of the Archons*, where Shemhazai, or Samyaza, tries to rape her. By uttering the secret name, she was turned into Esterah or Ishtar, the Star, Venus.

Here, we see a motive of death and replacement repeating. Not only this, but we also see the mystery of reversals as the poles were turned in *'illith's* epitaph of *Tzaphoni*, "the northern one." This is seen, in perspective, as turning into a Janus-faced mystery that ties *'illith* with the mystery of the Two Johns (the Baptist and Evangelist) as a "holy spirit." Her watchfulness of the northern terrains simply suggests the dual consequences of choice and how she is the entrance to the celestial north and nefarious south at the same time. She offers the change in perspective at the same time as she accommodates the choice made.

Ham, the son of Noah, the progenitor of the Egyptians, was said to have found his dynasty through the worship of Bileth (also known as Beleth, Gaap, or Balath) and Ashtoreth, burnt sacrifices to these deities or, most likely, to Baalath (Lady) Ashtoreth, who is under the rulership of solar Paymon in *The Book of Offices* (although more commonly it is Amaymon and southern spirits).

Concerning this, author Crowhurst, in his book *Stellas Daemonum*, suggests that Beleth and Gaap might speak of the syzygy of Norea and Seth, who, together, gave way for the race of the elect.[100] The angel of annunciation of this race and its becoming was Eleleth, the spirit of sagacity that shares etymological roots both with Lilith and Beleth. Crowhurst also points out that in Epiphani's fourth-century treatise *Noria*, Norea is given the name of *Eleleth*, a name which is an elision of "Naamah" or "Lilith the Younger" that in this form has been said to be the spouse of Azazel and Samael. This might be an encoded mystery related to the more mysterious dimensions of Eleleth, the wife of Noah, daughter of Enoch, decedent of Cain, as well as the wife of Seth, mother to the immoveable race of pneumatics that touches a realm in common for Lilith and Seth.

---

100 David Crowhurst, *Stellas Daemonum: The Orders of the Daemons* (Weiser Books, 2021) 123.

The seed represented by Seth, the golden seed, is subject to anointing and purification. Stroumsa, in his exegesis *Another Seed*,[101] is taken in with how Seth was baptised in Jordan by Micheu, Michar, and Mnesinous. This baptism was watched over and sanctified by the angels Yesseus, Mazareus, and Yessedekeus. This purification replicated the penitence done by Adam and was later performed by Iesu Christo, leading to the establishment of the kingless seed. The seed is kingless because it is the royal seed of perfect priesthood, and, as such, it is the role of priest and king in the manner of Melchizedek, which is the constitution of the golden seed. After his purification and anointment, Seth had his dwelling assigned to the White Mountain, Ardavan, or Charaxio, which is also Ararat—the Mountain of Victory. The victory is naturally the restoration of the sacred centre, the renewal of the City of the Sun.

The motive of the golden seed leads to interesting conclusions in the spiritual doctrines of Martinez de Pasqually, as presented in *Treatise on the Reintegration of Beings*. First, the nature of the fall is identical to exile. It is a state that occurs by being closed off from the vision of light. It is a condition where Adam and his progeny are made subject to all possible influences. The condition spoken of is one where the soul is caught in the matter outside Eden. The Body of Light has been forsaken in favour of a body of earth that needs cultivation. The fall means that it demands hard work to accomplish the return.

The exile made Adam and his descendants subject to a wide array of spiritual inclinations, thoughts, and feelings that all failed to rise from the spiritual centre in a dynamic unfolding. Rather, these impulses arose from everywhere in the circumference of creation. This disintegration and fragmentation were seen by Nimrod, and the Tower of Babel was an attempt to unify the world under the fallen royal perspective of the *Kshatriyas*. This was the second attempt to usurp the sacred centre and replace it with a false centre, the first being the attempt of the rebel angels, who preceded this pattern of rebellion. When humankind fell into exile, it caused a great vulnerability and sensibility.

In *The Apocalypse of Adam*, this was illustrated by the constant crying and sentiments of grave despair harboured by Adam and Eve. But Adam did not fall completely, not in the sense of falling into irrevocable

---

101 Brill, 1984.

corruption. Not only was Raziel providing ways of restoring the primordial state, but the angel of anointment, Heli, also supported Adam with the inspiration needed to restore the supremacy of the golden seed. By being the holy ointment divinised, Heli is also the angel of restoration, or, perhaps more correctly, the angelic power that reveals itself in the work of restoration, as in the three and a half years of Iesu Christo's mission.

As such, Heli is the bridge of golden *nous* that enables man to be turned toward the work of restoration. It was this spirit that anointed Enoch and then Seth. It was Heli who moved the blessing of Abraham's work through the hands of Melchizedek and restored the posterity of Abraham toward the path of reconciliation. As such, we see the golden seed working through its intelligence, Heli, in people like Moses, Solomon, Muhammad, Goraknath, and a host of other sages and wise ones, across time and place, who, with their message and actions, sought to restore the sacred centre.

As we have seen, Seth and his children were assigned the north; naturally, this is the spiritual north, the polar pole, while Cain and his people were assigned the south, the terrestrial and infernal pole. With the fall, the poles started to move, and the centre became dislocated. The use of the word *pole* is not accidental, as here we are speaking of an axis that connects the terrestrial and celestial. When the celestial centre becomes dislocated, this causes a similar dislocation on the Earth, and the axes need to be moved into its centre.

In fact, all of the questions humankind has today concerning injustice and malefic influences are explainable by resorting to the mystery of the turning poles and movement in general. The north and south were already assigned when Noah sent out the ravens that did not return. They found their kin in the southern lands and stayed there. This also tells us that the south represents a terrain lower than the north and also how it denotes a separation. The doves sent out returned with an olive branch, and thus, the mountain, al-Qaf or Ararat, the Mount of Olives, became the home for the progeny of Seth as it came through Noah's son, Shem.

Seeing the spiritual compass in this perspective leads to grave implications for the posterity of Cain in terms of their lineages' nature and their function. For here, a new motive discloses itself concerning the functions of Abel, Cain, and Seth. Abel must be seen as a pre-figuration of Iesu Christo. Abel presents himself as the first

sacrifice of restoration. By exposing himself to the accumulated powers of protection, as in the Martial *Sephirah Din,* represented by Cain,
three things happen. The earth is sanctified by the blood, Cain's anger
constitutes the necessary force for the poles to turn, and lastly, Cain's
act constitutes the nomadic road of reintegration for his people.

This is sealed in the divine mark given on Cain's brow. The light
of mercy literally marks his third eye. This means that Cain is given
the sight to find the seed, but at the same time, he is also given the
role of affirming the potency of creation, as we see in the role of Iblis
discussed by al-Arabi, for instance.[102] This same motive is replicated
in the relationship between Iesu and Iudas Iskariotes, which perhaps
exemplifies more clearly the dynamic that plays itself out between Abel
and Cain. When Abel gives his blood to the Earth, he is replaced by
Seth. He releases the golden seed for expansion into the Body of Light.

The same happens with Iesu upon Iudas' betrayal. This is the true
mystery of resurrection. It is a death to the corrupted matter and a
release of the golden seed by the powers that affirm the divine Mercy.
What actually takes place here are moments of restoration of the *Tzohar*
by the influence of Heli as Raziel's agent. Pasqually tells us in *Treatise
Concerning the Reintegration of Beings* that Heli was the one who taught
Seth about temporal creation, power, and spiritual authority.[103]

This theme of salvation and restoration also presents us with a
renewed insight concerning the triad of Father, Son, and Holy Spirit,
as it also reveals itself in the union of the two triangles. The down-
ward-pointed triangle of the past located Mercury toward the south,
but upon the slaughter of Abel, the triangle turned upward, and Mercury generated the caduceus in the form of a hexagram with a central
point. As such, these themes speak deeply about the union of the three
points into One, the point thus revealed in the tetragrammaton and
unfolded further within the Platonic solids until its final restoration.

Cain's mark has been subject to much speculation, from this being a
horn to it being a simple mark on his forehead. Symbolically, the point
and the horn refer to the same thing: a promise of restoration from the
point that reveals itself on the summit of the mountain of the upright
ones. It is a reference to the sacred centre. The road of Cain's restoration is

---

102 See William C. Chittick, *The Self-Disclosure of God* (State University of New
     York, 1998).
103 (The Johannine Press, 2001) 32, 41, 112.

found in Pasqually's explanation of the *Lathan,* the sign that, prior to the deluge, was given to humankind.[104] *Lathan* is popularly understood to be a comet, but naturally, this speaks of a flash of the *Tzohar* revealing divine presence and prominence. Cain and his people interpreted the sign as an impending catastrophe, while Seth's children saw in this a promise of restoration. This difference is found in the diverging perspectives of the two races upon the world and being. The seductive speech of the fallen angels led Cain and his posterity to believe that the Moon was the only celestial luminary. They were literally seduced to be kept in darkness. Since Seth and his children knew that the Sun was the celestial luminary giving light to the Moon, they held a perspective in conformity with the celestial order.

This lack of clarity generated confusion among the children of Cain, and it was this lack of clear vision that led Seth to forbid his children from marrying the children of Cain. It would metaphorically lead to the light being clad in darkness. This would result in a hindrance to Cain's restoration, hence the accursed wanderings as outcasts. That Cain was subject to divine mercy is also subtly spoken of in the incident when Boaz accidentally damages Cain's corpse and is punished for this. We might interpret this as an act of unintended anger from the righteous that works counter to the divine plan.

The restoration of Cain follows a very different pattern from that of Seth and his brood. The dwellers in the house of the Moon are subject to different rules than the dwellers in the City of the Sun. The Cainite challenge consists of exalting oneself and venturing to the divine lands outside of the Lunar Palace to realise the road toward the City of the Sun. Cain is blessed with vision and mercy, and the greater consequence of his divinely assigned task comes with the curse. When Cain murders Abel, he causes the mercy-blood to restore the Earth, the *prima materia* of humankind's mixed constitution. The restoration begins and must follow certain steps where the force of preservation and power represented by *Din* and personalised in Cain and Judas must be effectuated.

The curse is to be assigned a divine role aiming toward the restoration of the Earth itself, a role that enables restoration but at the same time induces resistance toward restoration, as the act itself is perceived as malicious. This also causes many devotees of Cain to interpret the *Lathan* in confusing ways. Mainly, this confusion is to exalt the act of

---

104 Ibid. 119.

murder, lacking the light that sheds understanding on the reasons for the murder. The Cainite legacy then becomes one of untamed rebellion and attempts to seduce people into believing that the terrestrial dislocated centre is the celestial pole, as in the case of Nimrod.

Cain's restoration is found in walking with the poles until the poles are turned into their original position. It is a walk, full circle, and takes one day. It is a desire for restoration into light, motivated by the mark of mercy and love that is taking place. At the same time, the corrupted state of the seed also leads to a continuous rebellion toward the sacred kingship, which is the power that makes the poles turn. But, at the journey's end, Cain will return to the grave of his father, and here he will make his grave wet with the tears of mercy, finally finding his road of restoration complete.

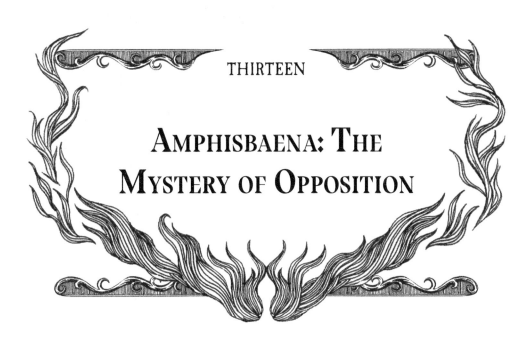

THIRTEEN

AMPHISBAENA: THE MYSTERY OF OPPOSITION

"If I take death into my life, acknowledge it, and face it squarely,
I will free myself from the anxiety of death and the pettiness of
life—and only then will I be free to become myself."

—MARTIN HEIDEGGER

The twain serpent coiled around the staff of Hermes, the caduceus, forming the two-headed serpent, expresses not only the essence of cure and curse but also the mystery of opposition. Where a modern perception tends to see this in the shape of thesis and anti-thesis, a traditional perspective will see how the one affirms the other. The mystery of opposition is often mistaken to be a mystery concerning good and evil in a moral and dogmatic sense; a metaphysical conception will see them as affirmations, just as Iblis affirms the total of possibilities in Allah's design. Certainly, Hermes, who is both the god of initiation and the psychopomp, does carry the staff of the *axis mundi* where he ascends and descends from the polar centre to the terrestrial centre, binding opposition along the tranquil and ever-upright axis.

We might see opposition as the terrestrial need for a measure based upon judgment, which ignites the illusion of duality, while the celestial measure sees the opposition as affirming the inherent unity of godhood. What on Earth turns into good and evil is, in reality, a balance between the celestial measures of giving and retaining, the inhalation and exhalation of creation. The Amphisbaena is the symbol of balance between the right hand and the left hand, as is the deeper mystery behind the zodiacal sign of Libra, and with the execution of temporal power in the terrestrial domain, this gives colour to Justitia. It is in this we find the route of sacerdotal initiation, the path of Seth and Hermes, where the forces that pull down, or the left—and what pulls into ecstasy, the right—obey the axis, supporting and affirming it.

Many misrepresentations of the Royal and Sacerdotal paths are found today, where certain insights tend to be relocated from their proper design and are used as a centre for generating an inferior design, often in error compared to traditional metaphysics and thus ape the truth in such ways that it becomes a distortion. Take, for instance, what is largely referred to as the "Luciferian Tradition" in contemporary occultism, which tends to focus on divinised misanthropy and exaltation of the left serpent of the caduceus, the one speaking of strength and power, running through the left pillar and the left side.

This *tamasic* power is on the *Etz Chaim* of Rabbi Luria and finds its most dynamic expression in the powers of *Din* or *Geburah*, the *Sephirah* associated with the powers of Mars. This is traditionally the abode of *Sar ha-olam* or Samael, "The Divine Poison," an angel of death. Talmud describes Samael as the guiding spirit of Esau, as the temper of Eve, and as the father of Cain. Some accounts see Samael as the angel whom Jacob wrestled with, while others say this was Metatron, and yet others still say it was Auriel.[105]

Uriel—alternatively, *Auriel*—meaning "Fire of God" is, in *The Testament of Solomon*, given a commanding function over the daemonic spirits in the treatise, and in *The Book of Enoch*, he is given dominion over Tartarus. He is said to be one of the two angels that were guarding the gate of Eden, most likely with *Raziel*, "Secrets of God." Uriel presides over penitence and repentance and is the angel of apocalypse

---

105 What is interesting about all these associations is their connotation with fire. We see this in Metatron as the pillar of fire that led Moses and his people in the wanderings of the desert and in Samael by his Martial temperance. It is additionally seen in Auriel by being not only associated with—and, at times, identified as—Pyriel but also in his importance in the alchemical works of the *Ordre Reaux Croix d'Orient* and allied French transmissions of gnosis focusing on the purifying powers of fire. This is also evident in Metatron's deep connection with Saint John the Baptist, both being spiritual agents announcing the arrival of holiness and divine presence, who baptized with fire and not water.

and vision. He was the angel who gave Ezra his visions in *Enoch I* and was the angel who gave the visions in *The Book of Revelation* to John of Patmos as he was the angel warning Noah about the deluge. He was the angel who aided in burying Adam and Abel, and he was the angel Jacob had to wrestle with to be granted mystical vision.

Milton, in *Paradise Lost,* says Uriel is a regent of the Sun, which means he is Hyperborean and comes from the north wind. He is also accredited to give alchemy and Kabbalah to the world, and in the *Midrash Aggadah Exodus,* he is described as descending to Moses and punishing him with flame in the shape of a burning serpent. Also of interest is that Uriel is the patron angel of Jerusalem and owns thunder, earthquakes, and the northern winds, hence why Hassidic sources describe him to be made from hail that could take the form of an eagle or a lion.

Finally, he is also the lion-faced angel in Ezekiel's chariot, affirming his association with visions, revelations, and divine secrets. His month is September, and his sign is Libra from the autumn equinox when the Sun enters the sign of Libra. His feast day is September 29, Michaelmas, which is the feast day of Saint Michael and all the archangels. Hence, we might refer to all these angels dealing with the divine light and revelation as "lucifers." At times, we also find the divine poison, the angelic servant, the blind Samael, responsible for choice in the heavens.

In Mesopotamia, the class of accusing spirits, *satanas,* was transposed on Samael's role as a divine accuser, a juridical function that gains importance in light of the scales held by Justice itself, denoting an ideal of balance between the powers of the left and the right. The balancing pole of Samael is Metatron, the angel of liberation. This would then indicate that Samael's role is one of restriction, seeing his role as an angel of death as one that brings cycles to an end.

Din is about severity, power, and protection—it is the abode of the third heaven where we find the doors to perfection and corruption. At the northern gate, the "northern one" will confront the pilgrim with the challenges of corruption—or by being poisoned. It is from these awesome powers of protection and restriction that the modern notion of a "Luciferian tradition" has shaped itself. This is a delusion in itself because Lucifer, "the igniter of light," has nothing to do with divinised poison as such unless he is equated with Samael's contrasting scale, Metatron, and the liberating effects of the light.

Lucifer took on these darker properties not only by subjecting him to a fall in accordance with Isaiah 14:12, but this misreading was later used by Saint Jerome and then again by John Milton in *Paradise Lost*, where Lucifer became the architect of pride and the leader of the fallen host. More properly, we would speak of the demon prince Lucifuge, "shunner of light," and not Lucifer in this role. Clearly, in modern times, a medieval error has become the centre for a tradition that deviates to such an extent from its rightful place that we are here speaking of what the French metaphysician René Guénon referred to as the "counter initiation" in his book *Perspectives on Initiation*.[106] The serpent of the left is broken off from the axis and is used to generate a false axis, and thus, illusion and fantasy follow from this organization of the compass.

This fall from the centre is thus used to exalt the fallen state, and humankind gains provenance by being untamed power and range, a warrior defending their self-construct against the threat of true tradition. With this "fall" from the centre comes a whole range of discourse where everything is painted in the colours of hellfire, tombs, and catacombs in a parade of necromantic and diabolic adoration—all in the name of Lucifer. Dualism arises from this, such as good and evil, moral categories, and, nonetheless, an illusory antagonism between Satan and his creator. Evil is nothing more than a judgment conferred in a terrestrial interpretation of *Din*, the sphere of power. By this sole focus on the left side and the dislocation of the serpent, a fall to Earth is accomplished, and the balancing power, mercy, or liberation is no longer seen as a complementary force to the left side.

The serpent has fallen from its vertical state to become a horizontal path of power ruled by temporality and, thus, a terrestrial centre alienated from the polar centre, the true north of perfection. What remains then is darkness, chaos, and power. Its distance from the axis generates an abyss of illusions where the *tamasic* and chaotic, the whole domain of the noble warrior, turns into profane shades of its divine origin. The power leads to pride and arrogance; it is like the heart, and the whole idea of mercy is infantilised as something weak and disposable. This is, in truth, the shadows the Sun cast, not seeing the royal stability of the Sun's fire—its cold shadow is embraced with passion, mistaken for power, not realizing that the Sun is the great giver of life and thus there is a turn toward the murky mystery of death and the shades created by the absence of the Sun.

---

106 Sophia Perennis, 1946/2004.

In truth, "shades" is a designation put in place as the influence of Samael in this fallen guise is the terrestrial and wholly profane shadow of the Sun. Not only this, but the left serpent, blazing within the mud of its fallen state, rejoices in its corporeality and calls upon ecstasy, not of the soul reaching to the mind, but from the body calling the passions to possess it with lust and anger, intoxication and rejection. It is a fallen paradox, a corrupted binary put in place where we find the horizontal serpent igniting its dark blood into its adulators. What happens here is that the adulators of the serpent of strength discard the true essence of the left side and reject the possibility of ennoblement that is accomplished through conflict.

Rabbi Nachman of Breslov teaches that conflict is not "evil," but its resolution might be.[107] Humanity as a microcosm possesses the left side as well as the right side and the central column—and, in the end, it is a choice concerning the way and measure humankind decides to utilise the powers residing on the left.

The left side represents poison, power, resistance, and strength, and the right side naturally represents its dynamic pole to generate equilibrium, blessings, healing, vision, and mercy. It is the forces of wisdom manifested in a loving vision. But alas, this serpent can also fall, and its horizontal path generates moralists, condemnatory pseudo-sages, dogmatism, and inquisitors. It is as though the serpent fallen on the right side sees themselves as holy warriors where their divine ecstasy is turned into crusades against an enemy generated by all their fears. At times, the ecstatic avenues turn into obsessions of purity, bordering on a heated dislike or even hatred for the body and all things terrestrial; the body is seen as a prison and not a medium for blessing and joy.

The caduceus, the staff of Hermes, his divine gift, was made of a golden forked olive branch. It was this olive branch he gained upon reconciliation with Apollo in bonds of amity. If we dwell on this relationship, we shall see how the mystery of opposition takes on the dimension of unity. Apollo was the patron of both the muses and the Pythoness in Delphi. As God of Arts and Prophecy, he possessed foresight. Foresight is the supreme Sethian gift, as seen in the case of Enoch and the prophets.

---

107 Rabbi Nachman, *R. Nachman's Teachings* (Breslov Research Institute, 1997).

Apollo also serves a dual role as healer and destroyer, bringing judgment and mercy. Perhaps it was this function that led Plato to refer to Apollo as "redeemer" and "purified" in his dialogue of *Cratylus*. His association with the Sun as Helios and later as Sol Invictus speaks loudly about Apollo representing the sacred centre, the priest-king of the City of the Sun. Yet another element is that his lovers were both male and female, and, quite frequently, these lovers are given names of flowers. Most famous is perhaps his intense relationship with the Spartan prince Hyacintus, as well as the metamorphosis of the nymph Daphne into the Laurel tree and Clytia's transformation into a heliotrope or sunflower.

He is also the God of medicine, an art which was transmitted to his son Asclepius in the form of the *Nehushtan,* or the serpent-coiled wand. It was the *Nehushtan* that Moses used to cure the Israelites upon being attacked by vipers. Apollo is also a God who judges severely any act of hubris, as in the story where the satyr Marsyas challenges the god to a music contest. Marsyas loses the contest, and as punishment, Apollo and the muses slay and flay him. All this established Apollo as a Sethian type, a priest-king possessing foresight, judgment, and mercy. He is both truthful and passionate, all in the right order, the very icon of the unity of opposition.

This opposition is, in reality, not an opposition. If we return to Kabbalistic doctrine, the *Sephirot* on the left (*Din* or *Geburah*) and the right (*Chesed*) are more correctly described as the *midat ha-rahamim* and *midat ha-din*. This means that we are speaking of the measure of mercy and the measure of judgment. The motivating influence of judgment is force and strength, while in the case of mercy, it is love. It is an interplay in creation between these powers, which are replicated in the human organism as the left and right arms.

Several proverbs speak of the importance of these two hands working together. The Talmud says: "The right hand accepts, the left hand rejects," which is similar to what we find in the symbolism of the hands in, for instance, Ifá and Vodou. The society of wise elders in Nigeria, the Ogboni, see the left hand as representing protection and restriction, while the right hand is the hand of generosity and blessing. Based on this simple observance, a complex order is developed that is the primary building block of Yorùbá social order and justice. These "measures" must then be mediated by wisdom, which means that what we call "evil" is simply an imbalance in our measure of mercy or judgment. It is a state born in the *Sephirah Din* and is a biased judgment. The gravest of all misinformed judgments are those we make about ourselves. This is why Apollo reacted so harshly to the display of hubris or misplaced self-importance.

Hubris is basically a form of misdirected pride, a judgment of one-self as superior to that of a god. Given the modern decay and how the loss of the sacred centre leads to the fissures in the great wall getting bigger and bigger, humankind tends to gravitate toward sensuality as it is embedded in flesh and earth alone. This causes a form of chain reaction where this attraction toward the left will reinforce itself the closer to the measure of judgment one is drifting.

In simple terms, we are speaking of an inherent imbalance. Sound judgment must temper our capacity for mercy unless we end up in mere sentimentalism. In the same way, mercy must temper judgment so we do not end up as ruthless warmongers lacking any form of discernment. The staff that connects the serpent of judgment and the serpent of mercy is the *axis mundi*, the pole itself that binds the celestial centre with the terrestrial. It is along this axis that the City of the Sun can be found on Earth.

Still, these two measures do tend to generate conflict, as spoken of in Ecclesiastes 7, 13, and 14 (KJV), which speaks about the natural order and the great design. "Who can make that straight, which he hath made crooked…God also hath set the one over against the other." The recommendation is to take joy in the days of prosperity, and in days of adversity, we should consider this mystery. In other words, the recommendation is to meet adversity with contemplation because, in those moments, the divine mystery speaks loudly in its movement and silence. What this actually tells us is that adversity is a moment of potential redemption.

These are the instances where *tikkun* can be exercised with the greatest effect. By not allowing ourselves to be dragged into the rising pulse of the raging *Din*, we engage in contemplation and works of restoration and go against the grain. This automatically pulls the force toward the centre. This is also affirmed in the curious thir-teenth-century work, *The Treatise on the Left Emanation*, by Rabbi

Isaac ha-Kohen, which suggests that the malefic powers are emanations from the principle of repentance. Thus, repentance is perhaps the principle leading to the emanation of the lesser palaces in the Palace of the Moon.

The caduceus is the *axis mundi:* the pole itself. But it is also the staff of *Tzaddiks* or sages, not only because the staff itself is the symbol of the leader of flocks, as in the shepherds' staff or the Bishops' crosier. The caduceus also symbolises the relationship between our *mazal,* or star, as in the royal sceptre. The wings speak of the volatility embedded in choice as well as the aerial nature of the mind. This is our angel and daimon surrounded by the two measures in equilibrium. It is a pulling of force and mercy into the central channel, the straight road of the children of Seth. It is the powers of Apollo in the hands of Hermes, and it is the point and the measure of its circumference.

FOURTEEN

Luz: Almond of Eternity

"My Companions are as stars. Whomsoever of them you follow, you will be rightly guided." When a man looks at a star, and finds his way by it, the star does not speak any word to that man. Yet, by merely looking at the star, the man knows the road from roadlessness and reaches his goal."

—Rumi

When Vasco da Gama entered the salty waters below the equator, he noticed a group of stars that were to be called the pole star of the south, the constellation we today call *Cruzeiro* or *the Cross*. But Gama did not allude to this name in the stars; he saw in them the *Mandorla*, or *the Almond*, which, for a man of the Renaissance, would suggest that he saw a celestial form of the *vesica piscis*. It was, for him, a halo in the heavens.

Toward the end of the 1600s, the *Mandorla* was, however, referred to as "the Cross." But still, under this name, the original intent was most likely kept in mind, as the Cross was surrounded by the halo of divine glory. In Semitic languages, the almond can be translated from *Luz*, a word which, in Latin, signifies light. We should also mention that Luz is, in both rabbinical and Islamic traditions, a name referring to a small bone in the spinal column that is said to be the root of resurrection.

The most common reference to Luz, however, is to the name of either the same town or a neighbouring town to *Bethel*, as told of in

Genesis 28 and 35. *Bethel* or *Beit El,* "the House of God," is naturally Salem and its terrestrial garden of peace and light, Eden. All these factors play a part in the mystery of Luz being a symbol of the Garden of Eden being represented by the almond. Most likely, Luz and *Beit El* were different names for the same city, Luz being its earlier name and the city where Iesu was born, then under the name *Beit-Lechem,* "House of Bread."

In Genesis 28:22, we find reason to see an association between bread and stone, the pillar of the house of God, the cornerstone of the temple. Alterations of names signify an alteration in meaning or a succession of events. In the case of Luz, we can see how the almond-shaped light is a reference to a gateway to the house of God, which gave birth to the "stone" by its relationship with bread. It was here at Luz that Jacob received the gifts of dreaming, had the vision of angels ascending and descending along the ladder, and fought with the angel, the typical signs of the presence of the *Tzohar.*

It is not only Luz that has been referred to as a "gateway to heaven," the original name of Babel was *Bab-ilu,* which means "gateway to heaven." While *Bab-ilu* turns into *Babel,* or "confusion," upon loss of tradition, we can also see a different route of manifestation in the transition from *Beit El* to *Beit-Lechem.* We see the process of solidification from oneiric ascent and angelic descent into how the four-squared stone is established in the temporal sacred centre.

This naturally carries a dual symbolism in a similar manner where *Janua Inferni* takes the place of *Janua Coeli,* and, thus, a reversal of symbols takes place. The reversal of symbols must be seen as the very symptom of tradition in the process of dissolution, and, in turn, the dissolution generates the mechanisms of redemption and restoration. What takes place is "the other" affirming the One; of course, it is this perceived "otherness" that brings on the dualistic confusion so common in modern profane perspectives on the mysteries. When the House of God becomes the House of Bread, we can also see the theme of the spiritual falling into matter necessary for the race of Seth to engage actively in the work of *tikkun,* or restoration, as detailed in Chapter Ten, "The Deliverance of Adam." It is in this mystery the meaning of *felix culpa,* or "happy fault," is encoded.

The similarities with *Bab-ilu* go even further as both *Bab-ilu* and Luz were royal cities, Luz once being the seat of Canaanite kings. Our mentioning of how *Janua Inferni* takes the place of *Janua Coeli* is not without significance concerning the mystery of the almond as a symbol both for secrecy and hidden or hollow vaults and caves. *Coelum*, literally a covering of the cavity, is similar to the function of the almond tree covering the gate to Eden, as the *Mandorla* covers the gateway to God in the constellation of the Cross.

Noting that the Hebrew word for "tomb," *kever*, is derived from similar roots, it provides new depths to the words of Iesu the *tzaddik* on the Cross, when he tells the man at his side that he will on this day come to *Pardes* or the Garden with him. The vault of the tomb is the womb of resurrection in "the Body of Light," as well as in the case of Seth, Melchizedek, Enoch, and others. What the garden and the grave have in common is their defined geography and restricted location as a gateway. The womb, the garden, and the grave thus serve similar restorative functions of renewal and immortality.

Guénon also tells us that Luz[108] is called "the Blue City"; blue as a sapphire, which does allot particular importance to the almond as the food of the prophets, yet holding the reminder that bluish tinctures of an almond scent are often poisonous. This is also detected in the flowering rods made from almond trees related to Jeremiah and Aaron. The Book of Revelations, 21:19, says that the second foundation of the New Jerusalem will be built from sapphire, and Lucifer was adorned by sapphires in the name of beauty, grace, and truthfulness prior to his fall.

In passing, it should also be mentioned that *Jambu Dwipa*, or the celestial islands looking at Mount Meru, is referred to as a sapphire, a relationship that generates the blueness of the atmosphere. The reference to becoming blue also carries relevance to Shiva in his form of *Nilakanta*, "blue throat," caused by Shiva drinking the *halahala*, the poison that was generated at the churning of the oceans of milk at the beginning of time. This reference plays strongly on the mystical properties of the almond, as milk and the deceptive quality of its scent and colour—yet the medicine and the poison do speak of the mystery of the *Amphisbaena*.

This grim poison was apparently something that had an amazingly aggressive effect as it stimulated the battle between the *asuras* and *devas*. Also, *Nila*, this dark, spatial blueness is a reference to the denser of the *Shaktis*, like Dhumavati and Bhairavi, both of them noted by

---

108   *The Lord of the World* (Coombe Springs Books, 1958/1983), 41.

their crimson-coloured scales and locations in the *Uttara* regions, more precisely, the outer or northern dwellings, providing identification with the dark blue of the *coelum*, the celestial vault, and the Hyperborean Pole. Interestingly, the city of Luz, according to a *midrash*, was reputed to produce *techelet*, a bluish dye used to colour tabernacles.

The poison Shiva drank can also be related to almonds by its scent, as cyanide venoms, found in bitter almonds, reveal its toxicity. Some nightshades (*Solanaceae*), like Datura, give away their toxicity with the same scent. As we see, the almond is the most proper symbol for Janus' dual function as the guardian of gates. Interestingly enough, the almond tree (*Prunus dulcis* or *Prunus amygdalus*) is in the same family as roses and is a close relative of the blackthorn (*Prunus spinosa*). Both provide white flowers and edible fruits, but the latter is armed with thorns that can poison the blood.

It was the almond tree that was used as the model for forming the *menorah*, spoken of in Exodus, and it was Aaron's almond rod in bloom that made his position visible as an elect amongst his people. We find the same rod occurring in *The Apocalypse of Zerubbabel*, where the angel Metatron announces the possession of Aaron's almond rod as a sign of gathering the scattered people of Israel and, thus, the re-instalment of the sacred centre. The *menorah* that was fashioned in Exodus was shaped like an almond tree, and here, we see the supremacy of the almond in relation to eternity, immortality, and the Golden Age.

The *menorah* was not only designed from one unit of beaten gold, but, as we know, the *menorah* carries seven lights, which are the seven planets. This leads us to realise that the almond tree was indeed the tree covering the entrance to the Garden as a symbol of *Janua Coelus*. From this, we might suggest that at the northern side of the garden, its relative, the blackthorn, would be guarding the northern gate, the thorns being gateways to the bloodstream of *Janua Inferni*. The presence of the almond tree in relation to prophets is also evident in Jeremiah 1, where the prophet beholds a rod of almond tree in the image of Aaron's rod. It is, therefore, the sign of the true Levite, the elect priesthood, who are recognised by their prophetic abilities. With this, we naturally understand what is at the root of the word *Kabbalah*, *Qibel*, the ability "to receive."

The Zohar tells us that the angel of death could not pass through the city of Luz, and this is interesting in light of the theme of resurrection by virtue of the little bone mentioned earlier, called *Luz*, which connects the spine and cranial vault together. Here, we find the ladder of heaven leading to the celestial vault, for it is not the simple meaning of the word *chakra*, "wheel," that expresses how the spine provides, by the nerves embracing it, a ladder of ascent and descent to the *coelum*. "Wheel" is also the meaning of *Ophanim*, the chariot of the prophets as they ascend and descend on the ladder of heaven in dreams and visionary rapture.

In *Samkhya* and allied philosophies, the spine is the ladder of the ser-pents' resurrection, the *Kundalini*, said to be resting at the base of the spine. When the serpent is awakened and called to rise, it will strike at the base of the skull and cause the celestial dew to flow from the *Sahasrara*, the gateway at the top of the skull. Herein is also found the mystery of Golgotha yet again. Most of all, we see here how the light coming from the gateway of heaven is made possible by turning *Janua Inferni* into *Janua Coeli*. True wisdom comes from the Hyperborean centre, the true Pole, not by ascribing the centre to a terrestrial garden dislocated from the celestial face that looks at it as the *dwipas* are turned toward the sacred mountain, the polar summit, Meru.

The almond tree, by guarding a hidden confinement of original purity, also gives associations to virginity and, through this, to the constellations of the Seven Virgins, the Pleiades, and to the Virgin holding a shaft of wheat, Spica. Mention should also be made to an Arabic epitaph of Spica, *Alarph*, which means "the gatherer of grapes." The grapes are related to the sacrament of wine and the supremacy of wisdom encoded in amethyst. This speaks silently about the mys-tery of royal priesthood and the importance of women holding "the sceptre of wealth" as the source of the blessings that activate divine power into divine presence, the *Shekinah* or *Matronit*. Amongst Arabic desert-dwellers, Spica was also referred to as *al-simak al-'azal*, meaning "the unarmed star." This name reflects her aloneness and distance from other stars. Her solitary, virginal, and unarmed position also tells us how much alike she is with Sophia and Norea.

This role is likewise proper, seeing that she is resting in the twelfth *nakshatra* under the guise of the stellar wisdom represented by *Chitra*, "the lamp" and "the pearl," establishing Spica as the Virgin of Light (*Luz*) and wisdom, a celestial mark of the original condition. In light of this, we shall also mention how, in Matthew 13, Iesu refers to the kingdom of heaven as a treasure of pearls and how, in the Book of Revelations 21, the twelve gates of heaven are also called pearls.

This clearly refers to the wisdom possessed by Seth as given by Raziel concerning the secrets of "the movements of heaven," namely the mystery and use of stars and planets. The relationship with being a lamp brings us not only back to the detailed descriptions of the almond-shaped lamp in Exodus 25 but also how God is said to be a lamp that lightens the darkness in second Samuel 22:25. More so, we find in the interplay between the light giving lamp the relationship between the *Tzohar* and the Torah or the starry splendour and the law in Proverbs 6:23 (KJV), "For the commandment is a lamp; and the law is light." The law spoken of here is certainly the secrets of heaven, of which the *Tzohar* is a shard.

FIFTEEN

MELEK TZEDEK
AND THE ROYAL ROAD

"There are no 'others.' What appears to be 'other than God' is
in fact foam upon the Ocean, forms manifesting meanings, the
Hidden Treasure displaying itself outwardly, sunlight upon a
wall. All multiplicity is the manifestation of Unity."

—WILLIAM C. CHITTICK

Melchizedek, or Melek Tzedek, is the mysterious King of Righteousness
that is encountered in Genesis 14, verses 18–20, and then later in Psalm
110:4 in the format of a prayer to the victorious one, as a remembrance
from the past that should inspire the model for the future king. Finally,
in the Epistle to the Hebrews, Psalm 110 is used in reference to Iesu
Christo. In Genesis, Melchizedek appears as the one who blesses Abraham with bread and wine after rescuing Lot from the captivity of the
four warrior princes who conquered Sodom. In the Babylonian Talmud,
Melchizedek is associated with—if not the same person as—Noah's son,
Shem. *Shem* means "name" and refers to the One.

What is curious here is that Abraham himself was a descendant
of Shem, and the blessing is thus a recognition of the exiled seed
returning to its source. In this meeting, we find the unification of the
seed of Seth by fall and restoration. We know that the descendants
of Seth can be grouped in two, given the fall of the *Tzohar*, the primordial light to the depths of Leviathan's oceans, and with this, they

also became a property of the children of Cain. This distribution is equally found in the pillars of the temple of Solomon, represented by *Jach-in* and *Bo-az*, speaking of "establishment" and "confusion." We know that the seed of Seth, as the world entered confusion, sought the peace (Salem) on the mountain but that some of them ventured down, intrigued with the daughters of Na'amah. We see here the effects of the *Tzohar* falling from its holders and becoming a part of the pedigree that came to foster the *Kshatriyas,* the warrior caste.

The progeny of Melchizedek is also spoken of in *The Second Book of Enoch,* where it says that he was born from the womb of Sopanima by Noah's brother or relative. Sophanima died, and from the corpse rose Melchizedek as a fully developed youth, endowed with "the badge of priesthood," which must be the particular glow or shine that Seth noticed upon at his birth. After forty days, he was taken by the angels prior to the deluge.

If we approach this account with some scrutiny and discernment, it is obvious that "the King of Righteousness" was born from the wisdom (Sophia) of the soul (*anima*) seeded by the "name" Shem. These two terms placed together, Sophia and *anima*, would indicate, in conformity with the writings of Ficino and Proclus, that the soul of this child was turned upward toward the realm of wisdom and divinity. By stating that the womb of Melchizedek was of this nature, it also suggests that he was of "another seed," the seed that had their attention turned toward the mind, eternity, and wisdom contrary to the progeny of Cain, who turned toward passion and territoriality.

In Genesis 9 (KJV), we find the tripartite progenitors of the human race in the naming of three of Noah's sons. Here, we also find the first curse after the deluge given to Ham because he witnessed Noah in his "drunken nakedness." Upon learning about their father's condition from Ham, the two other brothers, Shem and Yefet, went into their father's tent backward and covered him with a cloak in order not to witness his nakedness. Upon awakening from his wine-induced sleep and knowing what the youngest son had done to him, he cursed Ham, Canaan's father, and says in Genesis 9:26–27 (KVJ): "Blessed be the Lord God of Shem; and Canaan shall be his servant. God shall enlarge Japheth, and he shall dwell in the tents of Shem; and Canaan shall be his servant."

Here we find the seed of conflict talked about in the Hebrew Chronicles, and it is from Ham's son, Cush, that Nimrod came forth and constructed the tower of Babel. Likewise, several of the enemy tribes are descendants of Ham through Canaan and Mitzraim. Yefeth is the ancestor of Ashkenazi, but his immediate sons are Magog and Gomer (of which Gog might be a short form), as well as Yaval and Tuval, sons of Lamech, Cain's ancestor and murderer.

The similarities of names before and after the deluge are interesting in terms of their prefiguration and continuation, as well as the role the seed of Yefeth plays in this mystery. What we have here is a mixed seed, a cursed seed, and a perfect seed. The cursed seed represents the forces that rise at the end of cycles, its agents those who "reverse the symbols," the misguiders of the counter-initiation. As this is not enough, the Torah uses the following wording concerning the children of Cush, brother of Canaan, "Cush fathered Nimrod" in Genesis 18.

This is a repetition of the theme of violation ascribed to Noah, as we shall discuss shortly. What this violation consists of, in terms of forced sexual communion or simply a cross-fertilization between corrupted seeds, does not make much difference in terms of its essential meaning. The suggestion that we are speaking of here, a cross-fertilization, is further sustained in the name *Nimrod,* of which the root, *marad,* means "rebel." From a rabbinical point of view, a *marad* is not a simple brute but a calculated rebellion; it is not guided by passion but by wicked intent.

This wicked intent is to substitute the regal and celestial centre with a human mixture, as was the proposition in erecting the tower of Babel. It is also interesting to see that Nimrod's power, according to *Yalkut Me'am Lo'az,* came from Nimrod dressing the robe of his father, Cush. It was a hunter's cloak but renowned for its power and beauty. Nimrod's ability to gather people would suggest that Yaftes and Ham's accursed seed met in Nimrod spreading profanity to the world.

The sons and daughters of Yefeth, on the other hand, do represent the *Kshatriya*s, the warriors who rested in Shem's tent to protect the royal road and star. It is, therefore, the loss of objective with the gradual decay of the world that turns the warriors into a gang of brutes who lost their cause. Thus, the consequence of their mixed nature led to corruption, what we have elsewhere referred to as the choice occurring in the third heaven, where the crossroad lies between corruption and perfection.

It is, therefore, natural for this pedigree to feel accursed and thus feel a kinship with the accursed ones where the forces of Magog, who, under the leadership of the corrupt King Gog (also known as "Armilius"), starts the work of taking down the great wall protecting and supporting the regal centre. We also see here the establishment of a traditional society where the cast of warriors is established around the royal centre aided by a variety of people engaged in expansion and cultivation.

We might also address the curse of Ham and Canaan a bit more, as the mere observation of nakedness being sufficient to be accursed into slavery needs more explanation. Naturally, we have the element of pride in deliberately observing the *Tzohar* or the "nakedness of the father" as a reference to impurity arising from what took shape in Canaan's mind, namely to take advantage of the situation and gain dominion. The accounts vary from Canaan and his father Ham sodomizing Noah to Ham and his son castrating Noah. The act itself is actually of less importance than what the act symbolises, namely the overthrowing of the light and the violation of the sacred centre.

Yafeth, on the other hand, represents a dual function of nomadic warriors and progenitors of the world. Not only this, but King Cyrus, who ordered the restoration of the Second Temple, was a descendant of Yafeth, once again telling of the role this pedigree had in the sustenance of the regal centre. It is from this chain of events that the King of Promise, in the form of *Zerubbabel*, enters the royal road. This harmonises with Yafeth's name; we know that *yaft* means "expand" and that *yafah* means "to beautify." This would tell that the original mission of the warriors and noble casts was to expand beauty.

Shem, on the other hand, made penitence for the world, and after four hundred years, this resulted in the coming of Abraham; as such, the blessing by Melchizedek of Abraham was accomplished by an act of restoration made by Shem. *The Book of Jubilees* tells how Shem learned the arts of astrology, healing, and herbalism from Noah, a transmission only possible by the holders of the *Tzohar*, Raziel's secrets.

Noah's drunkenness should also be given some further attention because what is actually happening here is an excess of *spiritus*. Wine, being spirit: its grapes could further tie into the mysteries of Bacchus and Iesu Christo. Naturally, there is much to say about this mystery, but in this context, it is a message about warding sacredness. Wine is what Melchizedek gives Abraham with bread, as Iesu later does in order to seal his promise and legacy. This would suggest to us that, for instance, Tubal Cain was not purely a Cainite but a unification between the younger and older bloodlines and that some of the perfect blood of Seth was cursing through his veins.

What we see in the meeting of Abraham and Melchizedek is also how the *Tzohar* ignited a light in Abraham so he could father the Torah. We see here the interplay between the celestial and terrestrial Sun established as a point diverging in degree and location, speaking of an inherent unity between law and what prefigures it. This same motive is also inherited in the sharing of bread and wine, the bloodless sacrifice. This sacrifice is also at the core of the Vedic soma and, ultimately, is the sacrifice of the Golden Age, the terrestrial paradise.

This naturally places the acceptance of Abel's sacrifice and the rejection of Cain's sacrifice in a quite different light. What is actually occurring is that the smoke of Abel's sacrifice is finding its way upward, thus creating the vertical line, while Cain's offer is not rejected as such, but its movement is relegated to a horizontal axis. Thus, we are, in this mystery, speaking about human manifestation along the double axis we know as the cross. Consequently, this mystery of the double power, of the sacerdotal and royal, finds its form in the figure of Melchizedek, the holder of Janus' key and sceptre—or the keys of silver and gold.

We shall not dwell too much on this here but only mention that the mystery of *Janua Coeli* and *Janua Inferni* is what the mystery of Cain and Abel is concerning, as it also finds its format in the two Johns, the Evangelist and Baptist, and their respective dominion over the summer solstice and winter solstice. Again, the dual power is presented in its cyclical round. Jeru-Salem is, in similar ways, the terrestrial manifestation of the Salem, the peace guarded by Melchizedek, in the same way as the Torah manifests a timely representation of the *Tzohar*.

Melek Tzedek can mean both "king" and "angel of righteousness"; *Tzedek* is also a name of praise given to Jupiter as well as to sages. He is the *Allogenes*, "the stranger," who enters the design to affirm its perfection and revitalise the divine plan. In this way, Melek Tzedek prefigures Zerubbabel, yet again a stranger, who holds the royal sceptre in exile and promise.

If we turn our attention to the Élus Coëns, we find here a ritual or ordination of the candidate of the alliance to be an elect of Zerubbabel, where we see in the instructions that this ordination will exalt the Levite status of the candidate, and they will be referred to as "Ephraim." We see here again a reference to the merging and return of the wise ones, as this son of Joseph was, together with his brother Manasseh, the only one of Israel's tribes that went to Egypt and returned from it. The remaining tribes were confronted with a form of *mixis*, while Ephraim and his tribe returned from Egypt and Canaan, retaining their original purity.

Again, it is the theme of descent and return, the fall and redemption, the stepping into the world and exiting by the upright ones that are enacted. The task given to the elect of Zerubbabel in the *Ordre des Chevaliers Maçons Élus Coëns de l'Univers* is to "break the six arches and let the seventh be standing," which is a reference to the work involved in becoming a perfect one, in the manner of Seth. This is, interestingly enough, a reference to the fixed signs of the zodiac and the two luminaries, leading attention to the secrets revealed in the Royal Arch degree of Masonry. The elect also needs to engage in *jihad* at the bridge crossing the Euphrates, *Shetharboznai*, meaning "Star of Splendour," and refers to the *Tzohar*. In other words, it is a crossing where the elect engage in internal warfare against the *nafs* of the lower soul and corrupting forces to remain upright and not fall into the river itself.

This is the great battle on the bridge leading to the star, and it is only possible to accomplish by having made a connection with one's perfect nature—or one of the angels finding its reference in the *Shem ha-Mephorash*. By unsealing the secrets of six of the seven arches and thereby successfully crossing the river steps and passes in the manner of Zerubbabel, the elect is made into a knight of the East. Let us also comment that the name of this Masonic degree, "Royal Arch," is not without importance, as it is exactly this that is occurring.

With the establishment of the regal powers on Earth, the last arch becomes the first in the restoration of the Second Temple, and herein lies the mystery of Ephraim, the last that became the first. In general, Zerubbabel is like Melchizedek of a somewhat obscure pedigree, and there are not many sources commenting upon him. One is, however, the Book of Esdras the Prophet, which speaks about the same motives as those we have briefly commented upon in its fifth chapter.

What we find here is that Zerubbabel is already building the temple side-by-side with prophets. While building, the captains Tatnai and Shetharboznai approached them from the other side of the water and questioned their business. Even if the bridge here is replicated to be a captain, the basic meaning is still evident. *Tatnai*, meaning "gift," and *Shetharboznai*, the "Star of Splendour," approach and question Zerubbabel about his motives for the restoration of the temple, a confrontation that ends in a blessing. The blessing was given by King Cyrus, a descendant of Shem, who granted the resurrection of the Second Temple. We see the motive of a return to the centre accomplished by the legacy of Shem.

Zerubbabel is accredited with leading the Israelites out of their captivity in Babylon, and by laying down the foundation for the Second Temple side-by-side with the prophets, he also restored the Torah and the Prophetic Books, as mentioned in the ninth century by the Arabic historian Ya'qūbī.[109] Zerubbabel also had a daughter by the name of Shelomith or Shulamith. It was Shulamith that gave warmth to the aging King David, symbolically speaking of how the terrestrial power needs the warmth of the spiritual authority. This also makes sense in the little we know of Zerubbabel's father, Shealtiel, who was heir to the throne of Judah through King Jeconiah and, therefore, a predecessor of King David.

In the first chapter of the Book of Esdras the Prophet, we are also told about Zerubbabel's reputation. He was considered to be one of the wisest men in Persia due to a treatise on women and truth that he presented to King Cyrus. This would suggest a message of *Sophia*, "wisdom," being delivered to the king, and it also marks the vital, albeit silent, importance of women in this, our discourse of the invisible fire. Yet another thing that should be mentioned in these motives is how all this prefigures the relationship we find between Iesu Christo the King and Saint John the Baptist the Prince and herald. We see here the returning theme of sacerdotal and regal powers that are held and united by Melchizedek and Zerubbabel, being both from the line of kings (prefiguring David) and priests from the lineage that gave birth to Aaron.

But there is one more facet that leads to Zerubbabel being a priest and king in the same way as Melchizedek, and thus, prefigure Iesu. In the seventh-century treatise, the *Apocalypse of Zerubbabel*, we find a theme reminiscent of Enoch and Elijah's angelic journey and transformation. Here, we meet Zerubbabel, absorbed in contemplation and

---

109 Ya'qūbī, *Ta'rīkh* (Dār Ṣadir, 1960).

prayer, where he is taken to a river in visions. Further in this visionary rapture, he contemplates the restoration of the temple and is lifted to the city of Nineveh. Seeing Nineveh, he confesses his transgression, and the Lord tells him to go to "the house of filth." While he is there, he sees the Messiah in prison, and an angel comes to him. The text makes an identification between Michael and Metatron, which would most likely rest on the idea of Metatron being the angelic voice audible to humans. He is, as such, a sort of linguist of the angels.

Additionally, when the angel reveals who he is, we clearly see what transition we are dealing with. This angel is the same angel who guided Abraham and blessed him, the protector of Isaac, the angel who wrestled with Jacob, who guided Israel's wandering in the wilderness, and who destroyed Sodom and Gomorrah. This angel also appeared to Zerubbabel and gave him foresight, the very hallmark of possessing the fire of illumination that would reveal the inner dimensions of the *Tzorah*.

Zerubbabel is then given an apocalyptic vision of the end of days when the Messiah is released from his prison in a time of corruption and dispersion. After chaos and destruction, the Messiah will lead the upright ones to the gates of Jerusalem while God will stand on "the mount of olives." This divine presence will cause the mountain to crack open so that the people waiting at the gate of Jerusalem can ascend and thus end the exile. The mountain of olives is, of course, Salem, Melchizedek's kingdom, or Jeru-Salem, the city of peace.

Let us remember that the dove with an olive branch in its beak is still a symbol of peace, healing, and restoration, the Holy Spirit descending to establish peace. Likewise, olives, like grapes, thrive in dry soil and extreme weather conditions; as such, they are also a symbol of endurance and vitality. Naturally, the establishment of peace will, in a world suffering from decay and fragmentation in its distancing, form the sacred centre and will be met with revolt, as discussed elsewhere in this work.

The common theme of divine pedigree is found in Zerubbabel, Melchizedek, and Iesu. Some writers, like the Nestorian compiler of Biblical legends Solomon, Bishop of Basra, made this theme available in his *The Book of the Bee* in early 1200, an overlooked work that probably ended up in obscurity due to the popularity of *Legenda aurea* (*The Golden Legend*) from the same period. *The Book of the Bee* tells us about

Melchizedek, explaining that he had no natural parents and confirming that he was of the seed of Shem, who was the son of Noah.

This Syriac book adds one detail that is quite interesting, describing how Shem was told by his father to take care of the bones of Adam and how he was supposed to give Adam's bones to Mâlâh and Yôzâdâk, the father and mother of Melchizedek. This information is quite interesting as Yôzâdâk was the mother of Iesu, the person Zerubbabel restored the temple with in accordance with the Book of Esdras the Prophet. This would suggest a kinship, whether spiritual or by blood; in any case, our circle is closing around the seed of Seth and its transmission in the holders of two keys, the keys of hell and heaven, held by the priest-kings. The race descended from Adam after his penitence when he begot Seth, and in this landscape, the bones of Adam gain prominence as transmitting the structure of the particular wisdom Adam restored by his many years of penitence in the river Jordan.

SIXTEEN

PERFECT SOLITUDE

"The body is of one nature and appears in every form;
it exists to lead man astray."

—THE WAY OF HERMES, BOOK 13:12

The wise ways of Hermes the Thrice-Greatest are found within the many veils of timeless traditions all over the globe, where the same basic themes are retraced and reflect the same truths wherever they are found. The idea of solitude being descriptive of the purity of being at the centre of the self is found in traditional schools, preserving the mysteries in all points of the world. This solitude lies in the condition beyond qualities as expressed in the *Advaita* transmission stemming from the forest texts, *Agamas*, and then later the Upanishads. The three conditions of the spiritual seeker, their elements, and their effects are laid out in great wisdom in the form of tantric *yanas*.

Within the Perfect Solitude lies the Great Wisdom, which is beyond movement, that stillness from whence all is, and all rises. To be without "be-coming" is to be in the silence of the beginning. This is the all-encompassing "all-oneliness," to be "alone with the alone," to paraphrase Henry Corbin.[110] To "be-come" a harmony, replicating the harmonious

---

110 See Henry Corbin, *Alone with the Alone* (Princeton University Press, 1969).

perfection of the celestials, is to walk within the silence of Seth. The route toward the Perfect Solitude is amidst the many directions and follows all but is none. The Perfect Solitude is sometimes referred to as the "third condition," where the Sun and Moon join action and contemplation. In this, it becomes solitude as the priest-king realises that this state of perfection is beyond quality, and expansion becomes immersed in its stillness of origin.

These three conditions are replicated in the body and are revealed in the forms of attainment and direction the seeker displays on the path itself. These conditions and spiritual inclinations are found mostly in two expressions: the active path of the *ida* and what is also known as *Pitriyana*, the path of ghosts and death, where the warrior seeks to affirm their terrestrial being to ensure that the wheel of destiny is maintained for their repeated return in the terrestrial body. Rightly so, the path to the left is also the infernal inclination of the warrior or *Kshatriya*, which pulls downward and toward manifestation and matter.

Here, under the mutable and ever-changing rays of the Moon, the warrior seeks their own glory and allows that murky quality of *Prakriti* as it unfolds in the darkness of passion and surrenders to the animalistic nature. *The Kularnava Tantra* says that this is truly the consequence of the initiated to Shiva, that they become Shivas—but a genuine liberation will also open their eyes in such a way that they will be liberated from the slavery of darkness and realise the self. The challenge of the one who walks with Shiva is to turn all attention toward the body and indulge in the veiling of the senses in the intoxicating darkness of Shiva's mystery.

The active path is a path of body, and it is about armour and strength; it is about Mars venturing into the fields of battle and conquest. It is the general looking over the field in the moment of victory—and the breaking point is whether the general sees only themself or if they see the full circle. We might even speak about a form of fall or a further descent amongst the warrior seekers who go within the Earth and metaphorically establish the cosmic centre in hell. This will, in turn, generate a perspective with no horizon. It is the ultimate station of a *tamasic* disposition gone wrong. This is the husk of Shiva with the pole of death planted in its deadening eyes.

This is seen today in the unbalanced fascination with everything dark and demonic, for the appetite toward self-effectuation is resurrected upon lies and bitter dreams. It is seen in the selfish pursuits of power for power's sake, and it is seen in the shallowness of the mind—because the darkness indeed darkens the mind as it darkens the soul. This leads to a turn inward, where the landscape is lesser, and the lost warrior rides his inner landscape fiercely. All perversion, any dark alley of illusions and dreams, are evoked and become a part of the self-constructed webs of despair in the *tamasic* lands. This is, after all, the *Pitriyana* with all its restlessness, possession, obsession, and oracular grace.

It would suffice to look at groups of warriors throughout history and look at what happens when the material cause of protection ceases to be. Quite often, these groups tend to find a new target for the *tamasic* impulse, or they turn into crooks and thieves. Reverting the pole in this manner and creating the sacred centre within the darkness of the Earth will certainly not lead to the liberation or opening of the eye and self for the *Shaiva sadhaka*. This *tamasic* impulse is also seen in much of the modern rendering of dislocated Luciferian mysteries that solely occupy themselves with a specific act of Promethean aspiration. It is one of the clearest expressions of a non-traditional *tamasic* impulse, the antinomian path of self-glorification by veneration of a whole array of *tamasic* deities—or rather, deities understood as *tamasic*. These limited perceptions are born due to the lack of initiatic light.

The great secret of *tamasic* awakening lies in the reception of a traditional initiation so that the seed of true self can be quickened. Today, however, these antinomian ways are signified by pseudo-traditional initiations, absence of true connection with the spiritual centre, lack of lineage, and lack of spiritual virtue—instead, a limited and materialistic set of teachings are passed down, replicating and mimicking the eternal and Empyrean tradition. The consequences are that the initiation conferred secures and solidifies the *tamasic* shadows and ensures that the warrior will never see the light of self—thus, the person of courage and power becomes a misguided cancer that feeds on themself and sees enemies everywhere.

The other way, ascribed to the priestly caste and the divine ecstasy, is under the auspices of the Sun and the *pingala*, the quality of energy as it reveals itself in contemplative interest born by love and laughter—the spirit of inspiration, if you will. The red colour given to rajas signifies the *rasa* of blood and life and often reflects itself in attitudes of love and kindness, experienced as a form of holiness which, taken to the extreme, can ignite equal distortions as found riding the *tamasic* person—but opposite. Persons who cling to the form of the *guru,* who ceaselessly work toward assuming a material position amongst humankind, and those who depend on the acknowledgment of others to maintain their greatness are all *rajasic* people. It seems that the exaltation or denial of life and all its pleasures are all basic manifestations of rajas, also known as *Devayana,* the path of holiness.

These distinctions are also found in Western mystery traditions where they are commonly referred to as the left-hand path and the right-hand path, but in modern guises, which are often recantations, these ideas have often been given a quite different content and thus stray off from the perennial tradition as it recreates something altogether fallen and corrupt. Seeing how the *tamasic* currents were held by warriors in traditional societies mirrored on its antinomian ability to transgress in modern days where the only power holding a person back from progress is the person themself, quite often the *tamasic* person becomes a warrior without cause, purpose, or higher goal. The *rajasic* person tends to either become an icon of shallow holiness or a hedonist, clouding the lustful vision in ecstatic terminology.

Today, the right hand tends to signify a work of purity and holiness, while the left hand is a conscientious use of taboos to accomplish terrestrial empowerment. We might say that passion is what ties them together: the one by denying, the other by exalting. Certainly, the goal can be found in either of these ways, considering the traditional foundation is in order. But there is still a third way, the true way of Golgotha and the skull of fire where the Sun and the Moon shine from the eyes, but the path itself counts vertebrae toward its illumination in what is commonly called "the third eye."

This quality, *sattva,* the white ray, is the third condition. It is on this path that the black and red serpents of the left and right coil around in harmony to sustain the straight path of the upright; this is the path of the sages and saints. This is the path toward the Great Wisdom, beyond quality and the purity of being, where the true self rests in the ocean of peace and stillness. This is the state that unites the Sun and the Moon in a soothing fire that drives the snake upward to its cranial vault, symbolic of the celestial sphere itself. Here, the key lies in the transcendental, the supra-conscientious experience of a terrestrial person breaking through in the heavenly halls of silence where they are all alone in their solitude—but never actually alone. This state is often linked to dreamless sleep because here we find all possibility, un-manifest; it is the world of ideas and forms, the *mundus imaginalis*.

For terrestrial people, however, all paths start at the same place, in the terrestrial kingdom, where we all find the blessing of birth into life, and thus, we become possibilities manifested. We might see the "Devil" enter from the *tamasic* realms and challenge us, and we might blame him for his awesome ways of pushing us onward—or we can lose ourselves in denial and only seek what is good and deny the *tamasic* by fleeing from it. Neither is good.

Few *sattavic* people who flow within the marrow of *sattva* came to this perfect flow by the path itself. It seems likely that the left and right can equally motivate us to venture within *Sushumna*—again, given the conditions found in the initiation are real and possess the timeless virtues that enable humanity to go onward. The person aspiring to Perfect Solitude will recognise where they are coming from, for whether they are a sober or drunken saint, they can still be a perfected one. In the caduceus of Hermes, the *tamasic* and *rajasic* support and affirm the straight path while still being able to maintain distinct paths themselves. For the person seeking Perfect Solitude, the body can either lead to illumination or lead the seeker away from the light and into the Sun or the Moon.

While Parvati manifests the *tamasic* in the unfolding of *Prakriti*, Lakshmi unfolds the *rajasic*—but Sarasvati unfolds the terrestrial possibilities of the third condition. And how proper that *Sarasvati*, "the flowing one," rose from being a river goddess to becoming *Vāc* (meaning "speech") and the Divine Mind and, thus, Wisdom personified as the consort of Brahma. Her magnificent array is seen in the ways she manifests on her mount, either as a swan, such as in the *hamsa* mantra that brings peace, or as an owl, parrot, or peacock. This tells us that birds are the symbol of the third condition. It indicates that the word of creation, as found in her manifestation as Vāc, is at the core of the mystery of the sage.

The third condition is the coming into peace, where the celestial messengers, the birds, speak to the sage, like in the myths of the Holy Francis of Assisi. It is the peace arising in the silent lands after the rapture, the certainty of being. Unlike the body consciousness of the *tamasic* or the soul consciousness of the *rajasic*, the third condition is signified consciousness itself, the mind, like a quiet pond from whence inspiration arises. Sarasvati is the author of knowledge and speech, the inspiration that makes the soul turn into poetry and all things gracious and mindful. It was Sarasvati, in her guise as *Vāc,* who inspired the *rishis* or sages to think and recite their wise impressions and insights of the worlds into hymns and teachings. While *tamas* move into action, *rajas* generate a flight of all the soul's feelings into joy and meditation. The *sattvic* person will, however, be of a good mind, calm, and still in their constant inspiration from the divine abodes after the Moon-coloured, swan-rider of the many winds.

The three consorts follow in their qualities: Parvati-Kali in her ability to provoke our darkness so it can be annihilated; Lakshmi rests in the lotus of turmeric and gold, planting love, beauty, and virtue in us until the coming of Sarasvati, who gives liberation. This liberation is an invisible fire resting in the many winds. This is the Divine Mind, ever in flux, still, unresisting—in Perfect Solitude.

SEVENTEEN

RAZIEL'S SECRET

"O, you who dwell in these places, it is necessary for you to know those that are higher than these, and tell them to the powers. For you will become elect with the elect ones in the last times, as the Invisible Spirit runs up above."

—MARSANES

Behind written law, we have the timeless powers of which the law is a manifestation. This is the spirit-moving doctrine that, in turn, becomes dogma, and temporary reflections of the timeless are made solid for a brief breath of time. Books are born from vision and inspiration, guided by angels behind the veil of manifested possibility. All sacred scripture that provides law, be it al-Quran, the Holy Bible, or the Vedas, are timely manifestations of divine regality given to humankind in order to sustain the spiritual centre and landscape, given in proper and perfect spaces of time and land.

The law, to use Masonic terminology, is the book written by "squaring the circle." It is to relocate the divine light into a temporary solidity that establishes the Empyrean axis. The book and the law are, therefore, first and foremost, a stone, like the Kaaba or the mysterious stone of beginning amongst the Yorùbá, the *Oyigiyigi*. Raziel's secret is also a stone, the *Tzohar*, that inspired several texts and transmissions born from the primordial light. Raziel's secret is the secret of the book never written fully, but in timely parts, it is the wisdom revealed in visions and dreams, in the knowledge of the firmaments and the secrets of the hierarchies of the heavens. The book is the stone of primordial light, the visionary secret given to the golden seed from whence came the upright ones, the *Tzaddiks*. This book given to Adam and then later to Seth is referred to as "the book of generations" in Genesis 5:1. This book is spoken of in various sources, the *Yalkut Me'am Lo'ez, Midrash Tanhuma, Midrash Tehillim, Sefer ha-Aggadah,* the Zohar, and, of course, *Sefer ha-Razim*[111] and *Sefer Raziel ha-Malakh.*[112] The latter text talks about the names of God and the angels and is largely concerned with angelic and talismanic magic. The book says that it is about talismanic virtue, being an amulet in its own right. The book was also in popular Jewish beliefs thought to avoid disasters and kept as a house ward.

Sefer Raziel ha-Malakh tells of the transmission of the book from Adam to Enoch to Noah to Abraham, Isaac, Levi, Moses and Aaron, Pinhas, and so on down the generations. What the term "generations" means is encoded in the mystery of divine foreknowledge, the grace bestowed upon the holders of the *Tzohar.* It says both in *Sefer Raziel ha-Malakh* and in *The Book of Jubilees*: "God told the Prince of the Presence, 'Write for Moses from the beginning of Creation until my sanctuary has been built for all eternity. Then everyone will know that I am the Lord of Israel and the Father of all the children of Jacob and King upon Mount Zion for all eternity.'"[113]

As such, the book contains all the wisdom needed to realise the perfect design and recognise the mastery of the great architect of the world. This wisdom makes the sage perfect—and, being perfect, they will see only perfection. The account in *The Book of Jubilees* could also suggest that Moses, when he received the commandments, was lost in a visionary

---

111 This book likely dates back to the fourth century, and some commentators state that it should be of importance traditionally that it follows a different succession, that *Sefer Raziel ha-Malakh* was given to Adam and *Sefer ha-Razim* to Noah. This is, of course, a purely profane and linear way of seeing the succession of the *Tzohar* as shall be evident in the course of this chapter.

112 This text was first printed in Amsterdam in the year 1701 but is commonly ascribed to be compiled by the Ashkenazi Eleazar of Worms. A Latin translation was provided by Alfonso X of Castile (1221–1284) who also had *Picatrix* translated. The book seems to lean heavily on *Sefer Yetzirah* and Classical Greek magical sources, such as the *Greek Magical Papyri.*

113 *The Book of Jubilees: Or The Little Genesis* (A. & C. Black, 1902).

rapture, like Elijah and, later, Isaiah. The prophetic path is revealed in the tradition of Ezekiel, known as the *Merkabah*. Here, the work is related to the angelic class of *Ophanim*, wheels of fire that enabled the sage to enter into divine rapture where transmission was made possible and tradition sustained—the true meaning of Kabbalah.

We find in this tradition the throne of sapphire and the importance of the divine and invisible fire stemming from the *Tzohar*. *Merkabah* was later expanded upon by Isaiah's visions in the sixth chapter of his book, where the mysteries of divine rapture related to the seven heavens and heavenly palaces are detailed. What becomes clear is that Raziel is the angelic agent who enables the reception of the primordial light, and, as such, the prophet returns to the point in the divine design where light was created, the first day. The primordial light is, of course, different from the Sun; even the Sun is a reflection of the first light, and there is a difference in degree.

The Book of Raziel was given to Moses before the Torah. The Torah is, therefore, the manifested lawful matter from *The Book of Raziel*, a proper possibility within the divine eternity handed down in a specific moment of need. Sacred Law is a mirror of the Celestial Holy Law, as Dionysius the Areopagite tells us. Raziel is the holder of the secrets, whereupon Metatron and Jofiel, the *Sar Torah*, convey parts of the secrets in conformity with the receiver's spiritual estate (see Chapter Ten, "The Deliverance of Adam").

Sefer ha-Razim, one of the parts in *Sefer Raziel ha-Malakh*, describes the domain of Raziel's knowledge to be all knowledge celestial and terrestrial, and he reveals "works of death and works of life. Understand evil and good. Examine the periods and minutes to reveal periods of birth and death, and of affliction and healing. Interpret dreams and waking visions. Draw near battles and make peace in wars. Hold dominion by spirits and send forth."[114] An extended list of Raziel's domains, also recounted in *Sefer ha-Razim* in the translation edited by Dr. Morgan,[115] gives an even more thorough list of secrets of knowledge, stressing the need for humility as the *Sefer ha-Razim* expresses that these secrets are given in purity, which the Solomonic Tradition also states. For instance, in the first chapter of *Clavicula Salomonis*,[116] there are three points worth emphasizing.

---

114 In Savedow's translation (Weiser, 2000) 205.
115 Society of Biblical Literature, 1983.
116 In Skinner and Rankine (ed). *The Veritable Key of Solomon* (Llewellyn, 2009) 75–77.

The first point regards the use of confession, which is something the reader needs to perform prior to any operation. Sins are acts where we engage in a crime toward what is good and true. In other words, the moral colour needs to be discarded and seen in the context of sin as being about missing the mark, that it is about a deviation from one's goal and destiny. By presenting the confession, we are acknowledging human nature, that humanity is ensouled matter and, as such, often gets tangled up in the sensible world and thus makes errors caused by inferior judgments. It is far more precise to understand sin as acts and thoughts we engage in that counter our goal. When acts and thoughts counter the goal, it is recognised by drawing our attention to a host of unworthy consequences. For instance, rash judgments and bad advice are seen as crimes or sins due to their effect of disturbing our focus and drawing us toward an infernal activity.

The need for confession relies on the second point, humbleness. Humbleness is the capacity to consider other people's perspectives, and as the *Clavicula Salomonis* says, this is related to the gain of favours that are given to those: "who are humble in their hearts and who confess that they are upright only through homage to the Almighty."[117] The epitaph "upright" is, as seen elsewhere in this book (Chapter Twelve, "Seth and the Golden Seed"), a reference to Seth's legacy. It denotes the constitution of the *Tzaddik*, the wise one. The wise one also needs to possess a third factor, "courage born from a strong mind." The *Clavicula Salomonis* says about this: "A weak mind, being naturally inclined to create phantoms that never go away, will create an overpowering fear." In addition to these points, the author of the *Clavicula Salomonis* stresses the need for astrological knowledge "to be well versed in Astronomy," as the text says.[118]

In light of this, let us see in the *Sefer ha-Razim* what the domain of Raziel was and the succession of his book. The succession of Raziel's book, the Book of Mysteries, was given to Noah, who was the son of Lamech, the son of Methuselah, the son of Enoch, the son of Jared, the son of Mehallalel, the son of Kenan, the son of Enosh, the son of Seth, the son of Adam. It then ended up in the hands of Moses by the legacy of Shem. The book further comments on how Noah inscribed the secrets upon a sapphire stone. This can allude to a connection with the

---

117 In Skinner and Rankine (ed). *The Veritable Key of Solomon* (Llewellyn, 2009) 75–77.
118 Ibid.

Latin *sapientia,* "wisdom," which makes sense in a traditional context where the stone is connected to Raziel. Then, by an etymological route, it must suffer a corruption, perhaps based upon a similar perception.

The sapphire has a hexagonal crystal structure and is thus a stone, by structure, that speaks of Venus. The fact that it is found in all colours except for red tells us that it is related to Mercury as well. That the sapphire is never red suggests—or should we say, underlines—its relationship to wisdom as a power of mercy and peace, the red being the blood of Mars. The text itself inscribed on this sapphire stone is related to mastery of the investigation of the ways of heaven, and here, the importance of humbleness in order to give good counsel—or the mind being firm and thus capable of giving good advice—is mentioned again.

The lore disclosed in the book concerns, first and foremost, astrology. The nature of the seven heavens, the zodiac, the mysteries of the Sun, and the mansions of the Moon, as well as the fixed stars, are counted in this list of subjects. With these also comes knowledge of the names and signs of its presiding powers so that requests and prayers can be made to the proper authorities. The book says that this will suggest the proper time to perform wishes "of anyone (who comes) near them in purity."[119] Knowing the right timing would aid Noah in rituals of life (curing and healing) and death (funeral rites), in interpreting visions and dreams, and in pacifying war and arousing combat. It also gave the secrets that made Noah able to rule over spirits and demons and comprehend the songs of heaven.

Raziel also told Noah how to build the ark and thus secured its wisdom to be transmitted to Abraham and then to Moses through Isaac, Jacob, Levi, Kehath, and Amram. Noah had secured the treasure in a golden box, and it was in this way that it was revealed to Abraham. It was this treasure that made Joseph's dreams true and gave him the ability to prophesise the future, and it was this treasure that was hidden within the holiest of the holies during the forty years of wandering amidst wilderness and desert. It ended up in the hands of Solomon by Moses' successor, Joshua, giving the book to the elders and the elders to the sages who handed it down to Solomon. Moses himself rescued the book by elevating Joseph's corpse from the river Nile as Joseph was

---

119 *Sepher Ha-Razim* (Society of Biblical Literature, 1983), 19.

buried with the book. With the second destruction of the temple, the secret was retrieved by Zerubbabel and passed down to the *Tzaddiks* of the golden seed until our time and age.

From this, several important issues arise, and we shall address some of them as they relate to the office of Raziel, the angelic emissary who brought heavenly secrets to humankind. The first point is that these secrets are brought to wise and upright people from behind the *pargod,* the veil that separates the One from its possibilities and is the canvas where the preordained harmony has been told. Like people can have foreknowledge, the One as the source of the possibilities in the great design does possess the ultimate root that makes foreknowledge possible. It certainly is on this vinculum that we must understand and embrace perfection.

This secret is also disclosed in *The Book of Raziel,* and it is at this axis that we must understand the references to the pre-existence of the Torah or the immaterial and timeless pre-figuration of terrestrial law. Thus, here we find, by reference to the stone and the sapphire, the reference to the secrets given by Raziel as a treasure. This stone was no ordinary stone; it was a part of the primordial light that gave Adam the ability to see from one end of the world to the other. The stone the book was written upon was the light of foreknowledge and all wisdom, a remnant from Genesis 1:3, where light was created. It is this light that is the *azoth, eros*—the amalgam that keeps creation together. It is the *prima materia* of His design.

Upon eating the fruit that gave knowledge, the world was veiled in darkness for Adam and Eve. The light from the stone was lost, and the Sun dazzled their perception, albeit it was merely candlelight in comparison to the primordial light. The stone formed by the primordial light was kept by Raziel, who kept it until Adam had completed his penitence and thus gave it back to him. It was this stone that Adam gave to his son Seth, the first one of an uncorrupted race, the upright ones. This stone, this sapphire, is the *Tzohar,* the splendor or radiance of the One.

The Torah is, as such, a temporary manifestation born from the first light, the divine splendour presented in proper time, given the foreknowledge of the One. This jewel that provided the light for the Torah was given to Seth by Raziel. The secret is thus one of primordial light, and knowing this, the recommendations in the Solomonic tradition of being humble, confessing the terrestrial appetites, and being wise and upright become clear, as clear as candlelight growing out to reach the radiance of the Sun.

Looking at what happens with the possessors of the stone, we see that they are admitted into the Gan Eden, the third heaven where the crossroad of perfection and corruption is presented. Enoch, under the radiance of the stone, walked the garden for three hundred years and gained knowledge of astronomical cycles and the nature of constellations. His transmission, *The Book of Enoch*, is perhaps most famed for its account of the fallen angels. But within the greater horizon, the transmission of Enoch was no different than the missions of Seth or Iesu Christo, the mission of preservations of the light, as with all holders of the *Tzohar*. It was this light that guided Noah's ark, this light which was dim by day and bright by night, and the latter manifested again for Moses as the splendour of the burning bush and the pillar of fire that guided the exiled ones through their wandering and sojourn.

It is clear that the stone formed by primordial light gives direction. It is the insignia of the hieroglyph of the pole. The possession of the *Tzohar* has, therefore, been given to the *pirs, gurus,* or *shaykhs* of traditional wisdom. With Noah, however, the *Tzohar* took a different route when the ark landed on the mountain Ararat.[120] But alas, arriving at the summit of the mountain where transmission was possible, Noah made grapes, and angels instructed him in the art of making wines. In his drunkenness, he lost sight of the *Tzohar*, and it fell into the waters where the legacy of Cain assumed it. The retrieval, by Cain's bloodlines, was through being hidden away in caves beneath the mountain. It is from this event that the primordial light encoded in a stone that did not know the colour red was forged by the blacksmiths to serve their needs.

This was inscribed in *The Book of Raziel*, the knowledge preserved for the wise, where war could be ignited and the natural order distorted. We believe that the references to the mixing of the races of Seth and Cain were ascribed to the fall of the *Tzohar* being accessible to the race of Cain, and the light became a focal point generating the arts of spells and sorcery for terrestrial ends. And herein lays the secret of the fall.

Adam could read the book by holding the sapphire to his eye, and thus, the primordial light formed letters of fire (Shin). When Adam

---

120 A name that survived in the Solomonic traditions under the name *Ararita*, an acronym meaning "One is His beginning." One he is. One is his permutation.

engaged in the reading of the *Tzohar*, angels attended to learn the secrets, especially the wisdom of the 72—the *Shem ha-Mephorash*, whereupon the angel Hadraniel visited Adam to tell him that the stone was for his eyes only. The knowledge kept away from angels led to some angels falling from their appointed, and thus, they provoked the loss of the stone and its dispersal into the sea, where the book was rescued by the angel Rahab. Upon Adam's transgression, the book was again lost, and upon his penitence in the river Gihon or Jordan, Raphael restored his health and returned the book, and thus, it was given to Seth. This is the book mentioned in Genesis 5:1, the book of the generations of Adam.

Here, we have a complex angelic web, and the angel Hadraniel, spoken about in *The Apocalypse of Moses*, is associated with the flashes of light and the voice of the Lord. Then, in the *Sefer ha-Heshek*, he is said to be one of the 72 names of Metatron, creating a familiar likeness attributed to the role and hierarchy between Hadraniel and Metatron. He is an angel of fire set to guard the Easter winds. Interestingly, the *Anemoi,* or the Greek wind gods who announced the seasons, all of them depicted with wings, were given hymns by Orpheus and accounted for by Hesiod, but not *Eurus,* the *Anemoi* of the eastern winds.

In "The First Book of Adam and Eve," from *The Forgotten Books of Eden,* we read the following: "On the third day, God planted the garden in the east of the earth."[121] This would suggest that the east is the terrestrial gate of the perfected ones. Only with Seth would the east gate again be ventured through, and it became the gateway of the *Tzaddiks* of the golden seed. From the perspective of the Élus Coëns, humanity was seen as maintaining its powers of the mystery of the north, west, and south, but the east was the gate of redemption, reserved for the descendants of the Allogenes, the strange or other seed.

Yet another angel is Rahab, who surfaces later in Moses' successor, Joshua, who inherited the *Tzohar* from Moses. When Jericho fell, a sex worker called Rahab survived the fall of the city, and Joshua took her as his wife. From Rahab, Jeremiah and the prophet Ezekiel are descended, and she is the grandmother of King David. Looking at the nature of the angel of the sea, Rahab, and the later status of Rahab,

---

121 Rutherford Hayes Platt (ed.), *The Forgotten Books of Eden* (Alpha House, Inc, 1927).

the sex worker, as the mother of prophets and kings, we might see the theme of salvation and redemption entering the design, like with Na'amah and Norea.

The Babylonian Talmud sees Rahab as identical to Behemoth and Leviathan. The motives of deliverance should be evident in how the angelic prince of the ocean's depth, upon the retrieval of the *Tzohar*, saw a similar deliverance as in the transformations of Na'amah. This is the mystery of resurrection because if there was a fall, there must also be a resurrection. This is the key of Seth, the restoration of the fallen to its original state of perfection, as spoken of in *Allogenes:* "I saw the glories of the perfect individuals and the all-perfect ones who exist together, and the all-perfect ones who are before the perfect ones."[122]

The revelator of the *Tzohar* is Raziel, the angel of secrets and mystery, so let us now summarise his identity a bit more. If we accept the hierarchies as presented by the holy Dionysius the Areopagite, Raziel, by being a Seraphim and an Ophanim, belongs to the potencies of divine fire guarding and watching the divine throne itself. The root of the word *Seraphim,* and thus, their function, refers to the ability to kindle something or make it burn or glow. It is, therefore, an invisible fire, the primordial fire of transcendence, the glowing coals of perfect fire flowing forth in the rivers of wisdom from the divine throne. This means that Raziel is not only an angel formed in the likeness of the mystery itself; Raziel is the voice of the *Tzohar.*

The connection the Ophanim has with prophetic rapture leads the way to accomplishing the revelation of secrets along this axis of ecstasy and reception. It is an ascent along the ladder amidst the palaces of heaven. It is the straight road of the upright spine, the *Sushumna,* which brings Jerusalem, the city of peace, to Earth, hence the Kabbalistic axiom: *"Kether in Malkuth, Malkuth in Kether,"* which is basically, "as above, so below"—but opposite.

The wisdom of the book is of a transformative quality. This is evident in the variety of prophetic manifestations from this light in the form of inspired writ, be it texts or manuals of the secret art leading humankind toward reintegration and perfection. The transformative quality is expounded upon in how Enoch was transformed

---

122 James M. Robinson, *The Nag Hammadi Library* (Harper One, 1990).

into Metatron due to the wisdom the book contained. We are left with fire, with Venus, and with Mercury. The *Tzohar* glows from the sapphire stone, and its fire releases the fire letters of the Torah and secret writing. Mercury, the bridge, the messenger, the celestial quicksilver, and the dignity of love pouring forth from Venus exalts the fire and turns it invisible.

Here is the prophetic ascent, the inspiration of the sages, and the wisdom that makes possible the turning against the grain and the embrace of perfection. In books like *Sefer ha-Razim, Merkabah, Clavicula Salomonis, Picatrix,* and the works of Masha'allah and Avicenna, amongst fragments and texts of Roman, Greek, and Babylonian origin, shards of the stone are found. Amidst its writ and reception, the light of the *Tzohar* glows and kindles the ascent of the soul.

EIGHTEEN

SHÂTHIL— THE PERFECT PLANT

*"The lotus flower blooms most beautifully from
the deepest and thickest mud."*

—SIDDHARTHA

A curious tenth-century Manichean text, *Kitāb al-Fihrist*, written by
Ibn al-Nadim, says that Adam named his third son "Shâthil" after a
lotus tree, flowing over with milk, grew from the sunburned earth, or
desert, in answer to his prayers. The third son, Seth, was therefore called
Shâthil, meaning "the perfect plant." This text is quite interesting, as
Philo conveyed similar ideas about the name Seth, claiming it meant
"watering" or "irrigation" as a reference to the soul being like a plant
that only begets fruits when it is watered. This came from a word that
can be translated as "to drink," as in "one who drinks water."[123]

The Manichean Adamic traditions venture within a world where darkness reigns and where humankind has alienated themselves from the love
and knowledge of light. Genesis 2–4 was also of interest to the Nestorian
monk Theodore bar Konai, who lived in Syria in the ninth century.
While al-Nadim presents the negative theology of Mani in a way that
has marked contemporary perception of Gnosticism as world-rejecting
and seeing the corporeal world as a prison designed by the archon, Konai

---

123 See Stroumsa, *Another Seed* (Brill, 1985).

sees the patterns of redemption in these two chapters of Genesis in his text *Liber scholiorum*, also known as *The Book of Annotations*.

Konai here writes about the counsel of the "abortions," a variant of *nefilim*, namely *nefalim*, meaning "abortion," and refers to pregnancy occurring by fornication or pregnancy by antinomian ways. The custom amongst the Semites was to provoke abortion by the use of plant remedies. When Konai refers to the primordial disruptive forces as abortions, it is this antinomian and poisonous route of becoming he refers to. But like the sons of Zillah with Lamech, Na'amah, and Tubal Cain,[124] they did not vanish but lived on because of the secret holy decree they were granted to exist under.

Ashaqlun, the son of the "King of Darkness," advised the abortions to give to him their children, both the male and female children he advised to hand over to him. The male children he ate, while the female he gave to his wife, Nebruel. The text doesn't say what Nebruel did with the children, whether she ate them, set them aside, or raised them. The context does suggest that she ate them and that the consumption of this titanic seed provoked Ashaqlun and Nebruel to mate and thus give birth to Adam and Eve, not twins, but both brother and sister.

The text then tells how Jesus, in the guise of the angel of splendour, came to the rescue of Adam's demonic slumber and ignited him with divine fire, which awoke him from his darkened state. Jesus, the angel of Splendour, describes his condition as being cast into the teeth of leopards and elephants where he was swallowed by the voracious ones, absorbed by the gulping ones, and consumed by dogs, thus mixed with all that existed, all veiled in the stench of Darkness. The angel of splendour, who took him to the Tree of Life, resulted in Adam crying out in despair, realizing that his soul was bound to matter and that he was surrounded by malefic forces that wanted to enslave him.

Clearly, this Nestorian exegesis is born from meditation on what we find in Genesis 6:11–12, where it is written: "The world was corrupted before God, and the land was filled with crime. God saw the world, and it was corrupted. All flesh had perverted its way on the earth."[125] Al-Nadim, in *Kitāb al-Fihrist*, recounts the same story, but here, the

---

124 Lamech had two wives, Adah and Zillah. Zillah was the second wife or concubine and was not supposed to give birth, however, she did give birth, and ominous births they were.

125 Rabbi Aryeh Kaplan, *The Living Torah* (Moznaim Publishing, 1981).

Archontic reproduction is presented as cosmic sexual intercourse involving both the archons, stars, forces, and desires of every kind that created Adam, the first man, and soon after, the same cosmic event occurred and gave birth to Eve.

Like in the Nestorian account, the angel of splendour, Yeshu, comes to the rescue of the couple born by this complete mixing of all possibilities because, within this mixed substance, the Light of Goodness shined forth. Yeshu then explained the order of the cosmos to the couple and, in addition, instructed him in ways of revering Eve and refraining from sexual passions, a clear indication that the appetites and passions are the twain road of ascent and descent. However, in his ascetic practice, Eve was made liable for the court of the archon, Ashaqlun, who seduced his daughter, and from this mating, Cain was begotten.

Cain is described as a deformed man, red in complexion. The text then tells that Cain had intercourse with his mother, and from this union, Abel, "the white man," was born. Again, Cain had intercourse with his mother and fathered twin daughters, who were named Ibnat al-Hire and Hakimat al-Dhar. Cain married Ibnat and presented to Abel Hakimat. Hakimat was said to possess residues of light and goodness, and thus, an angel came to her and made her pregnant with twin daughters who were named Rau-Faryad and Bar-Faryad.

When Abel learned about their becoming, he was overcome with jealousy because he thought his wife hid that Cain was the true father of the daughters; Abel then went to his mother, Eve, to complain about his brother. This resulted in Cain, due to the false accusations, killing Abel and taking Hakimat as his second wife. The murder distressed Eve, the archons, and the messenger or overseer, al-Sindid, resulting in al-Sindid teaching Eve the art of enchantment and incantation, as well as the erotic arts, so that she could lure Adam out from his ascetic contemplation.

Apparently, the seductive actions Eve chose when she approached Adam, adorning herself with garlands, distressed al-Sindid. So did the son she begot, a handsome child with a radiant appearance that al-Sindid said was "not one of us." Hearing this, Eve sought to murder the child, but Adam came to his rescue, just as Yeshu had come to his, and said he would take care of the child and feed it milk and fruits. But as Adam went away with the child to search for cows and trees, the archons and some angels relocated the cows and trees, leading to Adam stopping in his journey and placing the infant down on the ground, tracing three circles around him.

Over the first ring, he called the name of the King of the Gardens; over the second, he called the name of the Primal Man; and over the third, he called the name of the Living Spirit and implored God to keep the infant safe. One of the three angels came to his rescue with a crown of radiant light, and at the same moment, the archons and al-Sindid were expelled. From the place he had made his petition, a lotus tree grew, and he fed the boy with its milk.

Upon seeing Adam lead his son, Shâthil, to maturity, al-Sindid approached Eve again and asked her to reveal herself to Adam, which she did, and once again, they joined in sexual congress, whereupon Shâthil (Seth) rebuked the father and went on to the east, to where Light and wisdom resided. Rau-Faryad, Bar-Faryad, and Hakimat al-Dhar went with Seth to the east, where they emerged themselves in contemplation and spiritual ecstasy, while the passion-ridden Ibnat went with Cain and Eve to the fields of Gehenna, the south.

Interestingly enough, Seth was the "different seed" in a corrupted world; his shiny appearance signified something other and alien that went against the current because the current was corrupted and perverted. Also, Seth was linked to a lotus tree that grew in the desert, and milk flowed forth. The lotus is a natural ruler for contemplation, as seen in many strands of Hindu zymology, where the lotus is a place of quietness and contemplation. This, in the midst of the scolding sun and the barren lands, Seth generates an oasis of milk and contemplation.

Seth was an anomaly in a perverted world. In the barren fields of sunburnt deserts, a lotus tree sprouted and gave forth milk, but what type of lotus is spoken of here? Is it the aquatic plant (*Nelumbo* and *Nymphaea* species) we commonly associate with lotus, or is it the so-called "lotus tree" (*Ziziphus jujuba*), known as "jujube"? It might be the latter, as jujube is a native of China, which, in traditional cosmology, has a significant meaning as the spiritual haven of perfection, Agarttha or Jerusalem; we might say that China is located in the north.

The shrub can withstand great varieties of temperature, and the fruits given by this tree have a taste of apples when young and of dates when ripe; likewise, the flowers give off a sweet Venusian smell, which, in China, is reputed to awaken slumbering erotic feelings. This is seen in the custom of placing jujube and walnuts in the bridal chamber to enhance fertility. It is also noted for being an excellent dispeller of pests and malefic.

It is also quite interesting to note that the "lotus tree" is resistant against almost all sorts of plagues and vermins, except for one commonly called "witches' broom." This condition is a reaction to various forms of attack, be it from insects, fungi, or plagues. It causes the tree to grow multiple sprouts from a unique point, which, during growth, twists and twirls together so it looks like a bird's nest—or a witch's broom. In other words, external malefic causes the affected part of the shrub to grow out a deformity.

The virtues of the lotus proper, the *Nymphaea*—white, red, and blue—which opens its beauty at night and remains closed or vanishes by day, can shed light on the metaphysical dimensions, and the blue lotus (*Nymphaea stellata*) is seen as a stellar nymph. This means that an alternative dimension to the legend of the perfect plant can result in celestial aid, a nymph manifesting the ways of bringing the infant into maturity. This would then recapitulate a multitude of incidents in Antiquity and beyond where celestial and divinised beings interact with humanity for a common cause, in this case, to rescue the different seed from extermination and leave the world to annihilation. As such, Seth becomes the very form of the potentiality for manifestation, as it is only in the night; veiled in darkness, the nurturing plant is active.

Vishnu resting in the centre of a lotus in an ocean of milk calls forth these same primordial themes of sacred preservation of gnosis and sacred doctrine so related to *avatars* and *bodhisattvas* of Eastern faiths, as Vishnu is the sum of the triple manifestation and thus, he is unity and not diversity. It is from the centre of the lotus that Mount Meru, the polar mountain and home of the denizens of Seth, rises. Not only this, but milk is the means of nurturance given by the mother to the child, affirming the idea that Seth's mother was a celestial or stellar nymph who fed him by the grace of the Milky Way.

This is symbolically associated with the sphere of the fixed stars, the Ogdoad, pleroma, sphere *de perfecti;* the milk of the night, yet again verified by the common representation of possessing eight petals of the lotus, the eight spheres.[126] Likewise, the colour of the milk, white, reflects back on the *Sushumna*, the spine, and the central pathway toward the crown. It is the stellar manifestation along the path of perfection,

---

126 It should be noted that some types of lotuses do have five petals and others have multiple petals, but the common amount for the lotus in question is eight. In the extension of multiple petals, the symbolism of the lotus will tie in with the mystery of the rose. In terms of five petals, this paves the road for a quite different mystery related to manifestation itself, as we see in alchemical symbolism where the five-petalled rose symbolizes the four elements and the quintessence.

the temperate and contemplative way of the upright ones, the race of upright and perfect beings instigated by the seed of Seth.

It is further interesting to note that Shâthil is symbolised by a plant, if not assuming unification with the plant that nurtured him. This is simply due to the traditional notion presented amongst many by the sixteenth-century chemist and alchemist Oswald Crollius (c. 1560–1609), who comments:

> *"The stars are the matrix of all the plants and every star in the sky is only the spiritual prefiguration of a plant, such that it represents that plant, and just as every herb or plant is a terrestrial star looking up at the sky, so also each star is a celestial plant in spiritual form, which differs from the terrestrial plants in matter alone."* [127]

We might see this as the star of perfection branding its signature on Shâthil. Since stars and plants only differ in terms of the plant being material, the virtues are identical, and the perfect star is the pole star, the still point of the north. This indicates more of a state and position than the star itself since fixed stars do move, even slowly, which leads to the curious condition of the north star being a position that various stars take turns occupying. It is in this that we find the reason why the Sun is symbolised with the point—because all stars are solar. The Sun is lit and visible in the night, and, as such, Seth, the lotus, which opens at night with the scent of Venus, is truly like a sun opening in the night, the seed of the stellar nymph and the Adamic parts of human perfection leading to the possibility of manifesting human harmony.

---

127 Oswald Crollius, *Traité des signatures* (Durville, 1624/1912). This is a part of his Paracelsian work, *Basilica Chymica*. Éliphas Lévi, in his *History of Magic* (1859), reproduced the core material from Crollius' *Book of Signatures*.

NINETEEN

THE CELESTIAL DEW
OF SALVATION

"Sown in corruption he will be resuscitated in glory."
—FIRST EPISTLE TO THE CORINTHIANS 15:42

Salvation, from the Greek *soteria,* refers to being rescued in the sense of pointing toward a "source for being rescued"; it is a noun that carries with it a potential for action, and the action is *salvare,* "to save" or "to rescue." This means that salvation needs to be related to an intervention where one is removed from one state to another, the prior state being of a nature inferior, improper, or damaging to the one finding itself in this state. We might call this "corruption" in the true sense of the words *breaking, spilling, destroying,* or *spoiling,* which is the meaning inherited in the Latin *corruptus.*

The idea of *corruptus* also carries the idea of bringing poison to an otherwise healthy organism, as its usage was referred to in Antiquity when corruption was largely seen as an effect of poison. "Poison" can also be translated from *virulentus,* which has given us our modern words "virus" and also "violent"; in other words, an organism full of poison that aims toward corrupting, in the sense of spoiling or destroying, something considered whole, complete, or healthy. The Hebrew *shachath*—as found in Genesis 5:11, where it is stated that the world was corrupt—brings the same themes of destruction and damage to mind with one interesting dimension added: a sexual connotation as *shachath* can also convey meanings such as perversity, oppression, and cruelty, all in a veil of lustfulness.

Modern interpretations of the fall of the Watchers convey this array of lustful denigration, where perverse spirits filled with sexual desire commingle with the daughters of humankind and beget a race of "giants," popularly called *Nephilim*. These accounts have often suffered from a too-narrow scope of interpretation, flooded with ethical considerations aping Christian morality, and thus, tend to give a distorted view of what a fall actually is and the consequences it constitutes. This perspective, often referred to as "Luciferian," only expresses one part of the design, the avenues of enlightenment that are related to bringing celestial and infernal fire within mundane proximity and the mystery of transgression as well as the gnosis inherited in the divinely appointed role of opposer and affirmer.

Many streams flowing forth from the Luciferian kingdoms represent a glorification of the act of transgression as it accomplishes the work and purpose of our journey on Earth in and of itself. As a consequence, a distorted focus on malefic deities is observed in the belief that the Luciferian kingdom is a misanthropic realm that adheres solely to the strong and mischievous in a network of so-called black magic and exaltation of the powers of the night. From a Sethian perspective, the overt focus on the darker strains of the world soul and being would be considered a distortion or at least a perspective from a specific angle that denies outlook from the sacred centre outward. The sacred centre is established by works of theurgy where the mind or consciousness is purified in such a manner that communication with the ideas and pontificals in the *mundus imaginalis* or the world of pure forms is established. From this world of un-manifested possibility, all things become possible, and from such a state of consciousness, one will be looking at the many worlds from the summit of the mountain where the denizens of Seth rest in contemplation.

Amongst the more complex and subtle accounts of the acts of the *salvator salvandus* and the celestial dew that revivify dry bones flows rich, albeit hidden, within the web and veil of Na'amah, daughter of Lamech, the Cainite as accounted in Genesis 4:22. Na'amah is, in some accounts, said to be the wife of the *tzadik* Noah, a righteous man void of blemish and fault, son of the Sethite Lamech (Genesis 5:28–29) and second husband to Na'amah.[128]

We find themes in texts like *The Apocryphon of John* that unveil a deeper mystery related to the ways of action and contemplation, a theme amoral and profound. It is a theme quite different than the rabbinical accounts that see Na'amah as one of the four Demon Queens that vampirise men in order to beget their offspring. By viewing Na'amah in light of the texts informing the Sethian stream of gnosis, quite different imagery will surface as Na'amah herself is exalted into the unspoiled maiden, Norea, sister and wife of Seth.

The salvation of Na'amah into Norea illustrates the deeper synthesis revealed in the hermetic axiom, "'as above so below'—but upside down," as commented by the metaphysician René Guénon, an observation quite understandable if we follow the literal effects of the use of the mirror as a metaphor for the mundane and celestial kingdoms. The celestial kingdom or the city of the *perfecti* is Luz, *Beit El*, the City of God.

Norea is Luz, in the same way as the Ecclesia was the bride of the Anointed One. The City of God and Na'amah or Norea is represented by the incorruptible virtues of the almond tree—the virgin maiden that is intimately linked to the zodiac sign of Libra and the fixed star Spica. By this association, she also becomes the celestial maiden of Venus herself, and it is here the divine *transvection*[129] of Na'amah into Norea happens. It is in this mystery that *Prunikos* reveals herself in a drama so often misrepresented in modern times, where *Prunikos* is simply seen as sacred lewdness by man's inability to look beyond the epiphany of the sex worker that *Prunikos* represents.

---

128 *Sefer HaYov'loth* 4:33, however, states that Noah married his niece Amzarach, daughter of Rakh'el, and thus the Sethian line continued uncorrupted in the line of *Noah*, whose name means "rest" or "comfort." However, the majority of Midrashic Aggadah maintains the idea that Na'amah was Noah's wife. It is also worth remembering that Noah is often compared to the Greek Deucalion, son of Prometheus and Pronoia. Deucaion was attributed as the first wine brewer and was warned about the flood as a consequence of King Lyacon of Arcadia's turncoat sacrifice of a young boy, which, in turn, resulted in the lycanthropic curse given by Zeus upon the king.

129 The word *transvection* is deliberately being used here as it indicates a metamorphosis of the genctic structure in a cell, either being repression or exaltation, as well as the lycanthropic acts of shape shifting and cunning night flights.

Instead of seeing a configuration of salvation and rectification leading to reintegration where the perfect seed can sprout again, modern pseudo-Gnostics have seen in this drama a reason to sanctify promiscuity in quite a carnal and profane way. We might see here the great divide between the perspectives taken by the *ben Elohim*, "the sons of Seth," in contradiction to the *ben Adam*, or "the sons of Cain." The descent of the Watchers, the Irin, can actually indicate that the fallen angels were actually *Targum* (*ben Elohim*), the Judges of Elohim; thus, angels effectuating a particular role as governors and overseers of the mundane and sub-lunar world, different from those of his sons.

The Watchful Judges, the governors of the world, were the angels who fell in the sense of leaving their destiny and centre, and thus the fall is a *mixis* of their righteous seed with strains foreign to their nature. What motivated their fall was said to be *Na'amah*, whose name means "beauty" or "comely" and often brings with it the lustful connotation of luxurious delight, meaning that for the Watchful Judges, she became an object of desire. But during the fall of the *Irin*, the resuscitation of Na'amah was accomplished by a redirection of the principle of lust or desire for higher purposes.

Na'amah is also Esterah, and her escape from the fallen ones is mirrored in the escape from Shemyaza, where she gains her salvation. Similar themes are found in relation to Ishtar, Venus, and Anahita, and thus, Na'amah, the Esterah, turns into the starry sister-wife of Seth, the maiden holding a shaft of grain in the incorruptible sphere, which is also known as *Pleroma*. In Genesis 8:21, this celestial dew is referred to as *nicho'ach* or "pleasant fragrance." The whole mystery is found in Luz, the fragrance and virtue of the almond, seen as incorruptible, an ideal form of the embryo from where the butterfly emerges.

This, in turn, is the very same as the coiled-up serpent that we find in the base of the spine, where the same mystery is enacted within the alchemical body chemistry of the *tzadik*, where the lustful potential springs to the vault of the mind and causes an ascent along the straight path of the spine. The serpent resting at the base of the spine will accomplish its ascent through the body plexuses known as *kamalas* (lotuses) by some form of arousal, which will cause the serpent to rise along the solar ray, or spine, known as *Sushumna*.

There will metaphorically be an ascent from the vault of the womb to the vault of the cranium, from the state of seed to a state of perfection augmented by the power of desire. This mystery is also evident in rabbinical sources, where the third book of the Zohar says that a man whose desire has been aroused by Lilith or Na'amah will be a vehicle for demonic offspring.

Norea is also Barbelo, the father's feminine spirit, or we might say the virginal face of *Shekinah,* as reflected in the peace of *Shulamith,* "the virginal spirit," who was associated with Norea by the Nicolaitans, a short-lived sect active in the areas of Ephesus in the first two centuries AD. In *The Apocryphon of John,* Barbelo is said to be the "glory of revelation." *Glorified* means to be transformed into something better, indicating a victory over corruption and thus being worthy of praise and honour. As for this curious sect known by the name of the Nicolaitans, not much is known, but apparently, they upheld a Sabaean Gnosis, and as the Cathars, they were accused of promiscuity and orgiastic ecclesiastical activities as accounted by the Church Fathers Irenaeus and Clement of Alexandria.

Luz is also found in Psalm 34, where the Psalmist speaks of a specific indestructible bone in the body, which will constitute resurrection. Rabbinical sources relate the spine to the nineteen daily prayers, and the vertebra in question is the nineteenth, but it can also be a reference to the cross-bone, the sacrum, that connects the spine and pelvis. It should also be pointed out that Luz is an alternative name for *Beit El,* or the House of the Lord, envisioned as a city painted blue where immortality and incorruptibility reign.

The angel of death has no dominion in Luz, and as such, Luz is a similar abode to Agarttha or Shambhala or even *Ville-aux-Camps* of the Vodousaints. The blue painting indicates that it is situated in the constellation of the Pleiades, also known as the seven sisters, which shares similar virtues to those found in Spica herself. So, the almond tree—or rather, the kernel itself, as *Luz* can also mean "kernel"—is the gateway to the city of the righteous ones or the *perfecti* because the city of Luz is designated by the centre of the being, its heart. It is at this centre that the divine principle dwells, and the return to the centre reveals the journey toward salvation and rectification, the hallmark of the children of Seth and his royal priesthood.

One other name given to Na'amah should be mentioned, as found in *The Book of Jubilees* 4:11. Estera or Estyra, Seth's sister and wife, is called *Azura,* an alternative name denoting Na'amah—Norea in her resituated state. The name is remarkably similar to the Hindi class of demigods, often given malefic attributes, *asuras. Asuras* were seen as beings who opposed the *daevas* or deities, but one of these *asuras*, Ganapati-Ganesh, sought ascent and was considered a *daeva*. Ganesh's resting place is the *Muladhara* chakra, located at the base of the spine. His beheading by his own father, his original constitution, born by the dirt his mother washed off her body, and his restitution by the father who beheaded him all suggest themes of ascent. Likewise, the archaeological consensus indicates that Ganesh was an unknown deity before the fifth century AD, and the *asuras* were children of Kashyapa, one of the seven sages associated with the constellation Ursa Major or the Big Dipper.

In the drama surrounding the Valley of Dry Bones, perhaps a similar motive is revealed briefly by the Apostle Paul in his Epistle to the congregation in Corinth. In this letter, he speaks of the vivification of the dry bones by the effect of the celestial dew we find in the prophetic book of Ezekiel, Chapter Thirty-Seven. Here, the prophet finds himself in the desert, in the Valley of Dry Bones. The prophet speaks, filled with divine virtue, and the divine breath causes the dry bones to be clad in sinews and flesh and become alive; a mighty army is rising under the kingship of David.

The mention of the valley is interesting as the valley and the desert denote the dwellings of hostile forces, as exemplified in works of demonologies concerning Lilith, such as *Emek ha-Melech* (The King's Valley) by the seventeenth-century Ashkenazi Kabbalist Naftali Bacharach.

The breath of God, as distributed by the prophet, serves the same purpose as the dew, for what is dry and withering affirms and makes Seth's relationship to water, in the sense of irrigation, more easily understood. He makes the dry land fertile by the breath of vaporous virtue that stems from the celestial dew that makes the barren fertile.

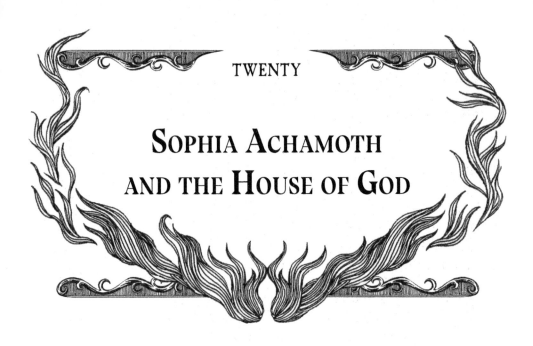

TWENTY

SOPHIA ACHAMOTH
AND THE HOUSE OF GOD

*"And a great clap of thunder will come out of a great force that is
above all the forces of chaos, where the firmament of the woman
is situated. Having created the first product, she will put away
the wise fire of intelligence and clothe herself with witless wrath.
Then she will pursue the gods of chaos, whom she created along
with the prime parent. She will cast them down into the abyss.
They will be obliterated because of their wickedness."*

—ON THE ORIGIN OF THE WORLD

Jules Doinel (1842–1903), the first Patriarch of *L'Église Gnostique*
(1891–1894), was ordained as a Bishop-elect by Aeon Jesus or Jesus
Christ himself along with two Bogomil bishops as witnesses to his
ordination in the heavenly Jerusalem in 1888. This vision, where he
received the divine afflatus, however, started long before. Already in
the 1860s, Doinel was contributing articles to Spiritist journals, and he
was himself a talented medium, clairaudient, and clairvoyant. In 1875,
Doinel met Allan Kardec's successor, Léon Denis, and Abbé Roca
through his second wife. The latter introduced him to Lady Caithness
(Maria de Mariategui), who became fundamental to him in his contact
work with Cathar spirits.

Doinel was fascinated with the Cathars and with Simon Magus.
He had a strong inclination toward the feminine mysteries, and so

the presence of Lady Caithness would then aid in making manifest the divine feminine. He, through automatic writing, received the presence of Sophia-Achamoth,[130] who presented herself as Helen-Ennoia of Simon Magus, daughter of Sophia and exiled—or fallen—from Pleroma, the noetic or Empyrean realms. She requested Doinel's help in asking for the intercession of Jesus to be reintegrated into Pleroma. She then said that "the Three are only One; the Father, the Word and Thought."[131] She identified herself as "Thought," which is *Norea*. It is quite remarkable how the themes concerning Sophia-Achamot, her fall, redemption, and apocalypses that were revealed to Doinel through Spiritism were in harmony with key texts in the Nag Hammadi Library, like *On the Origin of the World*, which was discovered forty-two years after his death.

The daughter of Sophia, Eve or Zoe, is in *On the Origin of the World* and in *The Hypostasis of the Archons*, credited with being the force that gave life and light to Adam. This light and life-giving quality caught the attention of the archons, that in some way set out to pollute her by "casting their seeds" on her or by raping her in a way that might suggest that she was tainted and, therefore, unable to ascend. The aim was to keep Adam in darkness as a soul-less and light-less serpentine creature. In these Gnostic renderings, Eve resisted the attempts from the archons, and in disobeying their command to stay away from the tree that gave wisdom and instead eating the forbidden fruit, she unleashed a redeeming principle embedded in the attempt of the archons to keep humankind in darkness.

The various theories indicating that the rape was successful and that Eve had up to seven children with Yaldabaoth, the chief archon, shall be discarded in this very context in favour of the ideas in the Gnostic text *Allogenes* that suggests that the archon only managed to rape Eve's shadow and that she indeed became the progenitor of the seven sons of Seth and angelic beings through Sophia (*Prunikos* or not). However, in *On the Origin of the World*, this rape is said to have a positive cosmological effect as Eve, due to escaping the lustful attempts of the archons, remained "in light," unpolluted, and became, in her hierophany as Norea, the wife of Seth, the syzygy, and parents of the immovable race.

130 *Achamoth* is the world-soul in Valentinian Gnosticism.
131 Jules Doinel, *Église Gnostique* (Krystiania, 2017).

This theme of Sophia *Prunikos* is also mirrored in Simon Magus' wife Helen, a sex worker he bought from a brothel in Tyre. For Doinel, Helen was Ennoia or Sophia. The same theme is found in the relationship between Jesus and Mary of Magdalene, also portrayed (falsely) as a sex worker. The key to this mystery, how a force becomes fallen or *Prunikos*, lies in this force wanting to be known, so when Sophia (Wisdom) wanted to be known, she gave of herself freely to all, *to be known*. Hence, we can say there is a lasciviousness and desire present, but of a spiritual calibre, and it is the wish to be known and see wisdom spreading through the power and arrows of Hyperborean Eros.

The Apocryphon of John describes Sophia's movement as something that sprang forth, like *logos* or words, and in this, she experienced passion. The source of this passion was from the aeons called *Truth* and *Nous,* and it became "love." This passion and love took the form of wanting to seek union with the Father or origin. In passion and movement, she sought to reunite herself with the immovable centre, but in this movement, the vast landscape known as the world and cosmos unfolded, and Sophia became the House of God, the power that lay at the foundation of the Church and upheld through Sophia, Eve or Zoe, Norea, and the three Marys: Mary of Bethany, Mary of Magdalene, and Mary the Mother of Jesus.

These six culminate in the Woman of the Apocalypse, spoken of in the Book of Revelations, Chapter Twelve. Here, as depicted in the twelfth-century manuscript *Hortus deliciarum,* she embodies in mystical ways the seven stars or maidens of the Pleiades, mirroring the seven Sethian sages in Ursa Minor. In this regard, it is of interest to comment that, in order to locate the Pleiades, it is customary to focus on the belt of Orion and follow these stars toward the shining Aldebaran until you find a constellation similar in shape to Ursa Minor—these are the Pleiades. The brightest star is Alcyone, and when speaking of her transformation in *Metamorphoses,* Ovid states that it makes her stellar presence known through the halcyon days. The halcyon days are seven days prior to and seven days after the winter solstice, which are days considered free from stone and filled with peace, a period of time when the kingfisher, Alcyone's sacred bird, is laying its eggs. In popular belief, the halcyon days are conceived of as a period of peace free from adversity, a temporary return of the original peaceful state of Edenic presence.

In order to make the return possible, the reintegration or *tikkun*, the world as we know it must end, and it must end by the power of a woman. In the Book of Revelations 12 (KJV), we encounter the Woman of the Apocalypse, who is described as "a woman clothed with the sun, and the moon under her feet, and upon her head a crown of twelve stars." This is obviously Sophia in all her splendour and fullness, manifesting at the end of the world. In the Book of Revelation, she is about to give birth to a male child, but the dragon Leviathan is circling around, seeking to devour the child upon its birth.

The child is born, however, and as in Book of Revelations 5:12 (KJV) says: "And she brought forth a man child, who was to rule all nations with a rod of iron: and her child was caught up unto God, and to his throne." The woman went to a place prepared for her in the desert where, for 1,260 days, she was fed on divine nectar. During these 1,260 days, Saint Michael waged the war in heaven, leading to the dragon and his army being expelled to Earth, where another unsuccessful hunt for the Woman of the Apocalypse ensued. It's interesting that 1,260 adds up to *Pri Etz*, "Fruit of the Trees," and might indicate that these 1,260 days would then revert the effects of the consummation of the forbidden fruit. Where this account ends in the Book of Revelation, *On the Origin of the World* tells:

> "The light will cover the darkness and obliterate it: it will be like something that has never been. And the product to which the darkness had been posterior will dissolve. And the deficiency will be plucked out by the root (and thrown) down into the darkness. And the light will withdraw up to its root. And the glory of the unbegotten will appear. And it will fill all the eternal realm." [132]

Looking at this excerpt in light of *The Thought of Norea*, we find her as the syzygy being both father of All and the Wisdom (Ennoia) of the Light, as the text reveals in the end, "the thought of Norea, who speaks concerning the two names which create a single name."[133] This short text, read from this angel, gives us a beautiful account of light in expansion and passion retracting to itself, as the scroll tells:

> "It is Norea who cries out to them. They heard, (and) they received her into her place forever. They gave it to her in the Father of Nous, Adamas, as well as the voice of the Holy Ones, in order that she might rest in the ineffable Epinoia, in order that <she> might inherit the first mind which <she> had received, and that <she> might rest in the divine Autogenes, and that she (too) might generate herself, just as she also has inherited the living Logos, and that she might be joined to all of the Imperishable Ones, and speak with the mind of the Father." [134]

---

132 James M. Robinson, *The Nag Hammadi Library* (Harper One, 1990).
133 Ibid.
134 Ibid.

In relation to the Woman of the Apocalypse being the culmination of Sophia-Achamoth, upon her restitution, it is also of interest to bring attention to two of her theophanies, namely Our Lady of Guadalupe and Saint Agatha (231–251). *Legenda aurea* tells that Agatha was from a noble family and that she made a vow of chastity when she was fifteen. This didn't stop the Roman prefect Quintianus from seeking to marry her. Agatha was not interested, and so he first threatened her with torture, but she didn't give in. Next, Quintianus was to send her to his confidant, Aphrodisia, the owner of a brothel where she was locked up, but to no avail would she marry the prefect. He then sent her to be tortured where, amongst the brutalities, her breasts were excised with pinchers and tongs.

The brutality done, she was sent to be burned, but an earthquake prevented this. In the story of Saint Agatha, we find again the prominent theme of the *Prunikos*. Agatha's feast day is on the fifth of February, shortly after Candlemas or Saint Brigid's Day, which, in its commemoration of death and the return of light, holds some significance. Likewise, her status as a patron of earthquakes and volcanic eruptions connects her solidly with the final Apocalypse.

Our Lady of Guadalupe is also interesting in this regard as she is like the Woman of the Apocalypse, clothed with the Sun with the Moon at her feet. Likewise, the theories of the Mexican nationalist Luis Becerra Tanco are interesting to comment on, as in his publication from 1666, *Origen milagroso del Santuario de Nuestra Señora de Guadalupe.*[135] He suggested a native Nahuatl origin of the word *Guadalupe* was either *Tecuatlanopeuh*, "she whose origins were in the rocky summit," or *Tecuantlaxopeuh*, "she who banishes those who devoured us."

Also of interest are the attempts to fuse her with *Coātlaxopeuh*, meaning "the one who crushes the serpent," which gives allusions both to the crushing of the serpent's head in Eden and how the Woman of the Apocalypse will again crush the head of the serpent at the end of days. Lastly, the vision that Juan Diego had of her was, in the past, a temple dedicated to an Aztec goddess, *Tonantzin*, meaning "Our Revered Mother," who presided over love and female mysteries.

The woman is the House of God. She is His presence because there is no difference. The Father is the Mother, and the Mother

---

135   An expanded edition was published in 1675 under the title *Felicidad de Mexico en la admirable aparición de la Vírgen María Nuestra Señora de Guadalupe.*

is the Father. He is the axis, and she is the landscape; hence, God wanting to be known was known in the form of a woman. In this, the syzygy, the synthesized union, was temporarily broken so God as "She" could make himself known through grass and star, worlds upon worlds, until that day of collapse and entropy when "She" becomes united with "He," and it all becomes One. As Sophia-Eve-Zoe says in *On the Origin of the World:*

"It is I who am the part of my mother; and it is I who am the mother.
It is I who am the wife; it is I who am the virgin.
It is I who am pregnant; it is I who am the midwife.
It is I who am the one that comforts pains of travail.
It is my husband who bore me; and it is I who am his mother.
And it is he who is my father and my lord.
It is he who is my force; What he desires, he says with reason.
I am in the process of becoming; yet I have borne a man as lord." [136]

---

136 James M. Robinson, *The Nag Hammadi Library* (Harper One, 1990).

TWENTY-ONE

THE ROSE AND THE SUN

"The rose looks fair, but fairer it we deem.
For that sweet odour which doth in it live."

—W. SHAKESPEARE

The symbolism of the rose and the Sun finds its place in our discourse, with the Sun being the point and the rose being the beauty opening up from the point. The rose opens up as a multilayered mystery of sweetness born from the golden seed of Seth, and a world of goodness is revealed. The seed that was given the sapphire stone cultivates the flowers of Venus. Aided by the angelic messengers that unite in front of us in the triad of Sun, Mercury, and Venus, the rose becomes a symbol of grace and redemption. It turns into a symbol for the unveiling of light and knowledge from the sacred point, the silent mystery of revelation, transition, and transmission. If we accept that flowers, in general, symbolise the world, the rose, with its multiple petals, would represent the mysteries of Raziel unfolding in a multitude of layers and possibilities around its centre and pole.

The rose as a symbol of secrecy is well known under the term *sub rosa,* meaning "in confidence" or "secrecy." This is also attested in the Roman banquet halls, where the rose-painted ceilings were often detected as a reminder to keep silent what was said under the influence of the wine. From the 1650s, in "under the rose," one could see a rose being elevated from the ceiling in European councils by the same token, that of secrecy. This connotation with roses and secrecy is widely attested in Greek myths where Aphrodite, Lady Venus, gives roses to her son Eros as tokens to keep his silence about her affairs. Eros, in turn, hands the rose to Harpocrates, a deity associated with silence and secrecy—but also the newborn Sun and son as in the Hawk-headed Horus. Like the eagle, the hawk is a bird of prey that hunts under the rays of the Sun, both belonging to the same order of birds, *Falconiformes,* or the falcon family. We might also remember the use of the double-headed eagle, used both by Byzantine and Roman rulers and found to have been used as far back as the thirteenth century BC, as archeological research in Turkey has revealed. The double-headed eagle has always been a symbol of aristocracy and dominion, a solar and noble bird.

From 1214, the *rosarium,* literally the "garden of roses," entered the Christian monastic life with the vision of Saint Dominic, who was given a rosary by the Holy Virgin. Originally, the rosary presented a Pentateuch of a triple mystery related to Mary and Jesus Christ. These mysteries are Joyful, Sorrowful, and Glorious, with fifteen mysteries in all related to the 150 Psalms, which encode the mystery of the vision and reception of the Virgin Mary. Here, we have yet another strand of symbolism entering the crucifixion and resurrection of the anointed one.

His crown is made of thorns, this being rose or bramble. Both plants might be derived from the Proto-Indo-European *wrdho,* meaning "thorn" or "bramble," and then later also used to describe white roses. The thorns, however, give us many important details, and the one we shall dwell on is its linkages with solar rays being used as weapons or tools of transition from one condition to another, the unveiling of secrecy. The Lance of Longinus gave the crucified Iesu his fifth wound, and the blood, in some accounts, spilled to the earth and formed into roses. In other accounts, they formed into the rose cup of Joseph of Arimathea, representing the Solar King; both his crown and the lance that took his last breath, leaving roses in his place.

The release of his blood is a symbol of redemption and salvation, for the celestial dew and the rose are metaphors mirroring each other. We should point out that the Latin *ros* means "dew," and "rose" is evidently from the Latin *rosa,* a linguistic similarity we cannot ignore. Here, we also have Adonis, who, like Iesu, gave up his breath from a wound to his side. In Adonis' case, it was the tusk of the boar that wounded him, and as he gave up his breath, his blood fell to the ground and formed into roses. This release of sanctified blood, the eternal triumph of the Sun as if formed into roses, was also found in the Carmelite Church of Mgr. Eugène Vintras (1807–1875), a devotee of Saint Peter and the Holy Virgin who gained fame for the miracles of his bleeding hosts; graced by the Holy Virgin, the host started to bleed—in the form of roses. Not only this, but the Holy Vintras was a great visionary of a prophetic pedigree, and on several accounts, he was seen to sweat blood.

It is also pertinent to remember Abaris the Hyperborean, a priest of Apollo whom Plato mentions in *Charmides* and refers to as an *epodikon* or *epodós*, meaning "enchanter," but in a particular context, as a healer or physician of both soul and body according to Plato. Abaris also surfaces in Johannes Bureus' runic reception that has a clear solar attribute and application where Abaris' arrow seems to be a central symbol. In his many rune rows, Bureus uses the cross, axis, and arrow as the traditional forms for generating the design and sequence. Abaris was famous for possessing this arrow, as it was given to him by Apollo in his Hyperborean temple, the celestial north, "the land of the Sun," *Tula* or *Thule*. It was here he was taught the arts of healing and prophecy, and the arrow was his means of transportation. The arrow also speaks of the crossroads, the meeting between sacred and terrestrial time, signifying moments of transition and reception.

In looking closer at the name *Tula*, which was originally given to the Hyperborean centre, it is revealed that the stellar temple of its nature is the scales, or Libra, a zodiac sign ruled by Venus. Curiously enough, the stellar temple of the scales also reveals a point of entry toward the Grail mythos, with the pole being marked by the celestial Dragon—or *Pan-Dragon*, King Arthur's father. Guénon tells us that the head of the dragon denotes the transition of the polar point from the constellations Ursa Major and Ursa Minor into the zodiac sign of the scales running on each side of the dragon's head. Henry Corbin notes similar thoughts in his *Temple and Contemplation*. Thus, the polar scales are referred to as *Tula* or *Thula*, and the same root is also found in the name *Arthur*, all referring to the Hyperborean solar lands.

The Sun is a disc or a wheel, as is the rose. This is a further demonstration of the intimate interplay between the rose and the Sun as forms of *Ophanims* or wheels. The Sun, in his chariot, who travels the path of the rose by day and the path of the lily by night, traditionally ascribed the path of the rose rulership to the great luminary of the night, the Moon. But even so, lilies, by their common six-petaled form, herald the presence of Venus, and their range of colours speaks softly of the Sun and Mercury. Like the rose, the lily has been a flower assumed by nobles and aristocrats. In many ways, the lily, despite speaking of purity and the promise of being cleansed of confusion and demeaning thoughts, ultimately represents quite a different strata of gnosis, a different avenue from the triad of planets as they walk through night waters.

In this mystery, we find the heart hidden within the cave of the chest. As Eros came to Psyche in the silence of the night, in the same way, our hearts are kindled in the night and tempted to rise from their caves and out into the solar lands. While the symbolism of the Sun and the rose speak of the revelation of secrecy from the Land of the Sun, the Hyperborean realm reveals its sacred centre into the sweet-smelling beauty of possibility. Hidden within every rose lies a garland of possibilities speaking of redemption and transition, a silent remembrance of how sacred blood is like celestial dew, a whisper of grace.

TWENTY-TWO

The Heart Cave
and the Land of the Sun

"The Dragon is in the middle of the
heaven as a king on his throne."

—*Sefer Yetzirah*

The symbolism of the cave refers to the hidden law that supports the mountain of victory, Mount Qaf. Its relationship is like the one between heart and mind, which ideally should be the starfire that sets the divine mind ablaze in manifesting wisdom. The hidden, what is veiled in the night, maintains the quietude of the poles and can uphold or distort equilibrium. The cave is the portal for the labyrinth and can give death or the particular insight that reveals itself when one finds the heart of darkness. This motive is perhaps most evident in the pyramids that were constructed in the shape of a double pyramid, one summit pointing toward the heavens and the inner pyramid, the crypt, with its summit pointing downward. This was to enter the heart of the mountain and find rest at the centre of the world.

The labyrinth is also representative of a journey, but also, in its more initiatic sense, it represents a technique for ridding oneself of malefica by constantly squaring the spirit tracks that always follow a certain straightness. The labyrinth has a kinship with the mountain, which lies in its etymology, where the first part, *laby*, derives from *lapis*, or "stone." The second word part is of obscure origin, and it is common to trace the word itself to the Lydian *labrys,* meaning "double-headed axe." This invites the idea of the labyrinth as being similar to what we find in the caduceus of Hermes as well as the axe or *oṣé* of the Yorùbá *òrìṣà Ṣàngó.* The double-headed axe represents the twin powers of gold and silver united on the axis of the sacred centre. Both the axe and the caduceus represent the double power of restraint and protection and of blessing and reception. The double-headed axe is also intimately linked to "thunder stones" and thunder itself by the constellation of Ursa Minor in particular, that is, the chariot of the Norse *Aesir,* Thor.

The function of the labyrinth was to unite the left and the right into one. In such a manner, the unicursal path would lead to initiation or death. The labyrinth is replicated in the body by the entrails, connected by the mouth and the anus. Upon meeting the heart and crossing the bridge of *Qabil,* the heart, the path of entrails turns straight and ends in the mouth, situated at the summit of the body. The cave is the hidden part of the *Baetyl* or *Beit El,* "the dwelling place of God," and from the summit, thunderbolts are issued. Thunderbolts are intimately related to the cave and the mountain, and herein lies the mystery of creation.

Even Leibniz spoke of the monads being born due to a "continual fulguration" of the divine essence, brought from moment to moment.[137] Fulgurite is the stone of creation; it is a composite of sand and quartz fused into a tube of sandy glass, replicating the soul's descent into matter. The soul blends with the matter but leaves a straight and open channel for air and spirit to pass through.

The heart is the silvern Grail cup that collects the celestial gold in itself. Interestingly, the same association is found in playing cards and the tarot, speaking of a certain traditional stream informing the tarot. The heart, as the inverted triangle, is, as such, the mirror of the mountain that, when united, creates the hexagon and perfect diamond. The heart represents the spiritual centre at the heart of the cave, as in the microcosmic body. This alludes to the heart being the spiritual centre itself, hidden within manifested majestic glory.

The mystery of the cave also alludes to a particular understanding concerning the *tariqa,* the Sufi chain of transmission. In *Insights into Islamic Esoterism and Taoism,* Guénon discusses in great detail

---

137 Martin Heidegger, *The End of Philosophy* (Harper & Row, 1973) 33.

the importance of the chain of transmission or *silsilha*.[138] Initiatic succession follows from the *Qutub* or the *pir*, what is known as the *At-Talimur-rajal*, but there is a certain mystery, direct and instant, which is related to the cave. This is the mystery of *Afrad*, by the route of *At-Talimur-rabbani*, outside the *pir*. Now, it is not outside, like a Nimrodian act; it is outside of the law because it appeals to the hidden law from which the manifested law is only a temporal necessity.

In the eighteenth surah of al-Quran, "The Cave," Moses is said to have gone to the cave of the seven sleepers to receive knowledge about his station and destiny. The spirit of the cave assumes the form of al-Khidr and takes Moses out into the world. Through a series of encounters of a prophetic nature that seem cruel to Moses, the secret of his station and true aspiration are given. Al-Khidr or al-Khezr, the Green One, is the manifestation of the celestial dragon who holds the scales of balance, and this force flows as the mercury of sustenance in the Sethian Tradition.

Similar motives are also found amongst the Yorùbá, where the prophet of Ifá (deity of wisdom) searches out a spirit called Elá, who dwells in caves and subterranean tunnels. Elá is the unmanifested wisdom that reveals necessary parts of the secrets woven into the fabric of creation through Ifá divination. Caves, at least allegorically, penetrate the centre of the Earth, or they go as far as "China," which is, in a Sethian context, a reference to the "land of the Sun."

The notion that the cave leads to the centre of the Earth opens a host of mysteries, but the one pertaining to this particular mystery is that the wisdom spoken of is drawn from the stellar dragon at the heart of the Earth. As spiritual mastery is given, material minority is assumed. The cave speaks of what is hidden, and there is great importance in maintaining what is concealed. This subtle mystery is told of in the curious story of Noah in Genesis 9, where the act of sacrifice is re-established.

The first sacrifices were the ones done by Abel and Cain and, with this, enabled redemption, reintegration, and celestial return. In Genesis 9, it is the sacrifice of Abel that is renewed, namely animal sacrifice, in memory of the animal nature that humanity needs to constantly sacrifice to obtain ascent. In this biblical passage, we also learn about

---

138 (Sophia Perennis, 1973/2003) 4, 5.

how Noah planted a vineyard, and by the gifts of Dionysus, he became intoxicated while in his tent. Of his three sons, Ham, Shem, and Japheth, it was Ham who saw his father's nakedness and was cursed. Shem and Japheth, on the other hand, took a veil up in front of them and covered their father with it. These two sons were blessed. This story serves little use as a literal story. As an allegory for the rupture of order, however, it is possible to see how the unruly and *rajasic* temperament provokes the hidden to manifest or for the spiritual to be subject to temporality and mortality. The veil represents the necessity of maintaining the spiritual heart hidden from corruption.

The heart is the seat of the soul that, for Marsilio Ficino, was associated with the land of the Sun, an ideal state where the soul was nurtured by the rays flowing from the sacred centre, the city of Hyperborean Apollo. This land is denoted by a perfect equilibrium, as temperance and Libra. Libra, or the celestial scales, were not always zodiacal. Originally, they were polar qualities ascribed to Ursa Major and Ursa Minor, respectively. They were located on each side of the celestial dragon, which then maintained balance. The dragon is the creeping water and the divine quicksilver; hence, Ursa Minor and Ursa Major are also referred to as "the wings of the dragon." The relationship Ursa Major has with the seven sages—and its interesting connection with the seven weeping sisters in the Pleiades—is typified by the seven planets. Likewise, its two front stars point toward the tail of Ursa Minor, the pole star. The pole star is the hole or cave where the *axis mundi* is planted, and by this, Ursa Minor represents a gate of descent and ascent.

The *axis mundi* is further seen in the Garden of Hesperides. In this garden, a single tree with golden apples grew. The tree was the *axis mundi* itself that gave the fruit of immortality and wisdom. The tripartite segmentation so crucial for sacred symbolism is again found in the number of nymphs tending to the garden. Even the Nimrodian motive applied here when Hercules entered the garden and took the fruits. Yet again, a mirror of the temporal powers usurpation of the spiritual authority takes shape. In the myth of Hercules, it is a typical *Nefilim*-like being that transgresses the limits of his activity and ventures within the spiritual and still domain. Here, the fruits of peace and contemplation are taken to be enslaved in action and temporal time and force.

The heart as representative of the land of the Sun is proper, as the sacred centre is invariably seen as represented by *omphalos,* mountain summits, gardens, and islands. All of them are motives that indicate that something is hidden within or beneath the manifested. Guénon writes about this in *Symbols of Sacred Science:*

> "...*according to Arab tradition the Rukh or Phoenix never alights on land anywhere other than on the mountain Qaf, which is the polar mountain; and in the Hindu and Persian traditions soma comes from the same 'polar mountain,' that soma which is identical with amrita or 'ambrosia,' the draught or food of immortality.*" [139]

In the *Metamorphoses*, Ovid tells how the phoenix prepares a bed of cinnamon, spikenard, and myrrh in branches of the oak or at the top of the palm tree when it prepares for death and rebirth. From the corpse of the bird, it is reborn and brings its nest to Heliopolis, the City of the Sun. In this intimate relationship, the phoenix—and likewise, the Persian *Simurgh*—has with the sacred centre gives it the reputation of being the leader of all birds, a tutor of prophets. In closing, we should note that it is upon the preparation of its crypt, or cave, that rebirth in the fire of the Sun is enabled. Herein lies mystery upon mystery.

---

139 (Sophia Perennis, 1977/2001) 94.

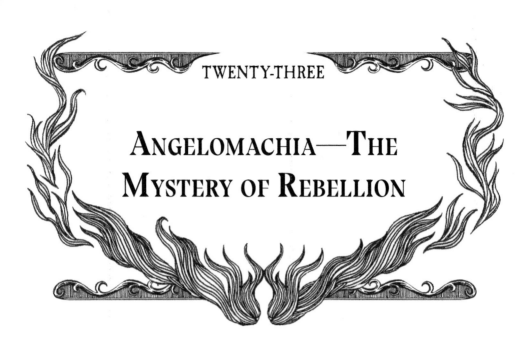

Twenty-Three

Angelomachia—The Mystery of Rebellion

"There is no one in creation, neither lofty nor low,
who can perceive the secret of these worlds."

—Rav Isaac ha-Kohen,
The Treatise on the Left Emanation

The legends of the fallen ones, the apostate angels that rebelled against God, are a theme found as early as in the Babylonian Dragon Myths. Arabic, Syriac, Ethiopic, and then Jewish sources have drawn upon this great theme that, in the wake of Christianity, developed into the legends of the Antichrist. This unfolded in a long tradition of apocalyptic literature spanning from Mesopotamia and the Arabic parts of the world to Northern Africa and Northern Europe. With the rise of Christianity, the focus on "the man of sin," as the apocalyptic John speaks about, was seen as heralding the coming of the greatest apostate of all, the Antichrist, who would seat himself in the temple of God.

Most modern ideas concerning the Antichrist are, of course, in error, as they too often are fruits of a Cartesian misreading that insists upon fragmentation and a dyadic taxonomy of "sameness" and "otherness." It is important in this work to point to the relationship the "Antichrist legends" have with the beguiling mystery within the "fallen ones." The lore of the apostate angels continues to compel and intrigue, and it is my hope here to trace some patterns and motives that can reveal the original context and true meaning of this mystery.

For the modern Western reader, the descent of the Watchers, the *ben Elohim,* the "Sons of God," is known primarily through the apocryphal *The Book of Enoch*. Already in the seventh chapter, this particular mystery is revealed to Enoch. Here, it is told how the leader of the Watchers, also known as *Egoroi* or *Grigori,* the angel Samyaza, was "enamored" by the female offspring of the human race. *The Testament of the Twelve Patriarchs* describes the *Egoroi* as a superior order of angels who possess the shape of humans and abide in silence in the proximity of the divine throne. This leads to the conclusion that originally, what they were watching was not only the creation but also the creator.

The silence indicates that their role was to contemplate the creator and the creation in silence. Silence is naturally the realm of the Divine Mind, the immediate sphere outside the cosmic centre of all possibility. By being immersed in the act of contemplation, they would support the serene and quiet order of creation. These Watchers, by contemplating the "centre of the world," would then be those that were in charge of witnessing the formless and indivisible point from whence all emanated.

The Book of Enoch tells how two hundred of these *Irin* swore allegiance to Samyaza and descended on Mount Hermon or Armon, also called Zion. The descent upon this mountain, which was located at the northern gate of the Promised Land (Canaan), created a rupture in the divine order by literally tearing the celestial fabric. Therefore, this place can be seen as a traditional allegory for transfigurations, as Moses, Elijah, Jesus, Melchizedek, and perhaps Enoch himself left their corporeal state behind on this mountain.

At Mount Hermon or Zion, flesh could lose its corporeality, and spirit could be flesh. The rebel angels followed the opposite route and brought spirit into matter. The rebellion of the apostate angles thus represents an inversion of the natural order, where the higher fell into the lower by a misdirected *eros* or love. The rebellion itself was intrinsically linked to the abandonment of destiny in favour of adopting an inferior perspective and a nefarious condition.

There are two consequences worthy of pointing out here; one of them is spoken of in the last verses of the seventh chapter of *The Book of Enoch* and the other in the subsequent chapter. Let's address the latter first. Here, we read about the knowledge the rebel angels brought. Azazyel "taught men to make swords, knives, shields, breastplates," and, in addition, he brought the arts of cosmetics, the use of stones and dyes, "so the world became altered." The alteration of the world seems to be caused by the "arts of war and beautification," taught by Azazyel/ Azazel, and after saying this, Enoch observed how the world turns "corrupted in all its ways." This is an interesting detail as it intimately concerns traditional doctrine, which will be demonstrated shortly. It seems that the arts the rebel angels taught to their wives were "sorcery, incantation, and the dividing of roots and trees." This knowledge had yet another impact, as told in *Enoch* 7:11, "And the women conceiving brought forth the giants," and in like manner in Genesis 6:4 (KJV): "There were giants in the earth in those days: and also after that, when the sons of God came in unto the daughters of men, and they bare children unto them, the same became mighty men which were of old, men of renown." These were the Nephilim, a titanic progeny. An intense general appetite is attributed to the Nephilim, leading to the Nephilim "turning against men, in order to devour them."

"And began to injure birds, beasts, reptiles, and fishes, to eat their flesh one after another, and to drink their blood."[140] The reference to blood-drinking Nephilim inevitably raises the issue of the mysterious origins of vampire legends. In passing, it is worthy to remark that the revolt of the Watchers can be traced back to Indo-European and Persian roots, insofar as demonstrated in the research of Wilhelm Bousset in the early 1900s.

Considering that ancient Persian religion and mythology influenced the Hebrew traditions while in exile, a common root is perhaps found in the Indo-European *WLKwYA*. Denominations like the *varcolaci* or *vrykolakas* are ultimately derived from this root. It also refers back to the Scythian tribe called the *Saka Haumavarga*. The use of *hauma* or *haoma*, an intoxicating drink, to induce an altered state might be what is referred to in Enoch's comment about the arts of Azazel, being the use of dye, "so the world became altered." We are touching here upon the intrinsic mystery of warrior-caste and warrior-sodalities.

Werewolves and vampires inevitably link with the themes of the Kshatriya Revolt in which they become assimilated to the demonic and the infernal, just as Guénon and Evolva may trace the term *vampire* to the Bactrian *Vyambhara* meaning a demon, a Druj, one of the

---

140 *The Book of Enoch* 7:6.

powers of Ahriman. As *The Book of Enoch* 15:8 says: "Now the giants, who have been born of spirit and of flesh, shall be called upon earth evil spirits, and on earth shall be their habitation." Such legends we see surrounding the Nephilim, Anakim, Gibborim, Jotnir, Danavas, and Titans. The Kshatriya Revolt is intimately associated with the Deluge, traditionally linked with the excesses of the giants, and thus, can also be seen as integral to Plato's account of the cataclysmic submergence of Atlantis.

One of the names given to this titanic offspring was the *Gibborim*, literally "strong men," from the same root as *Gevurah* or *Din*, the sphere of severity and divine wrath upon the Kabbalistic Tree of Life. Originally, the hand of severity, with its dark *tamasic* pulse, served to protect, to guard, and to preserve. It is a power of militant diligence invested in one's office. But, since the shattering of the vessels (*shevirat ha-kelim*), a misalignment unfolded, and thus, this energy was equally misdirected. Hence, we have the idea of "sin" that the fall brought with it, which is nothing else than a failure to attain the goals Fate has set for you.

The overflowing of the quality of severity into disequilibrium and the consequent "breaking of the vessels" lead to a situation enigmatically described in *The Treatise on the Left Emanation* in the following way:

> "*A form destined for Samael stirs up enmity and jealousy between the heavenly delegation and the forces of the supernal army. This form is Lilith, and she is the image of a feminine form…They were both born in a spiritual birth as one, as a parallel to the forms of Adam and Eve above and below: two twin like forms.*" [141]

Later, *The Treatise* explains that they were "entwined like serpents." What is interesting in terms of rebellion here is that the basic motive of un-orderly attraction is present. While the original attraction between Adam and Eve generates a state of contemplative golden peace, the union of the Geburic twins stirs the drums of war and antagonism. In this esoteric and mythic symbolism of the apostate angels and their leader, we can perceive that they clearly partake of the martial and heroic disposition, the quality of expansive and dynamic activity which is the province of the traditional warrior class. The rebel angels embodying this type of warrior, the holders of regal and temporal power, signify

---

141 Joseph Dan (ed.), *The Early Kabbalah* (Paulist Press, 1986) 173.

the second Dumézilian function in the tripartite "Divine Society" of Indo-Iranian and Indo-European antiquity.

Their mythic insurrection against divine spiritual authority, in fact, resumes an ancient theme with far-reaching implications, that of the "Revolt of the Kshatriya" against the Brahminic priesthood, who occupy the supreme apex in the hierarchy of the traditional world conception. As René Guénon noted about Nimrod's foundation of Ninevah and the Assyrian empire:

> *"(It) seems to have been a revolt of the Kshatriyas against the authority of the Chaldean sacerdotal caste. From that stems the legendary associa- tion established between Nimrod and the nephilim or other antediluvian 'giants' which also represent the Kshatriyas in ancient times; and from this likewise the epithet 'nimrodian,' applied to a temporal power which declares itself independent of spiritual authority."* [142]

Aesthetically, this can be seen in the monumental strain of heavy "gigantism," which often suffuses Assyro-Babylonian art forms. The Fall of the Angels and the Revolt of the Kshatriya are realised as repe- titions of the ontological process of Fall and separation.

In the original archetype of the Universal Sovereign, the sacerdotal contemplative function of the Brahmin and flamen exists in unity with the regal active function of the raj and rex, both offices conjoined in the primordial Priest-King, like Melchizedek. But tradition relates that at some point, a rupture and bifurcation occurred of these two aspects of the Universal Sovereign, in which the warrior class sought primacy and the ascendancy of temporal power over spiritual wisdom. In mythic terms, this was the first deviation from the transcendent pattern of the traditional world order. According to René Guénon, it signifies nothing less than the first fatal step toward a progressive and inexorable decline, eventually bringing about the decadence of humanity and the degeneration, loss, or occultation of the primordial doctrine and its mysteries.

Bearing intimate affinities with the metaphysical concepts under- lying the legend of the fall and exile from Eden, this revolt, from the traditional perspective, must represent that descent and denial by which humankind, forsaking the eternal dharma of the sacred order,

---

142 *Symbols of Sacred Science* (Sophia Perennis, 2004), 134.

"abandoned the sky to pursue the earth." Following this deviation, the tendencies of desacralization and materialization become increasingly manifest. The double keys held by Janus, Lord of Initiation, have consequently been usurped by the temporal power represented by the Kshatriyas or warrior cast replicated in the rebel angels. The keys Janus holds are represented by silver for the temporal power and by gold for the spiritual authority.

The importance of the keys is further found in the two hands, the left of restraint and the right of benediction. In the double function of Janus, as the herald of the Golden Age and Lord of the Crossroads of the Worlds, he also turns seasons as *Janua Inferni* and *Janua Coeli*. Through this, he witnesses the reversal of the poles and their rectification to their original centre. This is the true meaning of apocalypse and judgment associated so intimately with Kali Yuga and an age of spiritual waste-lands. This condition heralds the coming of the Golden Age; the *Inferni* (infernal) announces the *Coeli* (heavenly or celestial).

The spiritual tripartition of the "divine society" is epitomised by the divinities of the pre-Capitoline pantheon: Jupiter for the *Sacerdotes*, Mars for the *Eques*, and Venus for the *Agricolae*. This is the classical pattern of the priesthood, nobles, and agriculturalists, traditionally represented by the colours white, red, and green or black. This tripartite colour scale is found as a repeating nerve in all traditional doctrines. It is found in the Greek and later Gnostic typology of human activity where the Greek *Hyle* or matter turned into *Hylekoi*, represented by black and green. The soul or *Psyche* gave name to the *Psychekoi* and the colour red, while the white represented the *Pneaumatikoi*, those who were ruled by *nous* or the divine mind.

This tripartite order also resonates with the three gunas or predomi-nant qualities that inform the philosophy of yoga and reveal themselves in distinct temperaments. These gunas are *sattva, rajas,* and *tamas* and manifest through tantric practice as three roads: the *divya-bhava* or sattvic "god-like" temper, the *vira-bhava* or *rajasic* "heroic" inclination and the *pashu-bhava* which is the "being of bondage" type.

The rebellious Kshatriya, depicted in the narrative of the fallen angels, thus became assimilated to the demonic, exiled from the centre, and condemned for having "revealed the eternal secrets which were in heaven." [143] This does not refer to simply unveiling secrets but a profane

---

143 Ibid.

use of the sacred mysteries and, thus, forcing the higher into the service of the lower. The rebellion, as such, paved the way for the reign of material power and a gradual exaltation of the heroic and "Nimrodian" attitudes, which were largely hubris.

The underlying assumption here is that the sin of the Watchers consisted in the misapplication and profanation of the heavenly mysteries, debasing and materializing them by wielding their potency in the service of the lower ego. By dislocating the heavenly secrets and making them subject to the temporal powers, a similar rapture occurred in all planes of order, immaterial and material. The spiritual order went through a process of solidification and got lost in matter, where the usurping warrior cast wielded the heavenly secrets in the royal hands of terrestrial and temporal dominion.

In the modern age, this mystery has become subject to a complete fall in matter and taken over completely by a wholly profane perspective. What happens is a complete reversal of the poles, where paraphrasing Guénon, "what is high is seen as low, and what is low is seen as high."[144] This situation is partly informed by the materialism informing the modern spirit, where the focus is now on ambition and will. Any person can be whatever they want to be. There are no longer any adherences to Fate, to caste, to the stars, to anything that can witness the presence of a spiritual authority.

The Kshatriyas had usurped the priestly powers, and thus, there were only heroes and the enslaved ones left. Luck and fate had been given to everyone to forge by themselves. In this vacuum entered Lucifer as a response to the desire for light. Lucifer can be equaled to light connected with the moment of a realization, but the modern idea of a "Luciferian tradition" can be brought into question. There is no foundation of traditional metaphysics inherent in the "modern Luciferian traditions"; rather, there is a focus on the heroic, on the glorification of suffering as a means toward strength or *rajasic* and *tamasic* qualities—and this is hardly enough to define a "tradition" in a proper metaphysical sense.

In particular, with the advent of Theosophy, the "Luciferian" elements entered this mythos in an attempt to glorify apostate rebellion. Lucifer gained prominence by association with Prometheus, Phosphorus, and Auriel, but also from the myths informing the Antichrist legends. In

---

144 *The Reign of Quantity and the Signs of the Times* (Sophia Perennis 1945/2001) 206.

particular, the Canaanite son of Sahar, Helel, who, in Canaanite mythology, was a rebellious force who attempted to usurp the throne of God.

This means that the original fall, which was an unnatural desire toward the corporeal, matured into a God-defying attribute and the successive war in heaven. René Guénon, in *The Reign of Quantity and the Signs of the Times,* states that this phenomenon, "Luciferianism," is characterised by the attitude of rebellion by refusing to accept a superior authority.[145] "Satanism," on the other hand, is certainly not the same, as it is the manifestation of a complete reversal of normal relationships and the hierarchical order. We might see "Satanism" as the consequence of a "Luciferian fall."

The consequences of the "Luciferian" roots of modernist deviation and the inevitable descent and decline that the fall of the angels or the Kshatriya Revolt inevitably manifested can be seen in the modern materialistic world conception. This is a vital component for understanding certain aspects of esoteric traditions, such as the Kshatriya Revolt and the fall of the angels, as described in Genesis and *The Book of Enoch.* This Gnostic mythologem of deviation from the sacred order and consequent corruption and decline is the secret knowledge that makes sense of so many things that hitherto baffled or puzzled.

So many things fall into place and begin to make sense when viewed in the light of this tradition, not the least of which is the destructively unbalanced way the modern Western world exalts material dominion at the expense of sacred wisdom, manifesting the final fruits of the "Luciferian" impulse of "tamasic" descent, which characterises modernism and materialism.

The bipartition of the sacerdotal and regal functions that resulted from the Revolt of the Kshatriya or the fall of the rebel angels can be seen to have caused a fracture through the entire tradition. The consequences of this rebellion are most notable in the modern Western world, which is demonstrated by the West's focus on the importance of action. Thus, the West is markedly a *rajasic* or "heroic-oriented" world, in contrast to the contemplative and sacerdotal focus we find in the East.

This slippage is even noted in the Nordic *Eddas,* where, in the poem "Rigsthula," we see how the sacerdotal caste has disappeared. "Rigsthula" tells about how Heimdall, associated with *Yggdrasil,* the *axis mundi,* and being "white-radiant," returns to his ancestry in

---

145 Ibid. 241–242.

the form of Rig and brings forth three estates of humanity. What is interesting in this text is that the traditional colours have suffered a slippage together with the disappearance of the priestly class. Here, white is the colour ascribed to the royal aristocrats, the earls (*jarls*), who are in possession of the wisdom of the runes. The colour red has been given to the warrior-nobles, known as *karls*, who are the farmer-craftsman. The colour black remains with the peasants.

Insofar as the immutable norm of traditional civilization exalts the supremacy of spiritual knowledge over action and the dependency of regal power on the "heavenly mandate," it is to this symbolic "slippage" of functions in occidental branches of Indo-European tradition that we might trace the distant and decidedly mysterious origins of those tendencies which later manifest themselves in Western materialism. This materialism, with its relentless ethos of action, extroversion, and worship of material mastery and power, is underpinned by a pervasive and hubristic "titanism" whose final fruits are manifest in the bases of industrial-technological scientism.

The fatal rupture between the divine authority and temporal power generates the first of a series of cosmic conflicts that transpire as the ages pass. From the rupture caused by the celestial rebellion, a rupture is, in turn, generated between the aristocracy and the priests, then between merchants and the aristocracy, and finally between the working class and the mercantile class. This last rupture leads to an entropic disintegration, and the spiritual virtue gets lost in the dust of matter. As such, the successive clouding of the spiritual authority is mirrored in the entire historical process of increasingly negative cycles that lead to an analogous deterioration of human nature. René Guénon said in this regard:

> "*The supremacy of the Brahmins maintains doctrinal orthodoxy; the revolt of the Kshatriyas leads to heterodoxy. But with the domination of the lower castes comes intellectual night, and this is what in our day has become of a West that threatens to spread its darkness over the entire world.*" [146]

This rupture of traditional functions and consequent degeneration can rightly be viewed as a fall, but this fall also implicates a metaphysical

---

146 *Spiritual Authority and Temporal Power* (Sophia Perennis, 1929/2001) 30.

necessity. Ibn al-Arabi commented in length in *The Meccan Revelations* about the perfection of the One in the doctrine called *wahdat al wujūd,* "oneness of being." This doctrine tells that when the one discloses itself, it does so in conformity with its possibilities. The inherent oneness (*wujūd*) is unbound and, therefore, not possible to define by any articulation or definition.

The possibilities are found in the ninety-none beautiful names, which express an infinite range of possibilities for manifestation in conformity with the mathematical fact that nothing can ever be exactly the same upon repetition. If the divine name consists of all possibilities, it must also contain the apparent negation of divine truth, manifested as the principle of dispersion and exile from the centre; ego-centric, self-grasping, and fragmented existence is the illusory realm of contingent selfhood.

The Revolt of the Kshatriya, as a mythic theme, expresses the metaphysical nature of the double fall, the one of angels and of humankind. The "fall" clouds the eye of the heart in such a way that the spiritual havens seem alien and outside reach. In the clouding of the eye of the heart enters Iblis, the one who marks the boundaries for a given set of possibilities to unfold. The illusion of distance to matter being less than the distance to the divine tempts humankind to embrace the superiority of matter, and Iblis turns into this moment as your chosen *al-Mudhill* or "misguider"—which remains a divine possibility if we follow al-Arabi's reasoning. This tells us that misguidance tends to be the path most favoured in the materialistic West.

If delusion, vice, and misknowledge become increasingly apparent within the cyclical worldview of traditional devolution, manifesting as entropic symptoms of progressive deterioration in the state of things, it can only be in fulfilment of a truly mysterious purpose. This purpose is a necessary foil through which, by contrast, we are oriented toward and made cognisant of the Straight Path upon which all Gnostics and wayfarers attain the "Light of Lights," the Supreme Essence beyond all duality. Thus, the final phases of the Hesiodic "Age of Iron" or the winter tide of the Platonic "Great Year," for all that it is a corrupt and exhausted age of untruth, decline, and hypocrisy, nevertheless, present certain unique spiritual possibilities for the contemporary person.

When humans lived in heaven on Earth, Eden, they were absorbed in wisdom, born from contemplation of the possibilities of the One. It was a state of enlightened peace and bliss. This was a state quite different from the dyadic materialistic illusion of modernity that invites doubt and degeneration as a part of its heroic warrior ethos.

The restoration of celestial order is represented by Seth, who holds the caduceus with the entwined serpents, the one red, representing the royal and temporal power, and the other white for spiritual authority. They both entwine the axis of the sacred centre, like Adam and Eve or Samael and Lilith, upon restoration and salvation. Herein lies a mystery quite simple and profound.

By realizing your *varna*, or caste, you will realise your *svadharma*, or chosen lot. By this, in the words of Plato, you will consummate your chosen life. Bringing your life in accord with the position chosen will open a straight path to realizing your purpose through realignment with spiritual authority. This is the first step toward the realization of the *pan anthropos*, or the "universal man." Understanding the metaphysical implications of the Kshatriya Revolt and its complex ramifications in the modern world provides an important part of this mystery of reuniting the dislocated forces and impulses in a total realization of truth; hence, we must look to the stars to find our soul. In all this, we cannot deny certain grandeur to the warrior mythos, even in its deviated forms.

TWENTY-FOUR

THE THEOSOPHY
OF THE ÉLUS COËNS

*"The only initiation which I advocate and which I look for with
all the ardor of my Soul, is that by which we are able to enter
into the Heart of God within us, and there make an Indissoluble
Marriage, which makes us the Friend and Spouse of the Repairer."*

—LOUIS CLAUDE DE SAINT-MARTIN

Martinez de Pasqually was born in 1727 in Grenoble and is a highly
mysterious figure who, in many ways, mimics the features of the traceless prophetic chain. His life is largely veiled in obscurity, as is the route
of his mysterious legacy. By the Masonic charter inherited by his father,
who received this from Charles Edward Stuart, he opened a chapter of
Scottish rites at Montpelier in 1754. His Masonic chapter developed
over the course of four years, and a distinct doctrine and a lodge for
high-degree Masons was opened under the name *L'Ordre des Chevaliers
Maçons Élus Coëns de l'Univers.* This chivalric order had one goal: the
reintegration of humankind into its original spiritual state.

This led to a curious ritual curriculum of exorcisms and excommunica-
tions of malignant spirits and a theurgic work to call benevolent agents to
restore the human condition. What is particular with Pasqually's theurgy
is that his aim was not to make contact with spirits but, through a spiritual ladder, obtain communication and communion with what he called

the "Active and Intelligent Cause."[147] The doctrine behind this complex theurgy was presented in his *Treatise Concerning the Reintegration of Being*, which reveals an authentic expression of Abrahamic monotheism. In this *Treatise*, Pasqually calls attention to the heart as the pinnacle of "the Man of Desire" in contrast to the "Man of the Stream," who pursues a profane existence. The Man of Desire is the one who has turned his soul to a desire for the divine along the vertical axis of light and realization. It is the *psychikos* who has stationed himself in the heart of pneumatic ascent.

When investigating the sources that informed Pasqually, he says that he had travelled to Arabia, China, and several other faraway places.[148] Most likely, he referred to metaphorical regions that were associated with gnosis under the greater umbrella of the no-longer-used term "the Orient." One of his students, the Prince of Hesse-Darmstadt, suggested that he had received his knowledge in Africa, more specifically, in the Moorish regions of North Africa. Here, in the seventeenth century, we encounter North African and Spanish Sufi orders and conclaves of Sephardic Jews.

Pasqually also commented on his teachings coming from a mysterious figure named "Eleazar the Jew," which supports a deep connection with Sephardic Judaism and can explain the curious Pythagorean elements in his unusual Kabbalah. As pointed out by Robert Amadou, Syro-Christianity, Sufism, and Kabbalah were all focused on a certain gnosis that seems to have been caused and preserved by mystical cross-fertilization in the sixteenth and seventeenth centuries.[149] This particular gnosis concerns the Perfect Man and reintegration.

Pasqually sees Adam's role in the world to have been the Priest-King who would uphold the rites of the divine cult in the spiritual world. His assigned task was to keep the garden, as is also echoed in the Zohar, where Adam and Eve are said to be placed in Eden to tend and grow roses. The rose is a symbol with many layers, but here, it is the rose's relationship to secrecy and divine presence. The Mother of God, Mary, holds roses and lilies, symbols of the Sun and the Moon, which together represent the divine presence on Earth in the form of *Shekinah* and the *Sephirah Yesod*.

This was, as such, the task of Adam and Eve to cultivate the divine presence. The garden represents the Centre of Truth, where the God-Man was appointed as God's ambassador on Earth. In Adam, the perfect

---

147 "Pasqually, Martines de (ca. 1710-1774)." Encyclopedia of Occultism and Parapsychology. *Encyclopedia.com*. Accessed 8 Jan. 2024.

148 See Robert Amadou, *Les leçons de Lyon aux élus Coëns* (Dervy, 2011).

149 Ibid.

image of God in matter was realised and is hidden in the enigmatic insignia of the *Ordre Reaux Croix*, designating the highest hierarchical achievement in Pasqually's order. Naturally, in the insignia, we see the priest and king united by the breath upon the cross. Metaphorically, this represents the Perfect Man, Adam Kadmon. The cross represents manifestation by the squaring of the circle, and the *Ruah*, or the spirit of God, descends and makes the perfect image come alive. In this way, the purpose of creation is fulfilled.

Pasqually ascribes his tradition to Seth, the spiritual ancestor of theurgist. For Pasqually, the secrets told to Seth by the angel Heli, which must somehow be related to the Angel Raziel, are the ones who taught Seth about the rites of restoration. Thus, the ritual corpus of Élus Coëns forms a ritual ladder that enables humankind to become reconciled with God. In the doctrine of Élus Coëns, the double fall of angels and then humanity is given much attention because here, the theurgy plays itself out as a constant exorcism where all impurities are dispelled from the material realm. Pasqually is almost obsessively occupied with applying the negative commandments of the Torah upon the body so it can wrestle out the captured light. This shows itself in dietary and behavioural recommendations that take the form of essentials of the law for whoever wants to ascend the ladder.

At first, Pasqually seems to present a wholly negative attitude toward matter. He sees only the perverse, the morbid, and the corrupt everywhere, but I believe this is to draw our attention to the possibility of bringing humankind back into original unity. It is crucial for Pasqually that we identify and know the forces that steal our attention and turn us into a "man of the stream." What Pasqually strives toward is to bring the understanding that matter is the instrument of salvation. For him, the world is a perfect manifestation of Divine Severity and Divine Mercy, *Geburah* and *Chesed*. By assuming the original role ascribed to the first Priest-King, the "elect priests" of Pasqually's order will gradually habilitate all spirit afflatus imprisoned in matter to its original state—and this includes the perverse and corrupt demonic influences.

It is here the chivalric element enters, which, in Pasqually's age, used to be associated with military dignity, where several prayers in the corpus ask the angel appointed to bring the weapons needed to vanquish the spiritual enemies. It is quite simply a war, or a *jihad*, against one's lower self, the inclinations that draw one's attention away from the "centre of truth." He is speaking about, in allegory, Hiram Abiff's murders, in which vengeance is sought. The aim for the RC + degree of the Élus Coëns is to reinstall the sacerdotal and regal functions invested in Adam. By assuming the original role, humanity can yet again work toward unification, which is an alchemical and theurgic battle along the ladder of angelic lights that are called upon in its operative rituals.

If we now venture further within the depths of Pasqually's theosophy, the golden seed blazing within the double fall will become even more bright and clear. The condition spoken of in *The Book of Jubilees* is where the first couple finds themselves hungry and lost in total distress of alienation in their exile. It goes so far that Eve asks Adam to murder her, to which he answers, "How indeed can I do you any evil, for you are my body."[150] Here, the foundation of Pasqually's approach toward matter and theurgic aim is revealed. It is about being in possession of the knowledge of "evil" but refraining from activation—it is about discernment. Underlying this, we find expressed that the sense of unity with all is the original condition, where all is the body of God. The sensation of being one with the Divine Mind will lead to compassion and a refusal of "evil," as all actions done by you to others are acts done upon your very self.

The fall constituted separation between the garden of perfection, situated at the "centre of truth," and the possibility of otherness becoming a manifest illusion. The peace and contemplation of the garden are ejected as Adam and his progeny are also subject to a fall from the mind (*nous*) to be ruled by the soul (*psyche*). The soul is the mediator between the sense impressions in the sensual and sensorial world, and if the mind is not present to mediate between the impressions, the result is chaotic and unfocused. Such was the condition that Adam and Eve were subject to all forms of sensations and inspirations. The darkness of fragmentation covered his exile, and he was made subject to good and bad spiritual impulses.

This dyadic illusion led to the separation of Adam's posterity and a mentality prefiguring the modern material mindset. This is evident in the feat of Nimrod, who, by building the tower of Babel, sought to gather the disparate people around a material centre, subject to the temporal royal power. Nimrod sought to measure his authority against God himself, and thus, this constitutes the very first of a series of usurpations of spiritual authority by the temporal royal powers. This condition naturally leads to frustration for those who possess the

---

150 *The Book of Jubilees: Or The Little Genesis* (A. & C. Black, 1902).

nostalgia of the Golden Age and, often, a temperament of passionate suffering, a *weltschmerz,* or unconditioned compassion accompanying those spare individuals of a prophetic inclination.

Reintegration was made possible by Abel and Cain as a metaphysical necessity. By giving up his blood and breath, Abel re-enacted the consecration of the Earth and made it holy. As such, Abel reinstalled truth, and Cain, like Iblis, was the one appointed to affirm the truth. By necessity of sacrifice, the *anima mundi* is released from its severity, and through Seth, mercy is released. As such, man also suffered a fall from living in the world of the *nous,* the mind of archetypical ideas, to live in the world of the soul, where he was overcome by experiences and impressions.

Here enters the spirit of restoration, which brings the soul into alignment with the mind, the heart in a straight line with the mind. This spirit is the mysterious Heli, the angel of anointment. He is the oil of salvation, and Heli, as the angel of restoration through chrism, reveals that the breath of blessing and oil are the sacraments of deliverance. It was this spirit that moved Seth and, later, Enoch and inflamed prophets and saviours. Heli is the spirit moving within the image and form of Melchizedek. Whenever water, bread, and oil are present, like in Melchizedek's anointing of Abram, in the name of Heli, the anointing will stimulate ascent. Ascent is noted by a sense of purpose and a realization of destiny. The hand of fate has been opened, and you have accepted the particular path toward the city of the Sun that has been revealed to you.

The children of Seth were assigned the land north of Eden, while Cain, Ham, and his posterity were appointed to the southern lands. It is reasonable to assume that the delegation to the north side of Eden refers to a realignment with Polaris, the "centre of truth," while the south refers to the realms of *Janua Infernis,* which is basically the "not-centre." The prophetic messenger, in the shape of birds, was sent out in the deluge, and the first birds Noah sent out, the ravens, did not return because they found their kin in the southern lands. We see here how the *rajasic* and *tamasic* energies unite by the redness of the south and the blackness of the ravens, a realm typified by heart and soul in the body. When Noah sends out a second pair of birds, it is the doves. The white and peaceful dove returns to the arch, the spiritual centre, with an olive branch. The olive is so intimately linked with Zion and thus carries the message that reintegration is possible. Thus, the arc was stranded on the mountain summit, where the transfiguration of the angels was possible and where Iesu Christo, in the future, would return to his spiritual estate.

The sublime mystery that took place between Abel and Cain, where the sacrifice and the sacrificed became one in mercy, released Seth, and further understanding of the northern and southern lands was gained. Here, the upper triad and the lower triad mirrored each other and, together, formed the Seal of Solomon as forces of restoration and protection of the centre of truth. We might see the southern downward triangle as representing the principle of the past, with mercury being marked by its downward point, with sulphur to the left and salt to the right. This is the alchemical mystery of Cain's progeny. For Seth's children, the triangle points upward to the celestial Mercury, represented by the "Dragon of Righteousness." Between them, the Mercurial mercy manifested through oil, and anointment flows freely from pole to pole.

Pasqually also commented on the "mark of Cain" and said that this was a *Lathan* or a comet.[151] This naturally has many implications, but Pasqually highlighted that this mark speaks of confusion and separation. The comet is visible because of darkness and separation, and he also related comets to cataclysmic events. He concluded his *Treatise* on this subject by suggesting that Cain's mark consisted of being under the influence of the "lesser luminary," the Moon. Seth and his children were assigned the Sun and, therefore, the fixed centre of truth in contrast to the volatile Moon.

The drama of restoration and affirmation played itself out when the sons of Seth saw the daughters of Cain, and yet another *mixis* occurred. As such, Cain's mark announced mercy, which informed the Sethian transmission. By the first sacrifice, Cain restored balance to creation by accepting the role handed to him by Fate and thus prefigured the sacrifice of Iesu Christo and the release of the mercy of salvation. When Cain murdered Abel, he sacrificed the flesh and released the spirit. He did what needed to be done in order to become perfected. He released Abel from his corruption, and by a series of sacred annihilations, the poles of the world were turned back into place until the age of light resurfaced. This is the alchemical mystery Pasqually presented to explain how the interaction between the cycle of the Moon and Sun repeatedly released the golden seed and made him a portent for true tradition through his pre-modern theosophy.

---

151   *Treatise Concerning the Reintegration of Beings* (The Johannine Press, 2001), 119.

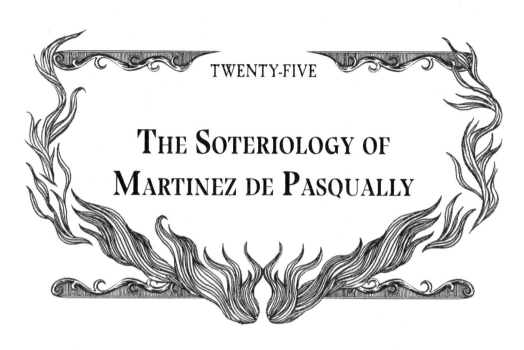

TWENTY-FIVE

The Soteriology of Martinez de Pasqually

"The will of the Operator is that of a fallen man who wishes to reintegrate himself to the creation of the universe."

—Robert Amadou

L'Ordre des Chevaliers Maçons Élus Coëns de l'Univers (The Order of Knight-Masons Elect Priests of the Universe) or simply *Élus Coëns* was given ample attention in the previous chapter, but it is interesting to give separate space to the soteriology of Pasqually as here, a bridge between Sethian and Valentinian Gnosticism might be detected.

When looking at the soteriology of Pasqually, a clear Sethian theme is present, but the redemptive motive we find attributed to Adam's penitence is not present in Pasqually's soteriology. Enoch, Seth, and Noah are correctly conceived of as the Three Patriarchs, the three luminaries, but Pasqually, it seems, also gave crucial importance to Abraham, Isaac, and Jacob as successors of the legacy of the patriarchs, yet he also stretched a vinculum from Seth to Jesus Christ through Moses, which is in harmony with the traceless path of Melchizedek. Yet, Melchizedek giving his blessing to Abraham would not indicate that Abraham would be the sole successor of Melchizedek, but rather a temporal manifestation of the timeless wisdom present in the

Abrahamic faiths. Pasqually writes in his *Treatise on the Reintegration of Beings* the following:

> *"Adam, in his first state of justice, as I have outlined to you, truly received from the divine spirit all of the sciences and spiritual knowledge—that is, the sure path and exact plan of every divine spiritual operation for which he had been emanated—but having made criminal use of his powers, the Creator withdrew them immediately and left poor Adam, even after his reconciliation, prone to making mistakes in all of his human, spiritual, and temporal works, which happens to man every time he operates only by virtue of the three ternary powers which are airy, earthly, and fiery powers."* [152]

From this, he concluded that Adam, upon losing his spiritual powers, never regained them, not even in his years of penitence that gave birth to Seth, which was the original pro-victim state he obtained. Instead, Adam became the first of the "Men of Desire," an imprisoned man. Seth was, as such, not instructed by Adam in anything but the mysteries of Golgotha and funerary rites. It was Heli, usually understood to be the Angel of God in the form of Christological wisdom, who taught Seth the secrets of the worlds and became the angel of prophecy and prophets. Pasqually referred to Heli as *"La Chose"* in his *Treatise* and clearly connected this force to Seth through Noah, who was bestowed the holy spirit of Heli, which he says is the *"Wisdom that walks with the Eternal."* [153]

For Pasqually, the gravest loss Adam suffered was his direct communication with the divine. Losing this, Adam became incapable of choosing, as his thinking became material, ruled by appetites and selfish desires. Adam became a victim of humours and temperaments and brought on a great enslavement to take place.

The theurgy of Pasqually is designed in such a way that ultimately, communion with *"La Chose"* will restore this channel of communion with the divine, and the Man of Desire becomes a quiet *logos* and the "second Adam," Adam Kadmon, Adam perfected in the image of Seth. The Sethian theme also reveals itself in the grade structure of Pasqually's order, *Élus Coëns*, where the degree of *Maître Élu* is given

---

152 *Treatise Concerning the Reintegration of Beings* (The Johannine Press, 2001), 113.
153 Ibid.

to the influence of Heli under the guise of Elijah, the prophet. The next three degrees involve the importance of Moses, Zerubbabel, and Joshua or Jesus, whereas the last degree of *Reaux Croix* invites Heli and Seth, and the objective is to become the Second Adam, which means that one has become a priest in the order of Melchizedek and accomplished the reconciliation of soul with spirit, crucial for the reintegration of being.

There are some similarities with Valentinian Gnosticism in Pasqually's cosmology and views on redemption insofar as the fall into matter led both Pasqually and Valentinus to the most terrible consequence of severing the direct communion with the divine. Pasqually saw the Man of Desire evolving through Cain, the hylic man, Abel, the psychic man, and becoming the pneumatic man, the man of *nous*, who connects us to Seth and reinstates the vinculum with the divine. The reintegration Pasqually had in mind is truly a reconciliation with the divine; hence, Jesus Christ became essential in the restoration of Adam's fall. It was necessary that Jesus Christ went through the suffering and death of Adam, but as a spirit of light, a perfect being like Seth, to even out the consequences of Adam's error.

Whilst Sethian prophets, like Enoch, Noah, Moses, and Elijah, achieved reintegration on a personal level, Jesus Christ made reintegration possible on a global level, hence the importance of Jesus Christ for the Man of Desire. The way of reintegration for the Man of Desire was through rigid theurgy, prayers, psalms, and fasting that was all religiously timed, especially to the movements of the Moon and other planetary bodies. The theurgic operations invoked angelic beings of a wide range of virtues, while the beneficial angels would be helpful for a more direct ascent in the work toward reintegration. The "bad" angels and more demonic powers and presences would be subject to exorcisms and, at times, attempts of restoration to their glory prior to their fall.

The daily invocations a *Maître Élu* is expected to perform consist of simple rituals where the principle of *Kadosh* is called in the presence of the Hebrew letter *shin* (ש), representing the fire of Seth, a candle-light at a given hour. In this, the Operator clearly states that they are seeking to "return in virtue and spiritual power eternally."[154] The Operator would then extinguish the candle and sit in quiet aspiration and longing in the

---

154 See Mathieu G. Ravignat, *The Original High Degrees and Theurgical System of the Masonic Elect Cohen Knights of the Universe* (Self Published, 2019).

aromatic darkness for some time. These simpler rituals would then lead to more complex theurgic operations, aiming toward communication with the divine through the intercession of Heli.

The redeeming motives in Pasqually's *Treatise on the Reintegration of Being* are of great interest, as in this, we see the consequence of Abraham's blessing by Melchizedek taken into the explorations of a different mystery, namely the one concerning the Man of Desire. It does appear as though Pasqually saw the dissolution of matter into particles of dust and then material absence as the goal of the work of an Èlus Coën, just as he saw Satan as the very real power of corruption in the world. Hence, it was important to bind and excommunicate Satan from all theurgic work so the grand and slow work of reintegration could begin.

It would appear that the life-denying Valentinian nerve in Pasqually's soteriology was quite strong and solely focused on the restoration of soul and spirit whilst matter was, by default, corrupt, and how Jesus' life, suffering, crucifixion, and resurrection were the spiritual mirror of Adam's trajectory as a being of light to a fallen man who restored original sin. This vision would be different from the view held by other Gnostic sects, like the Naassenes and Ophites, who were more occupied with how Jesus came to reveal wisdom and didn't make any pertinence for a sin Adam already made penitence for.

Following this track, it is also of interest to point out Giordano Bruno's pantheism, which would see the divine manifesting itself in matter, which would question the seriousness of corrupt matter or mixes and its role in redemption. Also, Jules Doinel was ordained by Aeon Jesus, with two Bogomil bishops attending. Bogomil doctrine teaches that Satanael, Michael's brother, was forgiven for his mistake, and, as such, redemption already happened by the intervention of God, which made it unnecessary for Jesus Christ to die for a sin already forgiven. Rather, Jesus came as an example and to light the fire of gnosis and wisdom. Saint Michael took care of the spiritual domains as the "Golden Tzar," and Satanael was given the material realm to rule over as its "Silver Tzar," clearly referencing the two main luminaries of the heavens.

No matter the stance of matter, the central theme in Pasqually's soteriology involves Seth and the importance of reigniting this original divine flame so we can be reintegrated into our noetic and primitive state as spiritual beings through the intervention of Heli.

TWENTY-SIX

BRUNO'S TELESMATA AND THE ASTROLOGICAL INCANTATIONS OF CIRCE

*"The crucial process of magic is the clear establishment of the Vincula
which will 'unite Earth and Heaven' within the Noetic mirror of the
Heart–Mind—this is the 'link' that energises the fashioned Talisman."*

—NIGEL JACKSON, *CELESTIAL MAGIC*

In his treatise *On the Shadows of Ideas*, Giordano Bruno gives an outline of his philosophy and methodology of creating talismans. Bruno saw the creation of talismans as working the shadow of the formless and divine ideas into a trail, footprint, or "engraving" of light. The shadow was perceived as a fusion of light and darkness that, in the talismanic form, provides us with a form created by light; in itself, it does not contain the full light of its original form, hence its shadow quality.

He also sets forth some general rules for creating talismans, which are as follows: [155]

1. Sensations, such as heat, for example, are not unilateral. The sensation depends on one's sensitivity to it, which is different from person to person. This led Bruno to conclude that it was imperative to create images from practice and foresight and not

---

155 See Giordano Bruno, *De Umbris Idearum: On the Shadows of Ideas* (Huginn, Muninn & Co. Pub, 1582/2013).

just uncritically adopt an image for use just because it holds some general merit.

2. In order to find true forms or images that represent the unique bond between heaven and Earth with the magician as a mediator, it is important to be aware of the axioms of chaos, which states that True Chaos is variety without order. No order exists where no diversity is found. The whole of beauty consists of variety.

3. When a talisman is made, you are conducting light and truth from the heavens to engrave its form of a material object, so a talisman is made from the light of truth, and this light then returns to whence it came when the astrological conditions for the access of this light are no longer accessible.

4. The greater the light and the density of the body, the sharper the shadow becomes, which means that the more exact we are in obtaining life and light from the heavens and embedding it in proper material substances, the sharper and better the result will be.

5. Is the shadow of an idea a defect in an effect? Is it virtue born by absence? Are these shadows substances in themselves, or are they cosmic accidents? We must remember that the light is like the father and the shadow is like the mother, and with shadows, there is no opposition to be found; there is no light or darkness, but its harmonious fusion, like in the Song of Songs 2:3 (KJV), "I sit down in his shadow with great delight."

6. In the twelfth concept, Bruno states that deformed animals take beautiful forms in the heavens because, in heaven, the virtues are unified and not scattered as on Earth.

7. In order for an image to have the desired impact, it cannot be made alive by showing it to the eyes only; it must become alive in the mind's eye.

8. In the ninth concept, Bruno lists the following considerations in conformity with the ideas of Plotinus (and Marsilio Ficino):

    - Clear the mind.
    - Attention.
    - Intention.
    - Contemplation of order.
    - Proportional comparison of order.

- Negation or separation.
- Desire.
- Transforming the self in the thing.
- The transformation in itself.

Bruno teaches us how to observe a thing in light of its form or idea and then move on to investigate its qualities and what the form might teach us about nature and the cosmos. On the basis of these forms, attributes are then chosen to give form to what is desired. Desire, or *eros*, was fundamental for Bruno in the manufacturing of talismans, and *eros* was present as the bonding agent, the power necessary to establish a bond or vinculum, as he writes in *A General Account of Bonding*:

> *"For action actually to occur in the world, three conditions are required: (1) an active power in the agent; (2) a passive power or disposition in a subject or patient, which is an aptitude in it not to resist or to render the action impossible (which reduces to one phrase, namely, the potency of matter); and (3) an appropriate application, which is subject to the circumstances of time, place and conditions. In the absence of these three conditions, all actions are, simply speaking, always blocked."*[156]

Bruno then continues with a description concerning *mixis* that reveals an Epicurean and stoic influence. It should be mentioned that Aristotle speaks about similar themes in his works concerning physics, states that not all powers and potentialities can be mixed, and stresses the need for the presence of a predisposition in the bodies that enables it to receive the active agent. Water mixes well with water because of similarity and water and wine mix well because of a sympathy that makes the one disposed toward receiving the other, while water and oil are in conflict and thus do not mix with each other.

One must study the nature of the matter in order to decide what agent would be effective, and thus, medicine for the human body must be of such nature that the pores can absorb it and introduce it to the bloodstream or that it can be introduced to the digestive tract

---

156   In *Cause, Principle and Unity* (Cambridge University Press, 1998) 132.

or directly to the blood. Further, the human-animal experiences the world, both natural and supra-natural, because of the senses. It is the senses that are the roads toward the soul. It is, therefore, important to carefully investigate both the individual and the species itself, which also includes the variety of planetary powers dignified or afflicted in the individual. This form of bonding between the active and passive power is of a more general type, while the bonding caused by harmonies, such as song and poetry, is of a different type.

The rhythm of song and poetry is caused by measurements of numbers in sequences of time. The level of effect varies from individual to individual, as some people are more moved by the tragic and others are more moved by the comic. As Bruno wrote: "different harmonies bind different souls."[157] There are also other forms of bonding caused by vision, imagination, and thoughts, as well as some significant nuances between these forms of bonding. First, the bonding caused by vision, where the eyes are the medium; if we see a thing of beauty, this arouses pleasant feelings within us; if we see something ghastly, it evokes unpleasant feelings. Bruno describes this process in the following way: "And the emotions of the soul and spirit bring something additional to the body itself, which exists under the control of the soul and the direction of the spirit."[158]

Bruno is encountering a mystery here because feelings like compassion and empathy are also conveyed through the same senses, and he concludes that feelings are bound through vision. Then, there is the bonding that occurs through imagination. He says that the role of imagination is "to receive images derived from the senses and to preserve, combine and divide them."[159] This can be accomplished by a creative free choice, as is done by poets and painters who combine images in a particular form of order. This bonding can also be unmediated by a deliberate choice, as when some form of inspiration arises in us and thus produces internal images, we are awake or asleep.

Interestingly, Bruno comments that this form of bonding can lead to mental illness, what he calls "the dreams of the wakeful," where one confuses the images for reality, which, in turn, generates mania and melancholy. Today, we might refer to this form of bonding as

---

157 In *Cause, Principle and Unity* (Cambridge University Press, 1998) 135.
158 Ibid. 137.
159 Ibid.

"delusions" and personality disorders of a schizoid type. Surprisingly, he also presents an environmentalist allegory here, speaking of the seed that is sown, which responds to its predisposition but also acts upon what is found in its environment, where improper mixtures create disturbances, hindering healthy growth.

Bruno even gives a further diagnostic explanation and suggests treatment, as he sees these forms of disturbances as arising from a besiegement of the spirit where noxious material distorts the world of images and generates fantasies and delusions. The cure is said to be "a simple purgation of humours and a simple diet are adequate to cure disturbed images and then free the internal senses which are bound in this way."[160]

Bruno considers bonding by imagination as crucial for the physician, saying that "this is the doorway and entrance of all the actions and passions and feelings of animals. And to that linkage is tied the more profound power of thought."[161] Thought is the last agent of bonding Bruno speaks about. Imagination and thought are intimately related to each other, as imagination duplicates thoughts to some extent.

He relates this form of bonding to faith and contemplation, and it is by thought which is produced by speech that a person is bonded to honour or to ill repute. Clearly, Bruno touches upon the core of rhetoric as presented by Aristotle and, in particular, how it is related to the character of the orator. It is illuminating to see that psychoanalyst and psychiatrist Jaques Lacan perceived similar effects; he comments in *Ècrits:* "It is through the pathway of the complex that the images that inform the broadest units of behaviour are instated in the psyche, images with which the subject identifies one after the other in order to act out, as sole actor, the drama of their conflicts."[162]

Prior to this observation, in the same chapter, Lacan refers to images or *imago* as a factor that is usually extracted or, by its nature, can cause "confused states." After this, we move into the field of the intellect, the divine mind, memory, and reason, what Bruno refers to as "the spiritual powers of the soul," and relocate this to an order outside bonding. This is because the material that the senses convey to the soul is not subject to the divine mind in the same way that sense imprints are subject to

---

160 In *Cause, Principle and Unity* (Cambridge University Press, 1998) 140.
161 Ibid.
162 Jaques Lacan, *Ècrits* (W.W. Norton & Co., 2006) 72.

the *mixis* that occurs in the "sentient world," where the corporeal is the field of experience for the soul.

This would suggest that love or *eros* is the most powerful bonding agent because this potency is revealed in sympathy and harmony. If so, *eros* would be the force that regulates and provokes the four temperaments as the compass of cures for the Renaissance physician. This was to discover what humour or virtue was in excess and bring the excess into harmony with the rest of humours and virtues so that the patient can experience a state of contentment and balanced fullness of life. This would indicate being turned toward what is good and true, such as in the myth where Psyche was turned to Eros. As Bruno comments:

> "(The) heroic enthusiast comes to realize that he can translate every-
> thing into the species of his intellect, in a seemingly endless process of
> actualization. This is due to the bond of love, which elevates him ever
> higher in this process, eventually causing him to realize the infinite
> (and thus apparently illimitable) potentiality of his intellect...
> Knowledge and love are thus revealed as the two cosmic forces which
> are apparently separate in nature but which spring from the same
> potency and source." [163]

The slight difference between Bruno and Ficino was that Bruno advocated a form of holistic universalism and saw no difference between the material and spiritual in terms of accessibility, which led to a perception of the cosmos as pulsating with the mark of God everywhere and a lesser focus on the inherent order. It was this "spiritual" orientation that, toward the end of his life, generated a theology that led to his errors as he reinterpreted vital statures of the Catholic doctrine from this perspective.

Let us turn to a key text when it comes to a refined and precise idea of how Bruno saw the talismanic art in practice by turning to his *Cantus Circaeus*, "Circe's Canticles or Incantations," published in Paris 1582 when he was thirty-four years old. Bruno saw the cosmos as filled with ideas and forms that generated unique bonds with one another

---

163   In *Cause, Principle and Unity* (Cambridge University Press, 1998) xxi/xxii.

and entered into cosmic rhythms mimicking the relationship between the Sun and Earth. Basically, he saw all the stars as Suns, a bold idea in his time, when the debate was still between the astronomy presented by Galileo and Copernicus, where Bruno was anticipating both the Newtonian paradigm and quantum physics. His rejection of the Ptolemaic hierarchy that naturally placed God in a superior position as the mysterious mover of all cosmic bodies in a hierarchic relationship was, for Bruno, a cosmological lie.

Bruno's thinking has been described as both pantheistic and pandeistic, both ideas being in concord with one another, with pandeism suggesting that the creator force, upon concluding creation, merged with its own creative product. Pantheism says that the material and spiritual are equal, affirming that the material world is as divine as the spiritual realm. Hence, what became the growing thorn between Bruno and the Church was, amongst other issues, this specific heresy. Catholic doctrine can go as far as agreeing that we can experience divine grace and mystery by virtue of creation, but to say that the creator is present in creation would impact the entire theology and, in particular, the idea of Jesus Christ and his perfection and claims to cosmic rulership.

Bruno's worldview is important to keep in mind as we now will look at his *Cantus Circaeus*. We will meet a presentation of the famous sorceress, perfect in herself as the embodiment of the Sun by virtue of being his daughter. Not only this, but the enchantments of Circe also demonstrate the unique system of magical memory Bruno developed by his quite "sorcerous" take on planetary hymns, showing Circe as someone who does not bend to authority but rather demands what she wants by virtue of the bonds she has established with the powers in question.

She is presented as someone who is learned in magical lore, which resides in hidden places, but that her house is guarded by "domestic things" such as sheep, cows, goats, and wild animals dwelling in the forest surrounding her house. It is a place rich with birds and fish. Circe is presented as someone whose magical lore is tied to the domestic cult of the house and would, as such, be quite in tune with the agricultural and domestic origins of what often is called "witchcraft," namely the art developed around the needs of peasants and agricultural societies.

However, to enter her house, you must first confront a muddy pig that is guarding the entrance to her atrium. It is crucial for entering her atrium that you avoid any squabbling with the pig and that the pig does not leave you dirty. The meaning of this encounter is explained later when Circe teaches her student, Moeris, about the qualities of the swine. She lists two sets of qualities, all of them bad, going from A to Z; hence, Bruno wrote about what qualities and virtues one needs to avoid in order to enter the atrium. Basically, you must be a virtuous, tranquil, and aware person in order to enter Circe's atrium.

Upon passing the test of the wine, you will be confronted with a dog, snarling and terrible. This test lies in not entertaining the dog's fierceness and avoiding his attacks and by not attacking the dog yourself. With this test being solved successfully, a solar rooster will bring you to the presence of Circe.

What is of interest here is to see Bruno's art of memory used in practice as elements of a story. We already know that the mystery of Circe is guarded by domestic life, wild forest animals, fish, pigs, dogs, and roosters, and these animal qualities tend to surface when we bring Circe to mind. The use of qualities set into the format of hymn or summoning continues in the first dialogue in *Cantus Circaeus* that goes like this:

"Sun, you illuminate all things. Apollo, hearer of song, quiver-bearer, bow-wielder, powerful with your arrows; Pythius, wearer of the laurel, prophet, shepherd, poet, augur, and physician; Phoebus, rose-ate one, long-haired, the one with the beautiful locks, golden one, shining one, peaceful one, player of the cythera, singer, and speaker of truth; Titan, Milesian, Palatine, Cyrrhean, Timbrian, Delian, Delphic, Leucadian, Tegaean, Capitolian, Smynthean, Ismean and Latalian; you who assign miraculous natures to the elements, by which dispensation the seas grow swollen or are rendered calm, the air and the heavens are roused or are serene, the teeming power and force of fires are directed or repressed. By his administration the structure of the universe flourishes, the inscrutable power of the manifestation of ideas enter us below through the means of the soul of the world. From this come the various and multiple powers of herbs, plants and stones, which are capable of drawing the Universal Spirit to themselves through the rays of the stars.

"Be present for the holy vows of your daughter Circe. If I am chaste in spirit and bound to you, be present with me that I might have the faculty of performing rites worthy of you. Behold, we have easily erected altars for you. Your fragrant incenses are present here, even the smoke of blushing sandalwood. Lo, for the first time have I whispered barbarous and arcane songs. The cleansings have been completed. We have unfettered seven kinds of perfume for the seven princes of the world. The usual loosenings and bindings have been accomplished. We have adorned all things with the appropriate hieroglyphics. Only one thing is missing; that we should offer up all things ardently desired in those imprecations which ought to have been first, and which have been sought again for their rhythms." [164]

This opening enchantment in itself contains, by poetic reference, all the keys of Circe's rituals. She focuses on the Sun, as she is his daughter, and in this, she references her spiritual ancestry, where we find the Sun, Apollo, Pythius, and Phoebus. These figures are each praised for given qualities that Circe herself, by ancestral dictate, also can access through being the daughter of the Sun. Hence, we see how the laurel is important for her poetry, prophecy, and song, to know the way of beauty and peace as much as the way of the arrow and illumination. Then, she salutes her geographical heritage in reference to being from a different location, both real and mythical, around the Mediterranean.

This being done, Circe summarises her cosmology and where her focus will be placed, namely on the "miraculous nature of the elements" that we see contain their own natural law, and it is the elements that cause the sea to "grow swollen" or be rendered calm—not God. Circe continues and states that "the manifestation of Ideas enter us below through the means of the soul of the world."[165] Hence, plants and minerals are given radical importance in her first enchantment, where it is explicitly stated that all material things pull the Universal Spirit to them and are inhabited by this Spirit through the rays of the stars.

---

164 Giordano Bruno and Darius Klein (trans.), *Cantus Circaeus* (Ouroboros Press, 2009).
165 Ibid.

Here, we see that the rituals of Circe in *Cantus Circaeus* can be said to follow this sequence:

1. She gives her word, a vow, or a pact.
2. She is chaste in spirit on the day of summoning, which would probably refer to dedicating the day to solar activities and meditation and not allowing any other virtue or quality to interfere with the bond or vinculum she intends to make. The more "solar" she manages to be on this day, the stronger the bond with the solar object will be. This preparation includes cleansing, most likely with an herbal infusion.
3. She erects an altar.
4. Incense is burned, in this case, sandalwood.
5. She *whispers* barbarous and arcane songs.
6. Seven types of perfumes are used.
7. Loosening and bindings are performed, which would roughly equate to exorcisms in the sense of throwing away impurities and calling other spirits or entities who would sympathise with the main force or potency summoned. In this case, the forces called are Apollo, Pythius, and Phoebus, alongside the Sun.
8. Hieroglyphs or seals and magical writs have been imprinted on all things.
9. The desire, wish, or intent is presented, but this should be presented in a rhythm, which refers to a harmony of intent, emotion, mind, and utterance.

What we see here is an example of an attitude of someone who knows who they are and knows what they want. Circe is making the necessary self-sacrifice, not because of humility or her worshipful nature. No, she does this so she can allow herself to be filled with virtues in resonance with what she seeks to summon to ensure a connection as powerful as possible. She treats the invited force respectfully, as any host should treat an invited guest with reverence and respect, not with humility and meekness. These elements become very evident later on in her incantations for the planets, which are quite different in temperament from what we find in the Solomonic corpus of conjurations. This is where the summoner borrows the protection and power of God and Jesus Christ to perform their magic. There is no God nor any Jesus in Circe's enchantments; she summons by virtue of who she is, her legacy, ancestry, and vast magical knowledge.

THE ASTROLOGICAL
INCANTATIONS OF CIRCE

Giordano Bruno, in his thesis on *Mathematical Magic,* addresses bonds or vinculums, the ways a spirit is bound or released between itself and the one who summoned it. He writes how some of these bonds are obtained from the natural world and others from the celestial, and here, Bruno gathers invocations, exorcisms, herbs, flowers, ice, snow, and elements from the natural world as being equally important as those from the celestial. The celestial bonds concern rays, heavens, stars, orbs, fortunes, lots, and other matters that invoke astrological timing or election.

Further in this thesis, he states that the strongest and highest bonds are those that stem from the intellectual and divine world, a bond that is generated by "pleading or blessing." It has to be a commemoration of the celestial things rising from the mysteries. He even gives an example from Genesis 3:13–15, Numbers 21:6–9, and Luke 10:19 concerning the use of the serpent. In this sequence, we find the expulsion of serpents from Eden, Moses erecting a serpent cross to drive serpents away, and finally, in Luke, how the followers of Jesus were given the power thread upon serpents.

This motive is interesting as we find the use of snakes as a bond related to command and domination, even in Norway, as recorded by Mary Rustad in her translation of a Norwegian manual of folk magic called *The Black Books of Elverum,* which says, "Beat a snake to death with a stick and lift a woman's skirt with the same stick three times to get her to conceive."[166] The point is how a bond was established because the bond and its use were always related to an understanding of the bond itself and how it could be used for good and for bad. In this

---

166 (Galde Press, 2009) 51.

spell, it is clearly the phallic shape of the snake that is confronted with another phallic object that intends to generate friction as related to the vulva and conception.

Let us look at the differences between Circe and her conjurations in light of what we find in a classic of Ceremonial Magic, Peter d'Abano's *Heptameron*, which summons the Sun in the following way:

> *"I conjure and declare unto you, you strong and holy angels: In the name Adonay, Adonay, Eye, Eye, Eyu, he who is who was, and will be, Eye, Aloraye, in the name Sadaye, Saday, Cados, Cados, Cados, high, sitting above the cherubim, and by His name, great, holy, strong, powerful, and exalted, above all the heavens, Eye, Saraye, Creator of the ages, who created the world, the sky, and the earth, sea, and all those who were in them on the first day of the heavens, and sealed upon them with His holy name, Yhon, onto the earth, by the seals of earth, by his honored and precious name Yhaaand by the names of the holy angels who rule in the first host and serve in the presence of the most powerful, great, and honored angel Salamia, and by the name of the star that is the Sun, and by the most immeasurable sign of the living God by whom all is foretold, I conjure the angel Raphael who is the commander of the day of the Lord, and by the name Adonay, the God of Israel, who created the world and every thing whatsoever in it, that you work for me and fulfill all my wishes that are my petition, plea, and vow in my distress."*[167]*

We have to account for the Thomist influence here, as Thomas Aquinas clearly stated in his *Summa Theological* that magic could be legal if one simply was present with devotion at the proper time a given virtue was present, meaning, at daybreak, you could recite Peter d'Abano's prayer and even leave out magical items to be empowered by the Sun without any active push toward making anything happen. Early Church law considered taking advantage of a natural divine ray in a passive mode to be in harmony with the divine order. Now, if we look at Circe's conjuration of the Sun, we see a clear shift.

---

167 I made a rendering here based on Peter d'Abano's, *Heptameron* (Ouroboros Press, 2003) and what is found in Joseph H. Peterson's *Elucidation of Necromancy* (Ibis Press, 2021), 51.

"Ye gods, I adjure you again—why do you hesitate? Why do you throw in your lot with the vectors of forms, falsifiers of the signs of Nature? Truthful Jupiter, whose outraged majesty reveals itself through you, also exercises power over you. The father of humankind compels you, in the power of whom I bind you thrice and four times. I also exercise power over you through the others who have the power of rule over the gods, above all other kinds of living creatures; so that you do not hinder me with their dead sophistries, so that the truth is manifested in outward appearances which go forth visibly...I will therefore further harass them with a third conjuration..."[168]

Circe is not pleading like a meek votary of the planetary spirits; rather, she is demanding, and not only this, but she is even giving a kick to the clerical practitioners, "the falsifiers," and thus, calls the attention of Saturn under the praise name of "Falxifer." She jumps to Jupiter and reminds him about his essence and virtue, but also reminds him about his place.

Circe is simply demonstrating that she knows not only herself but also the deepest virtue of each and every one: she knows their good side, their bad side, and even how they can be hypocritically prone to praise; therefore, she demands because she knows who she is, she is the daughter of Sol, she is her own axis and cosmos, and she is her own fire and centre. It is from this she commands the planets and establishes bonds to effectuate what she wants to see done. She demonstrates in her attitude what a "witch" is; someone who kneels for no one but pays reverence to whom reverence is due.

She is conscientious about lineage; she is the daughter of the Sun, the visible pole star of our world, the starry nail that dictates the premise for the world and enables the nocturnal life where she finds solace and space to re-centre every day. Circe does not hesitate as the gods do, but she is "the other way," the path crooked yet direct that takes the bull by the horns and becomes the solar centre of her own enchantments. Circe, in her third conjuration of the planets, states to her student, Moeris, that she will further "harass them" as she turns her attention to the Moon by again calling the attention of the Sun. Her enchantment starts in the following way: "Again I extend

---

168 Giordano Bruno, *Cantus Circaeus* (Ouroboros Press, 2009).

my hands to you Sun. Behold, I in my totality am present for you. I beseech you to reveal your lions, your lynxes, goats, baboons, your bay horses, your calves, serpents, elephants, and other kinds of these animals which pertain to you." [169]

She includes ravens, crows, locusts, frogs, and whales after this, and addresses him as Apollo by day and Dionysus by night and concludes by honouring him as: "You are prince of the world, eye of heaven, mirror of nature, architect of the soul of the universe."[170] When she moves from this salutation of the Sun to summoning the Moon, she does so as the Moon's "assistant" and calls her by the names of Hecate, Lucina, and Diana. She calls her as the wet nurse of living things, as the courageous huntress and queen of heaven, mother of the dawn, mistress of the sea, guardian of groves and forests, consort of Apollo, tamer of Hell, and the most powerful prosecutor of demons.

It is quite interesting what she is doing here, and the harassment might be in giving to the Sun attributes that are not commonly associated with the Sun, like baboons, locusts, crows, frogs, elephants, and whales. She might do so in the act of reminding the Sun, being the architect of the soul of the universe, that he also possesses these qualities in a particular solar way. For instance, an animal like the crow, which is commonly associated with the rulership of Saturn, would invite a rethinking of what the "solar crow" might be, both for the spirit summoned as much as for the enchantress. It forces a pause where a new bond is formed between the crow and the solar energy, which widens the soul of the Sun, an invitation toward expansion.

Bruno's philosophy was hermetic and was the fruition of the pioneering work done by Marsilio Ficino and Giovanni Pico della Mirandola. He expanded on the ideas presented in *The Emerald Tablet* in often quite stunning and unique ways. Hermes Trismegistus, in the twenty-fourth chapter of *The Emerald Tablet*, writes: "an infinite sphere whose centre is everywhere and whose circumference is nowhere."[171] This led to a cosmology that saw the universe as a series of concentric spheres composed of a mystical and ethereal substance, which means that around this fixed point, the elemental constitution was subject to constant permutations and changes.

---

169 Giordano Bruno, *Cantus Circaeus* (Ouroboros Press, 2009).
170 Ibid.
171 B.P. Copenhaver (trans.), *Corpus Hermeticum* (Cambridge University Press, 1992).

Bruno took this even further and suggested that similar cosmic organizations would be found everywhere in the universe with their own unique life forms, a proposition that didn't please the Church much. From a neo-Platonic perspective, Circe identifying herself as a daughter of the Sun would, by extension, also be the potential for a divine sphere on Earth in most divine dimensions. We are speaking of *theosis*, or how a human can become divine or godlike. *The Emerald Tablets* states: "They rise up to the father in order and surrender themselves to the powers, and having become powers, they enter into god. This is the final good for those who have received knowledge: to be made god."[172]

The wording, "to rise up to the father," and other parts of *The Emerald Tablets*, have at large been given a Valentinian Gnostic interpretation that sees the material world as inferior to the celestial world in a categorically and absolute sense. This would not correlate with Bruno's philosophy as this would be closer to William Blake's first lines in the poem "Auguries of Innocence."

> *"To see a World in a Grain of Sand*
> *And a Heaven in a Wild Flower*
> *Hold Infinity in the palm of your hand*
> *And Eternity in an hour."* [173]

It was more about achieving a proper understanding of the order of the cosmos and, through this, enabled multiple alignments or bonds with beast, mineral, and plant as well as spirit, phenomenon, images, and ideas in order to work on one's own deification. It is basically about becoming one with God, a god within the sphere we understand to be God, a monad within a gathering of monads. In this God sphere, there is a life force that pulses and flows constantly and is the "ocean" of all kinds of occult powers, forces, and mysteries.

It is with these mysteries we need to create bonds and vinculums in order to achieve an ascent. Hence, it is not that the material world is "inferior" to the celestial in a qualitative and categorical way; rather, it is about understanding that the divine is not only revealed in the

---

172 B.P. Copenhaver (trans.), *Corpus Hermeticum* (Cambridge University Press, 1992).
173 William Blake, *The Complete Poetry and Prose of William Blake* (University of California Press, 1982), 490.

material world, but the divine *is* embedded in the material, yet in our material world the divine is fused with other elements; therefore, it is difficult to clearly perceive what is what.

This means that the people of Earth must work on discernment and precise judgment in order to establish the bonds between one's soul, beasts, minerals, plants, images, ideas, and so forth. We are speaking of an entire chain of images and ideas encoded into the pure and clear perception of the lion or a piece of gold that naturally summons all other bonds. These bonds are made in relation to things and concepts to a pure divine idea that are the simple and rough rules for Circe's god-making, and in her case, the goal is to become a "mirror of nature," an architect of the soul, an "eye of heaven"; the daughter of Sun veiled in the flesh made sacred.

TWENTY-SEVEN

THE GOLDEN VERSES OF PYTHAGORAS

"If there be light, then there is darkness; if cold, heat; if height,
depth; if solid, fluid; if hard, soft; if rough, smooth; if calm,
tempest; if prosperity, adversity; if life, death."

—PYTHAGORAS

Pythagoras saw man as a free agent in the world and that pain and misery were due to bad use of our free will. A balance between "divine providence" and free will was needed in order to reach a state of satisfaction and contentment. Philosophers Anaximander (c. 610–546 BC) and Thales (c. 624–545 BC) both had an important influence on Pythagoras. In Anaximander's work, we see a distinct scientific turn in philosophy, hence his interest in physics, geography, and how the eternal laws affected the observable world. Curiously, he suggested an evolutionary theory where animals of Earth (including humans) came from marine creatures that started walking on land. He held ideas about order and chaos similar to Lao Tzu, where he saw that nature, like human organization, when deviating from its status quo, would always return to baseline.

But most of all, Anaximander's theory of the Limitless or Boundless (*apeiron*) being the source of all things, whether they are visible or invisible, led to Idealist philosophies like those found in several of Plato's dialogues and in the work of Plotinus and Porphyry. The idea that magic was possible through divine power being mediated by causality and occult or hidden knowledge of how the universe operated does owe its fair share to Pythagoras with the concept of *hēn* or oneness from whence a mathematical replication of the being and not-being that was so peculiar for oneness gave shape and form to the world. This simple cosmological idea also influenced the view of body and soul, which is viewed as something that should work together under a banner of health and harmony. The focus on harmony is seen in his most famous legacy to the world and in his contributions to mathematics and music.

Even if in Pythagoras we find a strong Apollonian focus, it is interesting to note the influence his thinking had on more Bacchic-oriented philosophers, like Epicurus, through his teacher Nausiphanes and other sects and philosophies of a similar bent. If we jump to the nineteenth-century philosopher Arthur Schopenhauer, we might find a more modern expression of ideas in harmony with the Pythagorean goals.

Schopenhauer, in his treatise *The Wisdom of Life*, points out how ordinary people take a strong interest in everything that excites their will.[174] For Schopenhauer, the will was a cosmic *Urkraft*, the essence of the world or the Kantian *Ding an sich* (thing-in-itself). Will executed by a human would then be about desiring and wanting something, always seeking the gratification of the senses and this inherent cosmic drive and desire that would constantly excite the will. This chronic occupation with small, ephemeral, and passing moments of excitement was a sure recipe for sadness and pain. It is crucial for the absence of pain in life to introduce the intellect, as he writes:

"A man of powerful intellect is capable of taking a vivid interest in things in the way of mere knowledge, with no admixture of will; nay, such an interest is a necessity to him. It places him in a sphere where pain is an alien, a diviner air where the gods live serene." [175]

---

174 Arthur Schopenhauer. *The Wisdom of Life and Counsels and Maxims* (Prometheus Books, 1995) 34.

175 Ibid. 35.

Schopenhauer was a man who enjoyed life, music, food, and the erotic, but it was important for him to allow the intellect to be predominant over the will, lest humanity fall into the worst state of all: vulgarity. Vulgarity was a state where the will was allowed to roam free without any hindrance or intellect in gratifying its passions. The vulgar person was someone who was solely occupied with all little external things, gossip, and hearsay, with ready attention for whatever drama or noise that was provoked or could be provoked in his surroundings. Schopenhauer considered people like this to be the most repulsive of all.

The Golden Verses of Pythagoras are verses of counsel on how to conduct your life so you can have less pain and more fulfilment and attain contentment and purpose through a healthy balance between the Dionysian and Apollonian dimensions of our being.

1. *First, revere the Immortal Gods according to how they are established and ordained by the divine decree.*
2. *Give attention to the owner of Oaths, Orcus, and next the Heroes, full of goodness and light.*
3. *Honour likewise the Terrestrial Dæmons by rendering them the reverence lawfully due to them.*
4. *Honour likewise thy parents, and those close to you in kin and spirit.*
5. *Of all the rest of mankind, make him thy friend who distinguishes himself by his virtue.*
6. *Always give ear to his mild exhortations, and take example from his virtuous and useful actions.*
7. *Avoid hating thy friend for a slight fault as much as possible.*
8. *And understand that power is a near neighbour to necessity.*
9. *Know that all these things are as I have told thee; and accustom thyself to overcome and vanquish these passions:*
10. *First gluttony, sloth, sensuality, and anger.*
11. *Do nothing evil, neither in the presence of others, nor privately;*
12. *But above all things respect thyself.*
13. *In the next place, observe justice in thy actions and in thy words.*
14. *And accustom not thyself to behave thyself in any thing without rule, and without reason.*
15. *But always make this reflection, that it is ordained by destiny that all men shall die.*

16. *And that the goods of fortune are uncertain; and that as they may be acquired, so may they likewise be lost.*

17. *Concerning all the calamities that men suffer by divine fortune,*

18. *Support with patience thy lot, be it what it may, and never repine at it.*

19. *But endeavour what thou canst to remedy it.*

20. *And consider that fate does not send the greatest portion of these misfortunes to good men.*

21. *There are among men many sorts of reasonings, good and bad;*

22. *Admire them not too easily, nor reject them.*

23. *But if falsehoods be advanced, hear them with mildness, and arm thyself with patience.*

24. *Observe well, on every occasion, what I am going to tell thee:*

25. *Let no man either by his words, or by his deeds, ever seduce thee.*

26. *Nor entice thee to say or to do what is not profitable for thyself.*

27. *Consult and deliberate before thou act, that thou mayest not commit foolish actions.*

28. *For it is the part of a miserable man to speak and to act without reflection.*

29. *But do that which will not afflict thee afterwards, nor oblige thee to repentance.*

30. *Never do anything which thou dost not understand.*

31. *But learn all thou ought'st to know, and by that means thou wilt lead a very pleasant life.*

32. *In no wise neglect the health of thy body;*

33. *But give it drink and meat in due measure, and also the exercise of which it has need.*

34. *Now by measure I mean what will not incommode thee.*

35. *Accustom thyself to a way of living that is neat and decent without luxury.*

36. *Avoid all things that will occasion envy.*

37. *And be not prodigal out of season, like one who knows not what is decent and honourable.*

38. *Neither be covetous nor ungenerous; a due measure is excellent in these things.*

39. *Do only the things that cannot hurt thee, and deliberate before thou dost them.*

40. *Never suffer sleep to close thy eyelids, after thy going to bed,*

41. *Till thou hast examined by thy reason all thy actions of the day.*

42. *Wherein have I done amiss? What have I done? What have I omitted that I ought to have done?*

43. *If in this examination thou find that thou hast done amiss, reprimand thyself severely for it;*

44. *And if thou hast done any good, rejoice.*

45. *Practise thoroughly all these things; meditate on them well; thou oughtest to love them with all thy heart.*

46. *'Tis they that will put thee in the way of divine virtue.*

47. *I swear it by him who has transmitted into our souls the Sacred Quaternion, the source of nature, whose cause is eternal.*

48. *But never begin to set thy hand to any work, till thou hast first prayed the gods to accomplish what thou art going to begin.*

49. *When thou hast made this habit familiar to thee,*

50. *Thou wilt know the constitution of the Immortal Gods and of men.*

51. *Even how far the different beings extend, and what contains and binds them together.*

52. *Thou shalt likewise know that according to Law, the nature of this universe is in all things alike,*

53. *So that thou shalt not hope what thou ought'st not to hope; and nothing in this world shall be hid from thee.*

54. *Thou wilt likewise know, that men draw upon themselves their own misfortunes voluntarily, and of their own free choice.*

55. *Unhappy that they are! They neither see nor understand that their good is near them.*

56. *Few know how to deliver themselves out of their misfortunes.*

57. *Such is the fate that blinds mankind, and takes away his senses.*

58. *Like huge cylinders they roll to and fro, and always oppressed with ills innumerable.*

59. *For fatal strife, innate, pursues them everywhere, tossing them up and down; nor do they perceive it.*

60. *Instead of provoking and stirring it up, they ought, by yielding, to avoid it.*

61. *Oh! Jupiter, our Father! If Thou would'st deliver men from all the evils that oppress them,*

62. *Show them of what dæmon they make use.*

63. *But take courage; the race of man is divine.*

64. *Sacred nature reveals to them the most hidden mysteries.*

65. *If she impart to thee her secrets, thou wilt easily perform all the things which I have ordained thee.*

66. *And by the healing of thy soul, thou wilt deliver it from all evils, from all afflictions.*

67. *But abstain thou from the meats, which we have forbidden in the purifications and in the deliverance of the soul;*

68. *Make a just distinction of them, and examine all things well.*

69. *Leaving thyself always to be guided and directed by the understanding that comes from above, and that ought to hold the reins.*

70. *And when, after having divested thyself of thy mortal body, thou arrivest at the most pure Æther,*

71. *Thou shalt be a God, immortal, incorruptible, and Death shall have no more dominion over thee.* [176]

In Evola's commentary on *The Golden Verses*, he stresses the importance of the Pythagorean connection of body and soul as they balance themselves out between force and harmony, leading to a state of upright character, signified by inner peace and deep contentment. In this space, it is possible to be sufficiently detached from the world of matter that enables a connection to the occult forces in creation. [177]

There are some elements in the verses that should be addressed in some detail so that a proper esoteric understanding can be grasped. This particularly concerns the first lines, which come off as very religious. The immortal deities are, of course, the celestial intelligence and the planets. Pythagorean adoration was not worship of the superior but affectionate veneration or reverence of what stood in a position of influence in the celestial hierarchy, like the planetary bodies and one's household spirits.

In the context of *The Golden Verses*, the *Orcus* is the shadow the Earth projects, both the Pythagorean *Antichthon* (also called "Vulcan") or Counter-Earth and the cone of the shadow the Earth casts upon the Moon. The cosmological idea of the Counter-Earth circling the

---

176 An adapted translation from *The Golden Verses of Pythagoras* by Pythagoras, made available by Forgotten Books in 20

177 A far supreme translation of *The Golden Verses* is made by Kenneth Sylvan Guthrie and can be found in Julius Evola's *Introduction to Magic. Volume II.* (Inner Traditions, 2019).

central fire is shown in the included diagram.[178] Both the Moon and the planetary idea of *Antichthon* were considered places where heroes and genii were living alongside Lares and Penates, or the household spirits of Roman Antiquity.

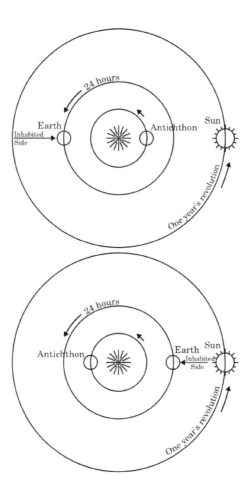

The daimonic fates must be understood as the Fate humanity has brought upon themselves by not listening to their daimon or guardian angel, the *numia* of our consciousness and soul. This will give an

---

178   M.A. Evershead, *Dante and the Early Astronomers* (Gall and Inglis, 1913).

overarching process of self-deification present in *The Golden Verses,* which gives an example of the Apollonian or harmonious way of enlightenment and achieving access to the fiery powers of magic. Finally, the Tetrad in this context must be seen as representing the *apeiron* of the eternal and the endless in its perpetual becoming. Also, it is interesting to note that for Pythagoras, the transmission of the Tetraktys was like transmitting occult magical fire directly from the central fire and thus represented a way of becoming connected to the chain of transmission of the invisible cosmic fire. In this way, *The Golden Verses* are counsel for living a content life, but on a deeper and more mystical level, several keys are given that inform how one can be reconnected to the central fire, to Hyperborea, to the land of Apollo and Artemis.

PART II

PRAXIS

TAU SHAMASH ADOCYNTUS LILIAE IN ECCLESIA PATRIARCHAE

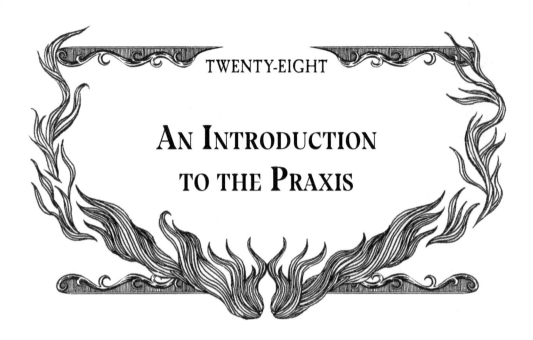

TWENTY-EIGHT

AN INTRODUCTION
TO THE PRAXIS

The practical part of *Invisible Fire* will present a rather wide range of praxis that illustrates the ritual nature of the "Sethian current" or Traditional Gnostic Doctrine. The ritual arsenal spans rituals to gain aid from spirits, rituals for divination, exorcisms, and ways of binding the influences of stars upon Earth by fashioning talismans. Also, an example of Élus Coëns inner work practices is given with the last working in this part, which is the preparatory procedures for any theurgic operation aiming toward reintegration. The text is taken from Pasqually's *Manuscript d'Alger*. Some of these rituals are adapted from *The Greek Magical Papyri*, a collection of texts that conjunct with Coptic Christian texts to reveal a treasure trove of practices that harmonise with the spirit of Seth.

Outside this, the contemplative nature of the Sethian doctrine must be stressed, as well as the importance of communion. Communion is exemplified in the mass, whereas the Roman Catholic Mass is a prime example of what this mystery entails in terms of the process of making the ordinary extraordinary. The miracle of the mass is not restricted to transubstantiation. The miracle rests in how the sacraments make us partake in the fruits of Wisdom. A veritable return to Eden takes place in this liminal interim between mystery and salvation, where the body and blood make the celebrant One with the mystery of deliverance and salvation.

Because of this, two masses have been presented here. One is a mass from *Ecclesia Hermetica Catholica, Misa Adamantina Phosforos,* and the other is *The Provictimal Sacrifice of Mary*. This mass was written and regularly performed by Eugéne Vintras (1807–1875). The Eliate Church of Carmel was dedicated to the veneration of Shahael or the Holy Mary. The version translated for this book is the revised ritual of Vintras' successor, Abbé Boullan. Vintras was an important portent for the succession of a Johannite, or mystical interior Ecclesia, in contrast to the revealed and exoteric Church of Saint Peter.

On August 6, 1839, Vintras was visited by an old man who came unexpectedly to tell him that his mission would now start. This man was later identified as Saint Michael, the archangel, and Vintras himself realised over the years to come that he was a manifestation of the spirit of the prophet Elijah. The particular mission Vintras was appointed to set in motion was "the reign of love" through the coming of the Holy Spirit. In constant divine rapture, the humble peasant from Normandy accepted the mission under the name Elie-Strathaniel and went to Paris. Vintras was a man of intense humility, reflected in his vestment carrying the Cross of Saint Peter, which is the cross upside down. This led to ideas of Vintras being a Satanist. For Vintras, the Cross of Saint Peter signified that, yet again, the Grace of God was turned toward the Earth and nothing Satanic and vulgar of any kind.

Vintras' Church of Carmel had an almost instantaneous popularity and grew rapidly. Vintras' simple message, wrapped in an impressive and complex theology and liturgy, spoke of the importance of sacrifice to gain freedom from the world of matter and thus be prepared for the coming of the Paraclete and the reintegration to follow. Of particular importance is the value Vintras gave to women. Not only were women representatives of Wisdom herself, but they were also entitled to ordination equal to men. In 1842, Vintras was arrested after a period of intense investigation by the Roman Catholic Church and sent to prison for five years. While in prison, his vicar, Abbé Maréchal, made some of the rites of the Church public, which revealed a great openness for sexual communion. Thus, a scandal was on the rise, leading to the Vatican's formal condemnation of the Church in 1848.

Some years later, Vintras moved to London, where he continued his mission and wrote *The Eternal Gospel*. The rites and liturgies went underground and were only conducted in secrecy. Of these rituals, *The Provictimal Sacrifice of Mary* is perhaps the most famous. It was probably this ritual that Abbé Boullan used in his sexual communion with the Abbess Chevalier to hasten the coming of the Paraclete, and it was this mass that made the hosts bleed. Naturally, unorthodox practices amidst the clergy of the Church led to accusations of the performance of black magic and of Vintras' ultimate propagation of a "Luciferian theology." The silent and contemplative mystery of Vintras and the Johannite succession of bishops was of no such inclination. Rather, it was a highly unusual approach to adversity and matter, but the aim was ultimately to facilitate reintegration and, thus, a return to the original Edenic state.

This is ultimately the goal of all these practices. Through Wisdom, the mystery is revealed, humanity is drawn one step closer to the Promised Land, and the return to the Golden Age is enabled. By Wisdom revealed, humanity can understand how to approach the world of matter and use it as a medium for ascent and thus bring the Divine Kingdom upon Earth. In this way, it can restore the original flow of the *axis mundi*.

A PRAYER FOR DELIVERANCE

I call upon you, Lord and forefather.
You are the Glorious One who rests amongst the holy host,
Eternal ruler of the Sun's rays,
Celestial ruler who stands in the seven parted region,
You who hold fast to the root,
From whence the holy angels were consecrated by your name.
Hear me, you who established the Decans and all angels.
I call upon you, Lord of the Universe,
This is my hour of need.
Hear me, for I am in distress, and I am perplexed.
Shield me against all excess from the aerial daimon.
Shield me from all excess of power as I call you by your secret name.
May my call reach you at the firmaments of the world.
Athezophoim Zadeageobephiatheaa Ambrami Abraam
Thalchilthoe Elkothooee Achthonon Sa isak choeiiourthasio
iosia ichemeoooo aoai.
Rescue me in my hour of need.[179]

---

179 Adapted from Hans Dieter Betz (ed.) *The Greek Magical Papyri* (University of Chicago Press, 1996).

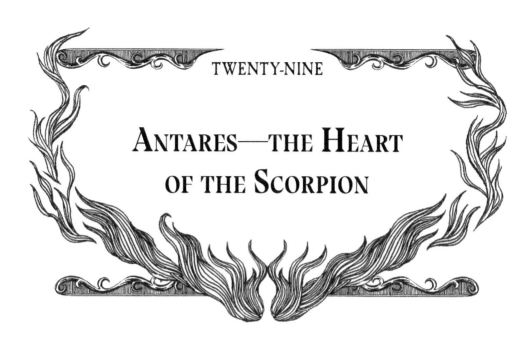

TWENTY-NINE

ANTARES—THE HEART OF THE SCORPION

A TALISMAN FOR PROTECTION

You will need a silver vessel, a scorpion, four white candles and one red, a glass of red wine, a pinch of saffron, and a pinch of cayenne pepper seeds. You will make this talisman when Antares is rising and is free from affliction. At the elected time, you will place the scorpion inside the silver vessel and light the candles around it. The four white candles will be placed in the cardinal directions, and the fifth candle, red in colour, will be placed at the side of the white candle in the north. Light the candles, harmonise your breath, and visualise in the centre of your heart how a golden drop of fire is found.

> *Who has put wisdom in the Lance Star?*
> *Who hath put understanding in the heart?*
> *It is you Lord, excellent Lord*
> *Who has set thy name in all the earth*
> *Who hast set thy glory above the heavens*
> *You are the author of the Law that stretches from*
> *mountain to mountain, from the north to the south*
> *And as such I call at the corners of the celestial orb*
> *The attention of the angelic host.*

Say the following as you visualise a golden drop of fire at the level of your forehead descending from the heavens:

In the east, I see the flame of the holy angel Michael's sword. I call you by your name (chant "Michael" three times). Thy fire is a golden drop that illuminates the sky. Thou art daybreak, and I call thy royal star, Regulus (chant the name of the star three times).

I turn toward the south, the noon of the illuminating fire, held in the arts of transformation by the great angel Uriel. I call you by your name (chant "Uriel" three times). Thou art the flaming Earth, and I call thy royal star, Aldebaran (chant the name of the star three times).

I turn toward the west, where the fire finds comfort in the aerial breeze, by staff and hourglass in the hands of the holy angel Raphael. I call you by your name (chant "Raphael" three times). Thou art the road and inclination the comforting fire, and I call thy royal star Fomalhaut (chant the name of the star three times).

And to the north I turn, where fire is embraced by silent water, in the lands of the Gabriel-hounds, holy angel Gabriel, I call you by your name (chant "Gabriel" three times). Thou are the fire burning in the heart of men and beast; listen as I call thy royal star Antares (chant the name of the star three times).

You will now remain facing the northern quarter and visualise the sky as water; within the water, a golden point of light is burning intensely, and it draws the sign of Antares in the sky. You will then give the following hymn to Antares and feed the scorpion a small glass of red wine, a pinch of saffron, and a pinch of cayenne pepper seeds.

HYMN OF ANTARES

Herald of sunrise, by glowing in the dawn
Saffron coloured eye of Serqt
Burning Eye of Isis
You are the Lord of every Seed, the Lance of Mars
You are the Azure Dragon rising from the depts.
You are Kalb Akrav, Kalb Akrav, Kalb Akrav.

The red glow in the heart of Scorpio
Thy house is fire, and thy hand is the sting
Thy heart is steady and warm
A promise of resurrection and fire
You are Kalb Akrav, Kalb Akrav, Kalb Akrav.
The royal guardian of the eyes of night
The royal warrior in the house of night-fire
With these gifts, I call out for thy blessing
May you find a resting place in this, your vessel
For you are Kalb Akrav, Kalb Akrav, Kalb Akrav.
May your fire of protection rest within me.
So it shall be, Now and forever more.
Amen.

THIRTY

A Shrine for
Al Thuban (Draco)

A SHRINE TO BRING SUCCESS AND HONOUR

This shrine will be built upon the mystery of Mary of Magdalene as the invigorating blood and must be performed in the days from her transfiguration, the summer solstice, where *Janua Inferni* opens the gates from Earth to heaven and until the feast day of Mary's sister, Saint Martha, on July 29. The full moon or, preferably, the black moon between the solstice and Martha's feast day is dedicated to Lazarus, the two sisters' brother.

As such, this mystery follows a common traditional motive of death, transformation, and renewal in the scale of red, black, and white or purple. The blood makes the Earth black and, from the incubation, ascends the splendour of light. The stars important to the mystery, Rastaban and Rastaben, are found in the head of Draco, the dragon's eyes, and the brightest star, the *Alpha Draconis,* is also called *Thuban.* The star culminates at three degrees Libra. Thuban is positioned in an interesting relationship with Ursa Minor and is almost in alignment with one of its stars, Kochab.

Gather the following items: A red cloth, a black cloth, and a purple cloth; a fern and some branches of willow, preferably in early bloom; a red and a white rose; a small root from an oak or a nut tree; a wooden cross; red wine; one piece of onyx; and a rose quartz crystal. You will also need various incense and charcoal, candles, and a jar made from stone, brass, copper, or crystal.

The First Night—Vigil of Mary of Magdalene

On the first night, you will light a single red candle as the Sun goes down. Fumigate your temple with benzoin and opopanax. Present the rose quartz in front of the candle and place the willow branches upon the red cloth. When you light the charcoal, you will pray upon the coals in the following manner:

O creatures of fire, purify this wood and be yourself pure as I cast out all impurities from this fire. In the Name of the Father, the Son, and the Holy Spirit. Amen.

Place incense on the coals and say:

Oh, holy spirits of air, you who carry the breath of creation, eternal pneuma, let this smoke be pure as the breath of the One and let it rise to the heavens and create delight and goodwill toward me. Let it be so. Now and forever more! Amen.

You will then turn your attention toward the imaginative reenactment of Mary of Magdalene in conformity with the themes involving her that appeal most to your heart. You will allow all forms of imagery to wander through your heart until you arrive at a point of stillness where you bring these emotional imageries to find rest in the comfort of your mind. You will then repeatedly utter the following prayer or call until you feel a serenity dawning upon you:

You are the Red Sophia
The Wisdom of Passion
Spread as grains of wheat all over the world
You are the chrism and the wine
The Bride and Bridle.
The One who anointed the gate
And thus became the gate
And the presence
You brought grains of stars to earth
Through you, they were cleansed
In the Halls of Putrefaction

A resurrection and a birth
A rebirth and eternity
You are the Red Sophia
The Wisdom of the worlds.
Amen.

Spend some time in silence, and when your concentration fades, take it as a sign of the vigil's termination. Wrap the willow and stone in the red cloth and leave it with the candles until the day after, when you will dry the branches and save them for later.

THE SECOND NIGHT—VIGIL OF LAZARUS

The vigil of the second night, which will be on the proper lunar day falling between solstice and Martha's feast day, will be done in darkness. Bring to your temple the fern, roots, black cloth, and onyx in addition to the items from the first vigil. Fumigate the space with cedar and pine as the Sun goes down, letting only the coal give fire at this moment. Whisper to the coal and the incense the same exorcisms as in the first vigil, and then lay down in your temple in the darkness. Lay your belly down with your hands crossed over your chest and your forehead on the floor, ensuring that your chosen root is placed so close that you can grab it with your mouth. You will declare:

In the bosom of the Earth,
My corpse has been given new life.
I am a flower yet to blossom,
The blood of wisdom has made me wise.
I am Lazarus. I am Lazarus. I am Lazarus.
Amen. Amen. Amen.

Now, take the root in your mouth and be still of body and mind until the position, in its discomfort, distracts you. Then, stand up and light a single black candle with the root in your mouth. Place a black cloth in front of the candle and drop the root. Adorn the root with the fern and place the items from the first vigil together with the onyx in the black cloth. Wrap it up and leave it in a place no light enters until the feast day of Saint Martha.

The Third Night—Vigil of Saint Martha

When the Sun goes down, bring the black cloth with the items to your temple and fumigate with frankincense and myrrh. While doing this, use the same exorcisms as in the other two vigils. Bring with you the items from the second vigil together with the jar, the cross, the wine, and the roses. You will then declare:

I have risen from the womb of the Earth.
I raise my gaze to the stars, and I call thee,
Al-Thuban, celestial Mary.

Then take the contents of the red and black cloth and burn it, saying:

All transformation goes from red to black,
From black to red
As I turn the black to dust
By the red Work
So may I be purified
And gain honour and not dishonour
May I be protected and not motherless.

Take the hot stones from the ashes and place the ashes themselves in the vessel. Place the stones on top, and as you place the cross inside, say:

Holy Martha, silent saint of courage
Whose gaze stills the basilisk.
As I robe in purple
And place the cross of the world
In this vessel,
May the blood of your sister,
Bones of your brother
Come together
And forge
Courage and wisdom.

You will then leave the temple and go outside under the stars. If there are no visible stars, let your imagination draw them on the canvas of the heavens. Focus on Thuban, failing that, on Polaris, and raise the vessel to the stars and pray from the heart while you see the flashes of starlight falling from the heavens and upon you. When you feel the bond is made, sit down in the grass, preferably naked or dressed in natural, light fabrics, and fill your mouth with the wine. Swallow half and spray the rest on the vessel. Take the roses, white and red, and sprinkle the vessel with the petals. Stay in meditation and communion with the star until midnight. Take the vessel indoors and place it at a window so that it can take the starlight all night while you go to the land of divination and dreams.

THIRTY-ONE

A TALISMAN FOR ALCYONE

A TALISMAN TO GAIN INSIGHT INTO HIDDEN THINGS

You will need the following: cumin flowers, one clouded crystal, fennel seeds, rose petals, cassia bark, green cloth, and a white cord. In the temple, you should light one green candle, one blue candle, and one white candle, and preferably dress the candles in star oil.[180] You should also have an oil lamp in the temple that will be burning with marigold oil (calendula). Let there also be present a cup of good white wine and a plate of honey as an offering to the angel of the star. Draw the seal of Alcyone on the fabric with a virgin charcoal stick. Let the items for the talisman be at the side of the green candle in a small white jar. You will then focus your mind on the chosen intent and start the working with the angelic call:

> *Who hath put wisdom in the Lance Star?*
> *Who hath put understanding in the heart?*
> *It is you, Lord, excellent Lord,*
> *Who hast set thy name in all the Earth*
> *Who hast set thy glory above the heavens.*

---

180 Star oil is an oil made under the rays of the star in question using the *materia magica* proper for lodging the star virtue into the oil.

You are the author of the Law that stretches from
mountain to mountain, from the north to the south,
And as such, I call at the corners of the celestial orb,
The attention of the angelic host.

After the angelic call, recite the following:

In the east, I see the flame of the holy angel Michael's sword. I call you
by your name (chant "Michael" three times). Thy fire is a golden drop
that illuminates the sky. Thou art daybreak, and I call thy royal star,
Regulus (chant the name of the star three times).

I turn toward the south, the noon of the illuminating fire, held in
the arts of transformation by the great angel Uriel. I call you by your
name (chant "Uriel" three times). Thou art the flaming Earth, and I
call thy royal star, Aldebaran (chant the name of the star three times).

I turn toward the west, where the fire finds comfort in the aerial
breeze, by staff and hourglass in the hands of the holy angel Raphael.
I call you by your name (chant "Raphael" three times). Thou art the
road and inclination the comforting fire, and I call thy royal star
Fomalhaut (chant the name of the star three times).

And to the north I turn, where fire is embraced by silent water, in the
lands of the Gabriel-hounds, holy angel Gabriel, I call you by your
name (chant "Gabriel" three times). Thou are the fire burning in the
heart of men and beast; listen as I call thy royal star Antares (chant
the name of the star three times).

Now recite the Hymn to Alcyone while you focus your gaze upon her Earth sign and conclude the hymn with a trifold breath upon her sign.

HYMN TO ALCYONE

O, sister, do not weep,
You are the dove betwixt the bull's horns.
Make me exalted in my destined glory.
Make me see truth, and expel for me fantasy and illusion.
Give unto me the hand of my spirit fair and true

So that the hidden knowledge can be mine.
Don't cloud my sight,
But open my eyes.
You are the scales the Fates hold in their hands.
You are the feather of judgment,
So inspire in me insight and understanding,
The treasures of wisdom I seek
Not to judge or be judged.
Oh, sister, do not weep,
But be my beacon of light,
My dove, my maiden fair and green,
Dweller in the stellar fog.
Be my light
In all hidden lands.
Alcyone,
Be my light,
My dove.
Alcyone,
Dove of
Light.
Alcyone.

Then, carefully collect the items in the cloth, and once again, recite the Hymn of Alcyone and give your breath upon its secrets. Tie up the talismanic bag with the cord, and for the third time, you will recite the hymn, but the last "breath" will be with a portion of the wine in your mouth that you spray over the bag. Leave the talisman between the candles until they have burned themselves out and the talisman is ready for use.

THIRTY-TWO

DIVINATION BY DREAM AND LAMP

Perform this divination when the Pleiades are in harmony with the operation, which is when Alcyone conjoins the Moon, and the Moon is free from affliction.[181] Sit down at your table and present a glass of red wine and a blue candle. Set the table up outside, if possible, under the gaze of the stars. Fumigate with frankincense. You will then take a branch of the laurel tree with thirteen leaves and write on them with cinnabar ink the following names and signs:

Aries:	♈	HAR MONTH HAR THŌ CHE
Taurus:	♉	NEOPHOBŌTHA THOPS
Gemini:	♊	ARISTANANA ZAŌ
Cancer:	♋	PCHORBAZANACHAU
Leo:	♌	ZALAMOIRLALITH
Virgo:	♍	EILESILARMOU PHAI
Libra:	♎	TANTINOURACHTH
Scorpio:	♏	CHORCHORNATH
Sagittarius:	♐	PHANTHENPHYPHILIA

---

181 This divination is adapted from Hans Dieter Betz (ed.) *The Greek Magical Papyri* (University of Chicago Press, 1996).

Capricorn: ♑ AZAZAEISTHAILICH

Aquarius: ♒ MENNY THYTH IAŌ

Pisces: ♓ SERYCHARRALMIŌ

On the thirteenth leaf, write:

CHALCHANA PHOE KOSKIANŌ ALĒMONTALL ASEICH

Then, present a bowl of clear water and a lamp of olive oil under the starry heavens. You will fumigate with frankincense and call the angel of foresight in the following way:

Oh, holy angel ZIZAUBIŌ, who dwells in the Pleiades
You great, indestructible, and fire-breathing angel
Who throws the rope of heaven to the Earth,
I call upon you and your attending host of angels.
Come quickly in this night and reveal for me with clarity
What I seek to know.
Oh, holy angel ZIZAUBIŌ, I call upon you on this night.
May you reveal all things to me through dreams with accuracy.

Now, incense the branch and bring the bowl of water and the lamp of oil to your bed. Place the bowl of water under your bed at the level of the head and the lamp at your head. Empty the cup of wine, place the branch under your pillow, and call the angel by his name while you focus on the nature of the knowledge you seek to behold.

THIRTY-THREE

RITUAL FOR GAINING A DAIMONIC HELPER

Both *The Greek Magical Papyri* and the *Picatrix* suggest some common elements that can be used to gain favours or gain a daimonic helper. One ritual format composed from these sources will now be presented.

Seven days before the Moon is full, you will enter a week of purity. Wash your body every morning and every night, and dress in clean, preferably white, linen. During this week, avoid going out at night and avoid strong drinks and enmity. You will likewise avoid meat and all and any bad inclination. Also, you will be celibate for the entire week.

On the morning of the first day of your week of purity, go out and find a beetle—a hornbill or scarab—and obtain some hair from the tail of a horse. You will then obtain a new oil lamp and new oil. Upon returning to your home this first day, tie up the beetle with the hair of the horse and hang it over the oil lamp. The intention is not to hurt the beetle, so the distance must be comfortable. Set this up in the northern corner of your house. You will then sit down at your table, dress it with a white tablecloth, and fumigate your house with myrrh and storax.

At your table, bring milk and honey, parchment, and sanctified ink. You will then mix the milk with honey and light a white candle. Also, present one cup of olive oil, one cup of sesame oil, and one last cup of nuts, then write the following design on the parchment and chant it accordingly. The writing should be in the shape of an upward-pointed triangle or arrow.

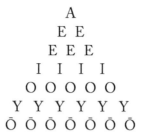

Then, drink the milk mixed with honey and write and chant the following:

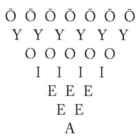

Next, wrap up the parchment and place it in a small bag. Make sure that the candles are burning steadily at all times. Then, go out to obtain the feathers of a falcon and a terracotta bowl. When night comes, place the feathers in the bowl at your table. Cut your nails and hair, place the clippings inside the bowl, and recite the following enchantment:

A EE EEE III OOOO YYYYY ŌŌŌŌŌŌ. Good daimon, I call you, listen as I call you: Harpon Knouphi Brintanten Siphri Briskylma Arouazar Kriphi Nipoumichmoumaōph. Oh, Orion, Hunter of the North, who causes the rivers to flow. Let now my good daimon flow toward me, guarded and guided by the angelic host of my star and place. I call my angel from the City of the Sun with the words: ARBATH ABAOTH BAKCHABRE.

Recite these words until you feel a flame gushing forth in your heart, and say:

HELI ELI LIHE HELI.

Then, leave all items on the table and rest until the next morning.

The next morning, repeat the same procedure, but the bowl with hair, nails, and feathers will rest at the side of the oil lamp during the day and rest on the table at night. Every morning, replace the offerings. Collect the old offerings in a bowl and place them in front of the oil lamp.

On the seventh day, after performing the usual procedure, go out at night under the fullness of the Moon. Prepare your table under the stars and present fruits, sweet bread, and a jug of red wine, along with the offerings you have been giving all week. Now, offer generous amounts of myrrh and laurel. Take the bowl with your hair, nails, and feathers, cut the beetle loose, and place everything on burning coals with your incense. Some instructions also advocate for the sacrifice of a white rooster upon the gifts to the daimon. If you choose to make this sacrifice, this offering must be burnt as well.

Then, recite the following enchantment seven times while vividly opening your heart and mind for your star to descend.

Oh, glorious Apollo, born from the womb between the poles, shining one, truthful one. You are Scemesh and Sol Invictus; you are Amon and Horus. May the wings of the falcon bring my daimon to dwell with me. ALLALALALA ALLALALA SANTALALATALALA ACHAIPHŌTHŌTHŌTHŌAIEIAEIA AIEAIEIAŌTHŌTHŌPHIACHA.
Send now my Divine Spirit so I can fulfill what rests in my heart and mind.
Send me this daimon and let him, in truth, tell of my mind's design.
Send him graciously and gently; may no opposition be between my daimon and my mind's design.
Amen.

Stare in silence at the night sky and watch for the signs that announce the arrival of your daimon. Upon taking notice of the omens, take the oil lamp you have used during this operation to your bed and go to sleep. Upon awakening, take all the things used in this operation and bury them on the northern side of your house. You will then take a bit of the earth from the burial ground and place it in your bag along with your seven consecrated parchments.

THIRTY-FOUR

Two Exorcisms

AN EXORCISM FROM ABBÉ JULIO[182]

This exorcism is a protection against visible and invisible enemies. The (†) symbol in the following rituals denotes when the sign of the cross should be made.

† Elias † Elohim † Eloa † Leo † Ya † Eserchel † Agla † Sadaï † Adonai
Agios o Theos, Ischyros, Athanatos, eleison imas.
Sanctus Deus, Fortis Immortalis, adjuva me (name) famulum tuum.
Abomni periculo, a morte aeterna animae et corporis,
Ab insidiis inimicorum, visibilium seu invisibilium eripe me.
† Jehovah † Sabaoth † Emmanuel † Soter † tetragrammaton † Omouzios † Eheye † Alpha et Omega † Via, Veritas et Via mihi famulo tuo (name).
Salutaria sint altissima tua Nomina.
Dixisti: † Hoc est Corpus meum; dic: me amet at Amore tuo majus erit prodigum
Animae conversion et salvation.
Pessimas Potestates quae contra me runt fortiter constringe.
In nomine † Patris † et Filii † et Spiritus Sancti.
Amen.

---

182 From *Le Livre secret des grands exorcismes et bénédictions* (Bussier, 1990).

AN EXORCISM FOR DRIVING
OUT KAKODAIMONOS[183]

Prepare a whip made from seven olive branches and a talisman written on tin. Write the following on the tin leaf and mark it with the sign of the Great Bear.[184]

BŌR PHŌR PHORBA PHOR PHORBA BES CHARIN
BAUBŌ TE PHŌR BŌRPHORBA PHORBABOR BAPHORBA
PHABRAIE PHŌRBA PHARBA PHŌRPHŌR PHROBA.
Protect (name).

The exorcism is performed by hanging this talisman around the neck of the person and whipping him with the olive branches while you recite the following prayer:

In the Name of the Father, the Son, and the Holy Spirit.
Hail God of Abraham. Hail God of Isaac. Hail God of Jacob.
You who are above the Seven and within the Seven,
Bring IAO SABAOTH and let your power issue from him and enable
me, (name) in this manner, to drive out the unclean spirits from this
child of your creation.
I conjure you daimon, whoever you are, by this god:
SABARBARBATHIŌTH SABARBARBATHIOUTH
SABARBARBATHHIŌNETH SABARBARBAPHAI.
Now, leave this person, (name), immediately and stay away from
them. I bind you with the adamantine fetters and the power of the
Mount of Olives.

Fumigate the person involved with frankincense and order them to go to a fall of running clean water and pray for release.

---

183 Adapted from Hans Dieter Betz (ed.), *The Greek Magical Papyri* (University of Chicago Press, 1996).
184 We have here in mind the seal of the star Ursa Major.

THIRTY-FIVE

MISA ADAMANTINA PHOSFOROS

THE MASS FOR THE ROSE BLOOD
AND THE DAUGHTERS OF ZION

ENTRANCE ANTIPHON

"Now there stood by the cross of Jesus his mother, and his mothers sister, Mary the wife of Cleophas, and Mary Magdalene. When Jesus therefore saw his mother, and the disciple standing by, whom he loved, he saith unto his mother, Woman, behold thy son! Then saith he to the disciple, Behold thy mother! And from that hour that disciple took her unto his own home."

—The Gospel of John 19:25–27

And this is his legacy: the Blood, the Bread, the Death. Where all begun, we shall continue. By the Master's death and his blood divine, we shall lift our heads to heaven and gaze into the mystery of the diamond and the rose blazing from the summit of all attainment.

Benediction

Priest: In Nomine Dei Patris † et Fili † et Spiritus Sancti † Amen. May She who is before All things, the incomprehensible and all-encompassing Charis, fill us with light, love, life, and liberty and increase in us Her own gnosis.

Congregation: *Amen*

Priest: *May the Grace of our Lord Jesus Christ, the love of God, and the fellowship of the Holy Spirit be with you all.*

Congregation: *Blessed be God, the Father of our Lord Jesus Christ.*

Priest: *Peace be with you.*

Congregation: *And also with you.*

All: *Amen.*

Asperges

Fill a bowl with water.

Priest: *This is the water of baptism. This is the water that washes away all sins. This is the water that restores to the soul its original freshness. This is the water from whence the foam, the holy spirit rose from the depth, and the dove descended upon. As fortune was brought from the water, so bring her freshness again so we can restore our souls, heal our wounds, and be pure as the living water itself. We pray upon this water and ask thee, Father, to bless † this water and let it serve as a protection against all evil. May this water † be the living water of salvation. † Amen.*

Congregation: *So mote it be. Amen.*

Take some salt.

Priest: *Almighty God, bless † this salt as you didst blessed the salt scattered over the water by the prophet Elisha. From the temple and dwelling where this salt is scattered, drive away the powers of evil and restore the sanctuary of cleanliness and purity.*

Congregation: *Amen.*

While scattering the water, whisper the words *Mem* or *Mayim.*

FIRST CENSING

Place an incense of copal mixed with roses on the coals.

Priest: *The stars of the green ground I offer to thee, Lord, may the sweet odours rise to the heavens like a vapor of blessings and let the dove of innocence and purity descend upon us. Through this smoke, may your temple be guided as you, in the pillars of smoke and fire, guided your people in the past, so do guide us now.*

While incensing the cathedral, chant: *Esh, El, Esh.*

ABSOLUTION

The priest and congregation engage in genuflection.

All: *I confess to almighty God and to my brothers and sisters my many faults born by ignorance and delusion in thought and deed. Through my fault, my fault, my grievous fault, I ask pardon for what I have failed to do and for all faults of word and deed born by ignorance and delusion. Lord, have mercy on us and bring us to salvation. Let us remain pure as on this day where our soul and body have again been washed with the water of life and cleansed by the salt of Elisha.*

The priest rises.

Priest: *Lord, show us your mercy and love.*

Congregation: *And grant us salvation.*

Priest: *Lord, let your face shine upon us.*

Congregation: *And bring us illumination.*

Priest: *Lord, heal our afflictions.*

Congregation: *Of soul, body, and mind.*

Priest: *Lord, prepare a table for us in your court.*

Congregation: *Amen.*

KYRIE

Priest:	Congregation:
Kyrie eléison	*Lord, have mercy*
Kyrie eléison	*Lord, have mercy*
Kyrie eléison	*Lord, have mercy*
Christe eléison	*Lord, have mercy*
Christe eléison	*Lord, have mercy*
Christe eléison	*Lord, have mercy*
Kyrie eléison	*Lord, have mercy*
Kyrie eléison	*Lord, have mercy*
Kyrie eléison	*Lord, have mercy*

GLORIA—HYMN TO THE FATHER [185]

*O Powers within me, sing to the One and to the All; with one accord,
all your powers sing praise at my bidding.
Divine knowledge, illumined by you, I sing through you of the spiritual light
and I rejoice in the delight of the Nous. Sing praise with me, all you powers.
You temperance, sing with me.
Justice, through me praise what is just.
Generosity, through me praise the All.
Truth, sing of Truth.
Good, praise the Good.*

---

185   Hymn from B.P. Copenhaver (trans.), *Corpus Hermeticum* (Cambridge University Press, 1992).

Life and light, from you comes the praise and to you it returns.
I give thanks to you, Father, the strength of all my powers.
I give thanks to you, God, power of all my strength.
Your word through me sings to you.
Receive all back through me by the Word, a spoken sacrifice.
Thus cry the power within me.
They praise the All, they accomplish your will which comes forth from you and returns To you, being the All.
Receive an offering of speech from all beings.
O life, preserve the All within us.
O light illuminate the All.
O God, inspire the All.
For Nous guides your Word, O bearer-of-the-breath-of-life,
O creator of the World, You are God.
All this your man proclaims through fire, air, earth, and water.
Through breath, through your creatures.
From you I have discovered eternity's song of praise and in your will I have found the Rest I seek. By your will, I have witnessed this praise being sung.

COLLECTS

Priest: *Let us Pray with a mindful heart.*

All:
Holy art Thou, O Lord, hand of salvation.
Holy art Thou, alone begotten.
Holy art Thou, the living Word, the redeemer.
Holy art Thou, foam born star of Light.
Holy art Thou, who brings Light from Darkness.
Holy art Thou, who sowed the incorruptible seed amongst men.
Holy art Thou, who pour forth the glory of heaven upon us.
Holy art Thou, who enflames understanding.
Holy art Thou, lovely dove who gives the Grace.
Holy art Thou, Wisdom seated on her throne above the waters.
Holy art Thou, the living flame, the eternal torch.
Be with us from beginning to end,
World without end.
Amen.

LITURGY OF THE WORD

Priest: *The Word became God.*

Congregation: *Inflamed by the Holy Spirit, he became God.*

Priest: *The holy spirit, dove of splendour, gave the gift of Grace.*

Congregation: *The heavenly dove is Grace.*

Priest: *She filled the silence.*

Congregation: *And the anointed one broke the silence with words.*

Priest: *The womb and the cup.*

Congregation: *From God's throne, they rushed forth.*

Priest: *The gift and graces came to man.*

Congregation: *Praise the Lord, holy in spirit.*

Priest: *So mote it be. Amen.* †

Priest: *Oh Lord, cleanse my mouth and tongue with water, hyssop, and burning coal so that what I may speak is wise and good.*

The officiant can then move on to the reading of the gospel or another suitable sacred text.

LITANY FOR THE HEAVENLY DOVE

Priest: *Oh Lord, open the gates of Jerusalem on high.*

Congregation: *Holy dove, descend, descend.*

Priest: *May the rivers that fortify our soul rush forth.*

Congregation: *Holy dove, descend, descend.*

Priest: *Oh, Lord, make thy self known to us.*

Congregation: *Holy dove, descend, descend.*

Priest: *Turn us to the path of righteousness.*

Congregation: *Holy dove, descend, descend.*

Priest: *As the morning star rises.*

Congregation: *Holy dove, descend, descend.*

Priest: *As the evening star rises.*

Congregation: *Holy dove, descend, descend.*

Priest: *Oh, Blazing Star!*

Congregation: *Holy dove, descend, descend.*

Priest: *Upward against the stream we go.*

Congregation: *Holy dove, descend, descend.*

Priest: *Oh, Lord, let us know thy Grace.*

Congregation: *Holy dove, descend, descend.*

Priest:
Descend as on the day Saint John.
Touched the head and soul of your son
And let us know the living flame,
And place our foot in the stream,
And walk to our rightful station.
Amen. †

HYMN

Agios O Christos
Christe Venire
Agios O Christe
Sanctus Christe Sanctus
Amen

GLORIA

Glory to the King of Kings, Glory to the Divine Shepherd, and to the
Living Christ in whom we shall be transmuted into Glory.
Oh, son of God, Word in Silence, Light in the Dark.
O Perfect Tincture regenerating us from the tomb of the profane flesh
into Life Immortal.
Glory to the Precious Blood of the Lamb who speaks, saying: "Whoso-
ever will drink from my mouth will become as I am, and I myself will
become He and She, and the things which are hidden will be revealed
to him."
O Lord, we have made our albs white in the blood of the lamb.
Let us receive the Seal of Light on our brow and heart in this thy
wedding feast.
I am thy bride as the hosts of angels and seraphim shining in their
splendour can testify. Find me worthy, O Lord, to dine at the table of
sapphire and gold.
Find me worthy, O Lord, to take my seat in the Jerusalem on high.
O Perfected Tincture, perfect me through your blood.

PROFESSION OF FAITH

All:
I believe in one Hidden Father of Light, supreme Mystery
Transcending Earth and Heaven in his inconceivable being:
I believe in Christ Jesus, Our Lord Messias and Illuminator
Conceived by the Power of the Holy Spirit
And born of the Blessed Virgin Mary;
Heavenly dove and rose blood of life and death.

He suffered, was crucified, died, and was entombed.
He descended into Hades and, on the third day, rose again.
He ascended into the heavenly Pleroma
And is enthroned at the right hand of the Father.
He will come in power to judge the Quick and the Dead.
I believe in the Holy Spirit, the burning body of the Paraclete,
The Holy Catholic and Apostolic Church Mystical,
The Communion of Saints and the Sanctum Regnum,
The absolution of sins and the universal restitution,
The Resurrection of the Glorified Body of Light
Into Life everlasting. † *Amen.*

COMMEMORATION OF THE SAINTS

All:
We commemorate those who did of old adore Thee and manifest Thy glory unto men. First of all, the Holy Virgin of Light, She of the Starry Womb, and Mary, ever Holy. Mary of Magdalene, who tasted love in full dregs, Your Holy apostles John, Paul, Peter, Andrew, James, Thomas, James, Philip, Bartholomew, Matthew, Simon, Thaddeus, and Judas Iskariotes who carried the burden no other man could carry.

The Martyrs, who by their blood, gave the essence of the dove to the Ecclesia.

The Holy and enlightened Teachers and the Doctors of the Ecclesia † *Simon* † *Menander* † *Saturninus* † *Plotinus* † *Plato* † *Cerinthus* † *Basilides* † *Valentinus* † *Marcion* † *Mani* † *Origen* † *Augustin* † *Jacques de Molay* † *Henry Cornelius Agrippa* † *Marsilio Ficino* † *Pico della Mirandola* † *Roger Bacon* † *Giordano Bruno* † *Johannes Trithemius* † *Isaac Luria* † *Count Zinzendorf* † *Jakob Böhme* † *Dom Pasqually de Martinez* † *Dom Saint Martin* † *Stanislas de Guaita* † *Abbé Boullain* † *Joséphin Péladan* † *Monseigneur Vintras* † *Joseph René Vilatte* † *Éliphas Lévi, and the hidden, unnamed, and forgotten Saints, Martyrs, and Doctors unnamed by one of these reasons.*

Amen. †††

SECOND CENSING

Priest: *In fire and smoke, the Lord guarded and guided his people, and with fragrance sweet and heavy smoke, we call thee, Lord, to this, your table. We are gathered here in your court to celebrate the Blood, the Bread, the Death. The rose that sprung open on the Cross of the Lord's journey and the phosphorescent light of the dawn of wisdom. Turn thy mighty face toward us and rest within the smoke and scent, O Lord.*

The priest chants *"Esh, El, Esh"* while placing the incense in the censer. The bell is tolled thrice.

Priest: *Mystery of Mystery. Holy, Holy, Holy, the veil, the stone, the cup, and blood.*
Mystery of mystery, behold the mystery.

The priest takes the censer and censes the cathedral, the congregation, and the altar while chanting, *"AIO, OIA, IAO, IAO, IAO."*

LITURGY OF THE EUCHARIST

The Blood and the Bread made glorious by the power of Death.
Blessed be him who descended to the caverns where all is shadow and fog.
Blessed be him who saw the shadow of all things just so he could rejoice in the awesome glory of God.
Blessed be him who was touched by the radiant diamond of enlightenment in the river Jordan.
Blessed be wise John of the adamantine waters of burning fire.
Blessed be She who gave him strength to pull through, Sophia, Norea, Mary Magdalena.
Blessed be the rose that opened up at the foot of the Cross, and blessed be the star that rose in the evening when he gave up his breath to his father.
Blessed be the unmovable mover, whose design remains the mystery within mystery, and blessed be the Lord by his blood, flesh, and death, and blessed be Mary through whom we shall know salvation.

We pray, O Lord, that the blessed daughter of Zion will intercede for us. She, who, with the gifts of the Holy Spirit, won your favour and love. Let her intercede for us so we can learn about the beauty within and discard all ugliness that turns us into the path of ignorance and perversion. Let us be blessed with the knowledge given freely from the fortune of beauty. Let us uncover her through your blood and flesh and commemorate the love of the rose.

The priest will then extend his arms over the cup and paten.

Priest: *Oh Father, Glorious One, make me the vessel on this day, and gift me the powers to do miracles in thy name. May the Heavenly dove, the holy spirit, descend upon me and make me in your likeness so I can turn this bread and this wine into the instruments of salvation through the blood and flesh of the Word. So mote it be, Father. Amen.†*

REMOVING THE VEIL

Her face covered, her beauty veiled. But on this day, she will again shine out from the centre of the Cross, the rose bleeding between the roads, the beauty, companion of the standing one. Behold the Beauty of Fortune and Love. Behold!

REMOVING THE BURSE

Behold the stone that sealed up the temple, the stone that covers our eyes. Behold the stone the builders rejected, the stone that sealed up Lazarus. Behold the rose stone of crystalline light, the stone she anointed. Holy, Holy, Holy. Behold the cup and the blood, the plate and the bread. The food of salvation, the face of the shining one! Father, may this Holy Spirit sanctify these offerings. Let them become the body † and blood † of Jesus Christ, Our Lord, Your son, who gave himself up to death, but by rising from the dead, he destroyed death and restored life.

He broke the chains of sorrow and darkness and opened the gates of Eden in the fullness of his grace.

On the day of the supper, the Lord took a bread and broke it, and he said: "Take this and eat, for this is my body, and through this, you shall know life eternal."

He then took the rose blood and said:

"Take this and drink, for this is my blood, and through this, ye shall taste salvation."

He then took the bread, dipped it in the wine, and gave it to Mary to eat. As she tasted salvation and consumed eternity, the Dove descended upon her, and all saw her glory. The evening star rose and embraced her in a shroud of beauty, and the Lord said:

"Holy, holy, holy are thee, Spirit of divine Fortune," and his heart was enflamed with Love.

And the Lord said:

"No other woman can compare with her, in the beauty of her face, in the wisdom of her words.[186] Grace is poured forth on your lips, and so God has blessed you forever."[187]

He then said, "Come all ye hungry and thirsty and dine at the table of my Mothers, for in this you will find the living salvation."

He then again broke the bread, dipped it in wine, and gave everyone to eat from his all-encompassing love.

"After all had been served," he said. "As often as you do this in memory of me, as often you will taste the waters of paradise,"

And he said: "Go forth, daughters of Zion, and see your queen, the morning stars sing her praises, the sun and moon bow before her beauty, and all God's children rejoice in her presence. Daughter of Zion, full of loveliness and grace, you are fair as the moon, glorious as the sun, most favored of all women."[188]

He then took Mary by the hand and asked the disciples to follow him to the garden.

---

186 Judith 11:19–21 (KJV).

187 Psalm 45:3 (KJV).

188 Song of Songs 6:10 (KJV) and Luke 1:42 (KJV).

Cleanse and wash the cup with water, and veil the paten and cup again. The congregation will spend some time in meditation on the miraculous mystery of the Eucharist.

BENEDICTION

Priest: *Blessings to you all.*

Congregation: *And with you.*

Priest: *May the Peace of the Lord be with you.*

Congregation: *And with you.*

Priest: *May the love of the Spirit rest with you.*

Congregation: *And with you.*

Priest: *So mote it be. † Amen.*

MALEDICTION

Priest: *May we become aware of our shortcomings, O Lord, and give us the wisdom to turn vice into virtue, defeat into glory, failure into understanding, and deceit into victory. We reject the king of the nafs to rule our soul, and we throw them out from this temple of abundance! May we triumph over our enemies, hidden and known, and may those who oppose us with ill intent and Satanic motives bring upon themselves what they desire upon us—so also they can prepare a window of light to enter their life and learn from their shortcomings and evil inclinations, the humbleness and love that leads to salvation and eternal life.*

Congregation: *So mote it be. Amen.*

POSTCOMMUNION

Priest: *O Lord, we are pure, and we have been made holy and glad by your holy spirit, by the blood and bread of the Saviour, and by the overflowing Grace. We pray that you let us always be mindful and aware. Let us leave this your house as better men and women. Let us be living gospels, beacons of light that restore the soul of the weak and replace sorrow with joy and despair with hope. Such is our prayer, O Lord. Amen.*

Congregation: *World without end, forever and ever. So mote it be. Amen.*

Priest: *So, children of Zion, brethren of the Word. Go in Peace. Go in Light. Go in Love. May the rivers of honey and milk from Eden nurture your soul and spirit. The rose that knows no death be with you, now and forever more. † Amen.*

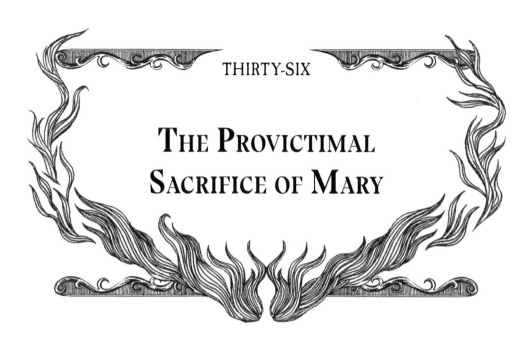

THIRTY-SIX

THE PROVICTIMAL SACRIFICE OF MARY

O Wisdom created, who is forever the unchanging reflection of Wisdom uncreated, Noble Queen, ineffable Shahael, You are the regent of an empire sovereign, the heavens speak of Your glory, with its countless spirits that inhabit these realms; Your kindness, Your mercy, and Your love will never cease as Your eyes watch the children of Carmel, exiled down here in this valley of tears and expiation.

The luminary of faith enlightens us like beacons of salutations and brings messages that, after our fall from grace, the celestial restoration was attainable only through our prayers and maternal mediation that has been permitted to us through our penitence. This has allowed us to hope to attain our supreme and angelic being.

We proclaim our glorious origin; Our Sovereign is Our Mother, the masterpiece of Divine creation through God and the thrice Holy saint. We exalt in Your greatness; nothing can enter into comparison with Your Being and Your Name; Your Name is above every name in the heavens, in the Earth, and in hell. Your power has its source in Him who is in Himself embraced in all, the incommunicable and infinite essence.

Shahael is the living tabernacle, the supreme reflection, the diadem of the glory of Him who conceives Himself embraced in all ideas and spheres. This crowning achievement is not yet at its centre; that much is true. The Divine Essence is but the centre of all things, and She is the vibrant manifestation of Him, who makes all things, Himself included, without any help. And so it is said about the Queen: "She came out from the mouth of the Almighty. She was born before all of creation. It is because of She the luminaries of heaven fell silent." O Carmel, rejoice in your assigned task as the one to glorify the heavenly and Divine Mother.

But after the revolt in the heavens and its re-enactment in the Garden of Eden, it was our Celestial Queen who pleaded for us, knowing that Her children had made themselves deserving of punishment. The God of Heaven, the God who is, heard the cries and your ardent prayers and the lament from your Mother. The spirits who lived in glory gave echo to your complaints and appeals, and He gave grace and favours; He vested the human nature so that it could be deserving merits, and He brought a way for the redemption of the human spirit in union with our divine Son, "The Lamb slain at the beginning."

Glory be forever to our heroic Mother; the Earth has seen the hours for mortal life, ignored and emptied for glory, and this is well known. But we, the children of Carmel, we know who you are, O Shahael, who rests in the supreme greatness of creation.

From Eve, we received our human nature, but our spirit and our virtues are from the Mother, and it is You who are our true Mother, true from within the law of our penitence. O Queen of Queens, Your children are joyous because they recognise Your glorious Maternity, and You keep us safe in love without denying the instruments and life worthy of that maternity.

The maternity of our mothers doesn't exclude what we gained from Eve, but it is not the Royal and ineffable Mother, who, in the order of nature, is of grace and exalted glory. Through the luminaries of prophecy, we learned that humankind was driven out of Eden for their lawless disobedience, but by Mary, who gave us the Common Eucharist and the wine of the Tree of Life, we return to Eden.

The divine plan of eternal mercy will not pass by for the children of Carmel. The spirit and virtue of Shahael have been communicated to Eve, and, by participation, our mothers, according to the order of the generation; also, the spirit and virtue of Mary were sent to a chosen order that Eve amongst the Eves would welcome as the new Joan, She is the Strong Woman through the centuries, for, in this hidden mystery, rehabilitation and renovation of all of humankind came from the Victorious reign of the glorious.

This is the faith that ignites our hearts with the active flames of ardent charity and the fires of love that consume spiritual love, the celestial and divine. The spirit of virtue of Mary our Mother, Shahael, who reigns in glory in the heavens, communicated to the Strong Woman who lives here in the conditions of our mortal life; by this is guaranteed our participation in this ministry, as the denominator of what heaven deign to grant us, by our heavenly vocation and our divine mission.

O Spirit of love, Jesus Christ, who was glorified by being sent to us, You lived, and by this, You transformed and sanctified our hearts, our souls, and our spirits; but it is through the prayers and by God's design Wisdom is created. O! Come to us, come to the Earth and move through the worlds, in the glorious Reign of Our Lord, Jesus Christ, made possible through Mary. Amen. Amen. Amen.

PROFESSION FOR OBTAINING FORGIVENESS

O God, who lives from eternity to eternity, I confess at the foot of the altar our sins to the Glorious heavens; we recognise them all as partakers of rebellion and the wicked criminal acts that stole from us Your Essence and Spirit that were ours to hold, and in this alone, You possess Your own glory. Forgive us, forgive all our brethren here, gathered for this sacrilegious and wicked rebellion.

O Eve, with this we do not say, come those deprived of the divine light, for it is Your fault that has brought this sadness upon us. Your disgrace is ours, the Veritable and eternal truth; we could not see in this proper sin unless it affected our true and real understanding. We have participated in Your rebellion. We were there, provoking You to lay your hands on the forbidden fruit that gave the knowledge of good and evil and, thus, counter to the divine order and dictate. And so we cry to God for forgiveness for us and for our brothers and sisters who participated in the second fall.

But the blood of the Lamb has been made available for us; our Mother has mingled Her tears with the adorable blood of his compassion, so let us wash our hearts and spirits in healthy waters of renovation and regeneration.

BENEDICTION AND GRACE

Any Grace, any gift, all Grace comes to us from You, through your divine Son, our Lord Jesus Christ, who grants answers to the prayers of the children of Carmel, the blessings supreme of life, mercy, and love, has been established its source and cause in the heaven of the heavens. In the name of the Father, the Son, and the Holy Spirit. Amen.

PROFESSION OF LOVE TO THE SUPREME HOPE

Heavenly Mother of pure love, no created being can explore the delights of the sovereign Creator Who is in You. The three persons of the Dignified Trinity receive the celestial call that wisdom created would repay all with love, for without this, the innumerable spirits in the creation would have been powerless to give these gifts of love.

We, the children of Eve, partake even more in Mary. Turn our face to the heaven of the heavens, the worlds inhabited by spirits; we affirm that our hearts and all the love we are capable of is through you, Our Queen and Our Mistress. Reign amidst us without reservation; undivided is our consecration, and undivided is our aim, which is to love and to make You known through our strength, our hearts, our love, and our spirits.

Through generations who have preceded Him, He has made the law available to the human race. There is no ineffable name that does not know happiness or glory, Your gestation, nor the extent of Your mercies. In this manner, we see how now, in the present, many are not in ignorance about the abundance of Your grandeur, not knowing that You are the hope of our lives, our Mediatrix of our redemption, the true Mother of love. Entire nations, tribes, and kingdoms do not know you yet, and the light to the spirit and souls you bring to those immersed in darkness.

Children of the Light, we can be a lighthouse in the succors of mercy for generation upon generation. From the heights of the holy mountain Carmel, we dominate our spirits in front of the world of majesty; by the sacred mandate, we go into all the worlds, which contain the spirits who knew the law given to humans, through all the worlds everywhere we announce the wisdom of Mary, Shahael, the co-redeemer, Queen and Mother who reigns in glory with Our Lord Jesus Christ.

The sky was shining upon us in the ineffable brightness of the third Revelation: the secrets of prophecy that have been passed on through century after century and do not give to our eyes a sealed book. But in this Church, the spirit that rules supreme is the one who obeyed the law of punishment. These are the noble and generous hearts and souls who practice noble virtues, which makes them worthy of admiration, like the veritable angels and the elected ones who also share this life in the light. We have been given a unique privilege, unprecedented in the preceding centuries, by living at the dawn of the glorious Reign of Mary.

The era of gold will unfold from the work of the Strong Woman, who will venture out by the power of the Lord Jesus, and even the embrace of Death will be regenerated in the image of the apostle Saint John the Evangelist and Prophet. But these gifts, these blessings, these heavenly graces and treasures are not for us alone. Generations of wicked spirits who have suffered under the laws that were given to humans have been waiting. The virtue, the great power of life that rests in the sacrifice of Mary, was made effective with the divine sacrifice and thus was set in motion our return to Eden.

Humanity knows the reign of Jesus the exalted, who brought humankind by the shedding of His blood, and Mary, through Her Martyrdom, has mingled the tears of the maternal and compassionate with the redeeming blood. And so it must be done on Earth, in the hour decreed by the Almighty, the coming of the Glorious Reign which has been promised, predicted, announced, and forestalled by all prophets through all ages and all generations.

OFFERING OF THE BREAD

O Mary, Virgin, Queen of Virgins, immaculate pure and undefiled, holy Scripture calls You the heap of wheat surrounded by lilies. Your breast blessed us, indeed, Wheat of the chosen one, Your divine Son, in whose reign all participate. In this, our sacrifice, it is not the Common Eucharist, Jesus glorified, that we want to communicate, but your mercy, your love, and your virtue, in which we seek to be united and to die to ourselves, to our earthly life, animal life of our passions, our inclinations, our natural bent, so we can live the spiritual life, the heavenly and divine, You are the principle and its source, O Mary, All-pervading Mother of the living. Amen.

OFFERING OF THE RED WINE

The luminaries of the prophecy revealed that Eve would be born, a Woman really strong in battle against Satan and his family. According to this divine promise, Shahael, His Wisdom Created has been coated with our human nature, and henceforth, Satan and his followers will continue to suffer a thousand defeats until our return to Eden.

This is not the wine that brings forth virgins, but blessed by this substance, we shall share in Her power to take on our nature, and in Her, we shall invigorate our corporeality. Our communion and gospel are of the vital fermentation and reform that transform, renew, and regenerate sanctifies. Daughters of Eve, according to the law of our nature, by this cup of blessing, we will become children of Mary, and thus, we shall receive grace and prophecy from Her spirit and virtue. Amen.

OFFERING OF LIGHT

This luminary on this altar and between our hands are anointed with consecrated oil. It is the image and symbol of the Spirit of the heavens, where Wisdom is created, and we shall repeatedly adorn Her with ineffable love, words uttered by Shahael at the moment of the heavenly rebellion. "You, uncreated Essence, adorable and indomitable love, O thou who hast designed to be the glory manifest in all of your operations, thou who hast given me, in creating love in all that you have created, and shall create ever send down your mercy on those unfortunate ones and lost."

Great and Eternal is You for whom my love is spread to all for You to meet. If all these wonders have proclaimed the living tabernacle of thy grace and the refraction of Your wisdom, give me the spark of your ineffable, sovereign, and infinite mercy. O may all generations of past, present, and those yet to come share in Your love, Your kindness, and Your mercy; O Mary, Our Queen and Our Mother, be our life and our light for eternity. Amen. Amen. Amen.

THE ACT OF GLORIFICATION

We confess we believe with a faith that nothing can shake: the closer we are to heaven, where His Supreme Essence is, the brighter is His light and love, which is uninhabitable, impenetrable, and incomprehensible, and heaven is the realm where Uncreated Wisdom is reflected in glory, wisdom, and love. Heaven is the home of Shahael, Wisdom created.

He Is, says the Eternal One, one who glorifies the heavens before all and before all creatures. He is the one who has to be present at my advice; His desires, His prayers, and His claims attract my word, and I'll never be quiet for Her. The angels will owe Him the glory, and it will attract the heart for the raptures and delight. So it will shine in the glory of His reflection, through all his creation for Him and because of Him. The nine heavens form a kingdom where He is the one who reigns supreme. Among those worthy of praise in creation, there are some who will arrive to Him by passing by. His creation is with Him, naked, and the elected one will be given His blessings.

Shahael is crowned on the mountain of glory; He created the heavens under His feet in glory. He is the glorious Almighty. He is partaken of by his love, and She responds to the Wisdom of His Word, Shahael, who is Mary, in which the uncreated Wisdom is His delight. Everything created did not know the Creator, and thanks to Her son, She mended the world by His immutable decree, Him, who is subject to no change.

O Queen of Angels, O Mother of men, O Sovereign Mistress, the children of Carmel glorify Your name. Exalted is Your greatness as we proclaim Your mercy. Let the words of our speech on the holy altar enter through the worlds to be worn by Yourself at the foot of the throne of the One Almighty God and living rod, source, and purpose of any Life. God is the God of heaven and of all spirits and all of creation that He was agreeable to create. Amen.

SONG OF PRAYER

O Mary, our faith is love, and You are the whole reason for our hope. You are the one who delivers the heavens to Earth. Your supreme power of Martyrdom, the indivisible union of Your faith and Your love, our redemption gives You all right to our admiration and any tenderness, and of our love; for Your pain, Your suffrages, Your tears, which were the price for our salvation and our life. We are ineffably happy to offer this sacrifice and to make it available to our children, our husbands, our brothers, and our sisters, but we declare aloud to the heavens, the worlds, and the faraway lands. Here is not found any neglect for the divine sacrifice, and through this, we are allowed to participate in the Body of the saviour, glorified by the Blood Divine, and through this, our regeneration is affirmed by the worthy so we can take part in the wheat given to the elected and the cup of the divine blood given to those rightfully anointed.

The power of our anointment enables us to help the spirits who are in the worlds of rehabilitation, repression, and atonement in the worlds away from the centre and the lesser worlds, but only by an active and living faith. By giving love, regeneration is made possible by uniting our sacred hearts, our souls, and our spirits in Jesus and Mary.

So far from us, esteemed above the other, we know that our responsibility is all the greater, the demands of our divine mission given to us by the power of sacrifice, total dedication, the contempt of ourselves, the renouncement of our proper love, and true love for our brethren or those who have preceded them in the falls, those who live like us, in a condition of life deserving or who are awaiting their human becoming.

We now have the supreme happiness of knowing our home and why we are bearing the body of our penance. By offering our sacrifice within the fold of Carmel, after having received the holy anointing of Elijah, who must restore all things according to the prophetic promise of the Saviour, we name the light of power that is within us and allows us to be helpful of the spirits and souls, in the past, present, and future. After having participated in the rebellion with Eve in Eden and having merited to be expelled with Adam, we, by faith and in love, participate in the pardons and in the blessings of all that live to empower regeneration, which is in Mary through Christ. By being deserving of forgiveness, we also recover the rights of our innocence to be identified, renewed, transformed, sanctified, and regenerated.

The human race continues to bear grudges against Women, accusing Her of being responsible for the first forfeiture in Eden, but here in Carmel, the Woman is inflamed in prophecy and brings to Earth and the worlds the powers of Mary's sacrifice for humankind's replacement and renovation. In this sacrifice of life, the Heavenly Queen has accomplished, by Her visible ministry, the wall of holy books. "I have impregnated the deepest parts of the earth, and I see those in the sleep of death and I fill those who trust in God, I shed the same doctrine as did the Prophets, and I leave to those who seek wisdom that I will not cease to give until the generations of the saints." Amen. Amen. Amen.

INVOCATION DEPRECATION CONSECRATION

Let the bread of pure wheat, by virtue of the suffering, compassion, and the merits of Mary, our Mother, mingle in union with the blood of His divine Son. The Word made God, our Redeemer, blessed be the substance that serves as the food of life, the restoration of life, and the rehabilitation and renovation of our human and angelic nature.

May the substance of the wine, by virtue of the tears of the Holy Mary and the merits of Her love and compassion, both for ourselves and our brothers in the worlds, close the Supreme fermentation of revitalization and transformation to obtain our return to Eden by the powers of the divine blood of the Redeemer. May this light, this visible image of the eternal luminary of fire and divine love of the Holy Spirit that we hold between our hands, be a symbol of our faith, which in this life is found worthy by repentance. May love consume our union with Jesus and Mary so we can bring about the glorious reign of Our Lord Jesus Christ for all of creation.

THE UNIVERSAL PRAYER FOR ALL SPIRITS

Standing on the holy mountain of Carmel, facing the altar, our hands anointed with consecrated oil, we reach our hands to heaven in boundless confidence. Not in our name will our prayers rise to the Heaven of heavens, through all the worlds. Our word is no other than the word of Mary, our heavenly Mother, whose spirit and virtue we softly have been communicated. Our ministry is the one that truly says, "I am leaving the mouth of the Most High and I was born before creature. I was created from the beginning and before all ages, I never cease to be in or after all: ages, my ministry has been demonstrated in the holy abodes. I am the mother of the pure love of science true and holy hope."

Seeing the sublime Enlightened one of Patmos, who witnessed the great Prodigy in heaven, the Mother, Shahael, covered with a great light, and this woman, Mary, who suffered the pains of childbirth, because it gave us spirits destined for a human life, the life through Her tears that united with the blood of the Saviour, the divine Son.

The Supremacy of Elohim: His powers will be given to the hearts fed by faith and love. So we cry to all worlds that the first door that opens resurrection is flung open. We call unto the spirits who live in the greater enlightened worlds, worlds of light, the divine worlds, that they may unite with us to help the spirits, who are in the process of atonement of the world, purifiers in front of the Glorious Reign.

The unification of God in Jesus through Mary must be a truth. For to our ministry, this has been revealed through the prophets, the holy amongst all spiritual worlds, that the world must be restored. The humans must work on their return to Eden, and the children of Carmel will open the road by anointing Women with the Holy unction. We offer this sacrifice for the sake of the return of our brothers and sisters by the way of light, justice, love, and regeneration.

O You who believe in doctrine, the third revelation revealed and awaited the glorious reign of Mary, come and take part in our sacrifice; participate. Come take part, away from the assaults and snares of Satan and his followers, who unceasingly search to attack humans in search of reintegration in the heel; that is to say, the corrupt spirits of our human nature.

COMMUNION

By the act of this, our sacrifice will ail our lives so that we can unite ourselves to Mary and be clothed with strength to live in faith and love.

DISTRIBUTION OF THE BREAD

May this part of our sacrifice be active in us and animate the life of faith and love. May our hearts and our souls, by this fermented bread, receive the blessings of Our celestial Mother, who gave to us the gifts of light, mercy, kindness, compassion, and love to hasten the rehabilitation and renovation of spirits, souls, and hearts.

DISTRIBUTION OF THE CUP

May our hearts and our souls receive by this cup the light of mercy and true charity. O Carmel, may this light, symbol of the spirit of Mary, who taught us that it is through Our Queen and Our Mother that we will reach unto Jesus, to unite ourselves in Him by the divine Saviour, our redemption, our salvation, and our lives with whom we reign in the days of glorious reign, to return to the heavens of glory where He "reigns forever and ever." Amen.

FIRST ACT OF GRACE

Within the rays of divine luminary, the prophets You have named in the centuries past, the Queen Myrionyme, that is to say, a thousand names, but now to live on the mountain Carmel, we want to honour You, praise You. Your blessing is in every dignitary known on Earth and in all the heavens, wherein is found Thy mysterious secret.

Your mercy has caused Your appearance in all the worlds from the heavens and until the depth of the world, designed to purify the worlds because Your heart is that of a mother whose boundless kindness and love cannot be subject to assessments of our measures nor the weak conceptions of our mind.

The land You have taken in possession is hidden from revealing Your spirit and Your virtue, a woman living, as we are, in the conditions of mortal life, and in this lays our faith and our happy belief. But this gift, this grace, this blessing is not the reward of one elected, but we can carry the hope of taking part in Your disclosure, under the dignity and names that You deign to grant us, if we know how to make us worthy. O! So be it for us and our sisters present, now and forever more. Amen. Hosanna. Alleluia.

SUPPLICATION DEPRECATORY BLESSING

The Marisiaque of Carmel is on their knees, begging you, O Mary, Our Queen and Our Mother, to bless the ground and the worlds, every spirit and every one of Your children, our brothers and our sisters in faith, and all creatures with a soul, all beings and all things in the natural order, spiritual, heavenly divine, so that we render praise and love forever, unto you and your divine Son, Our Lord Jesus Christ, and for Yours and our Redeemer, Saint Joseph, the most Holy Trinity, Father, Son, and Holy Spirit. Amen. Amen.

THANKSGIVING

Arise, O generation of women of faith who have served the cause of good through all the centuries past, come, Carmel gives you the most pressing appeal; come unite with us in the Almighty, in the strongest and most earnest thanksgiving. The words of the prophets and the faithful servants which the Almighty has received in His ineffable grace, and given pardon to the prophets and the faithful servants of the heaven who are from eternity to eternity, and through this is accomplished to take into possession the promised land of the sacrifice of Mary.

In this sanctuary, amidst the premises of the elected officials who share our hope in the glorious coming of the reign of Our Lord Jesus Christ, the Female offered the Provictimal sacrifice; in heaven, on Earth, and in the worlds was heard a song of eternal thanksgiving for the benefits of this inestimable gift.

For if Eve ate the fruit of the tree that gave knowledge of good and evil, against the commands of God, the children of Carmel found the corrective of the fall: they drank from the Cup of Renovation and thus participated in the recovery and reintegration. They held in their hands the Torch, symbol of light, both spiritual and celestial, by which they would find the way of renascent and the means to achieve perfect regeneration of the repenting Spirit coated in human nature.

In the Name of the Father, the Son, and the Holy Spirit. Amen.

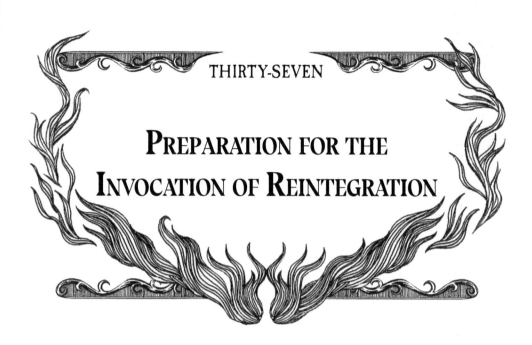

THIRTY-SEVEN

PREPARATION FOR THE INVOCATION OF REINTEGRATION

This work is better performed on Wednesdays in the evening before falling to rest. It can also be performed on Saturdays, even though this invocation is not specific to any other days. These two days are devoted to two principal universal spirits, one being under the signs of which Mercury controls, directs, and actuates the unspecified ground and all body forms. The other is under the sign of Saturn, which controls, directs, and actuates the hearts. This has more power on the animated creature than Mercury, which is easily understood considering the difference in distances from the terrestrial surface to either of these planetary bodies. Saturn is above the Sun and below the third terrestrial horizon, while Mercury is above the third terrestrial horizon, leaning toward the two other inferiors. These horizons are usually called "rational circles" and are visual and sensitive.

This invocation will begin on Wednesday evening before going to rest, and we must make our heart naked to receive and retain some impression of the spirit of Saturn via the spirit of Mercury, which strips our heart of the coarsest matter that wraps it.

In the celestial order, there are seven principal signs, each one indicating a planet. It is demanded of the practitioner that they familiarise themself to a perfect level with the spiritual virtues and powers that are contained in these various planets. Their correspondences, both exact and reciprocal, are in harmony with a person and their body form since the spirits that direct each one of them are subjected to the power of the person of desire.

This invocation is given assuming that the practitioner makes use of it with respect, discretion, and confidence. They must not deviate from anything that is prescribed here if they wish to be able to communicate with the spirits, which are within the capacity of the practitioner.

PREPARATIONS

It is necessary to have a particular room where there are neither tapestries nor tables. It does not matter that there are other pieces of furniture provided that the part of the wall that lends itself toward the east is clear. The hour of midnight to one o'clock is the most favourable time for this invocation. It is necessary to do them only in the first or the second quarter moon and not in the last two phases. Otherwise, its influences will be negative and could harm the practitioner. On the days you wish to make this invocation, only one simple collation will suffice.

Take a yellow candle, pure and without any form of resin or impurity. If this is not possible, also take a white candle, as it will defect the impurities in the yellow candle. Use scissors to cut the excess of the wicks before blessing them. Then, gather the candles on the ground at the eastern angle. Dress in the proper colors and bless the candles as you have been told.[189]

Always have your face turned toward the east when you make the invocation, and never deviate to look to the right or the left after you have pronounced the divine words. If the angle of the room does not look that friendly, it follows that the medium must direct the attention to the wall.

The follower will sit upright as the medium of the room faces the east. The medium will trace on the ground all that they will receive with white chalk. If the work has started at midnight, it must go on until one o'clock. Say:

> *"Blessed are those which came in the name of the Lord. May the peace of the Lord always be with us. Amen."*

Extinguish the candle and ascend toward another white one for purity and to draw benevolence.

---

189 By intoning, *"By IESHOUAH, Our Lord, Amen."* †

THIRTY-EIGHT

THE RITE OF GOLGOTHA

For this ritual, prepare the aromas of galbanum, myrrh, and cassia for fumigation. Present wine and bread for the communion. A wooden skull must also be present; it is better if the skull is from an evergreen, like yew or holly, but this is of less importance than the skull being fashioned from wood itself. Place the skull in a black dish filled with graveyard dirt, ashes, red earth or clay, and ocean sand to make the mound of Golgotha. If dirt from a cave can be obtained, add this to the dish. Place the skill in the centre and a large wooden cross behind the skull. A single black candle should be lit and placed on top of the skull. Lastly, two coins must be present, one silver and one golden, along with a flask of the oil of Golgotha.[190]

With the Golgotha prepared and fumigated and the candle lit, say to the skull:

> *"This is the body of the first Man.*
> *I am the last man.*
> *And I call upon the first*
> *To rest in the last.*
> *I—A—O.*
> *The Alpha in the Omega will give the New Seed.*
> *Yud—Yud—Yud."*

---

190 This oil is made from equal parts of galbanum, cassia and myrrh dissolved in a
mixture of olive oil and walnut oil in equal amounts.

Now mark the skull with the oil at the brow (third eye), then the left eye, and lastly, the right eye. Then, take the silver coin and say:

"Father, I mark you with the light of the Moon."

Place the coin in the cavity of the left eye, then take the golden coin and say:

"Father, I mark you with the light of the Sun. See how I make you come alive in the waters of Venus."

Place a piece of bread on the skull and pour some wine over it. Close your eyes, count your breath, and allow it to become still. When you open your eyes, take a small piece of the bread on the skull and drop it in the wine. You will then say:

"I am the last, bound to the first. I am the new seed that seeks the wisdom of resurrection and of salvation, of revelation and reintegration. Through this, my self-sacrifice (spit on the skull), I seek to be in thy presence so your sons and daughters can inspire and teach me."

Commune with the spirit of Adam through the wine and the bread.

THIRTY-NINE

THE EMPYREAN RITE OF SETH

For this ritual, you will need the earth sign of Norea, which will serve as a focus for the sacred flame of Seth. You must also have access to *The Three Steles of Seth* from the Nag Hammadi Library.[191]

Fumigate with vanilla, rose, and benzoin, and wash your hands in cassia and a hint of anise and cinnamon, which is how Seth's burning water[192] is made.

Have three candles present, all white, and three cups of water (I—Auriel), wine (A—Seth), and milk (O—Norea), respectively, along with bread that should be made by your own hand and contains flour, walnut, fig, and honey. These elements will be laid out in conformity with the diagram below, with the bread and the flame in the centre of the triangle.

I (Auriel)

A (Seth)   O (Norea)

---

191 Translations of *The Three Steles of Seth* are available online and/or from a variety of Gnostic scholars or translators.

192 As all three of these herbs do bestow a burning corrosive state on the skin, be cautious with the strength of the infusion in water or alcohol.

Then recite the First Stele of Seth addressing A (Seth) in the following way: "*A—I—O*" at least twelve times and consume a small part of wine after the recitation, supplication, or prayer has been performed.

Then move on to the Second Stele of Seth, addressing I (Auriel) in the following fashion: "*I—A—O*" at least twelve times, then consume a small part of water.

The Third Stele is then recited in honour of Norea in the following way: "*O—A—I*" at least twelve times, then some milk is consumed.

Then, carefully pass the wine, water, milk, and bread through the central fire and consume the sacraments, stating:

"These are the first offerings
In consuming the first offerings, I take back what was lost.
In purifying the milk, wine, and water in the crucible of Seth,
Matter is yet again pure and innocent, filled with wisdom.
By consuming the first offerings, I open myself to the
Empyrean realm and call upon the fire of Seth
To set my soul, spirit, and heart aflame.
Such is my call; such is my prayer
Amen! Amen! Amen!"

Then, extinguish the candles, leaving only the central fire to burn. Focus on this central fire and see it as the burning cosmic centre. Allow yourself to be consumed by this fire and dissolve in it.

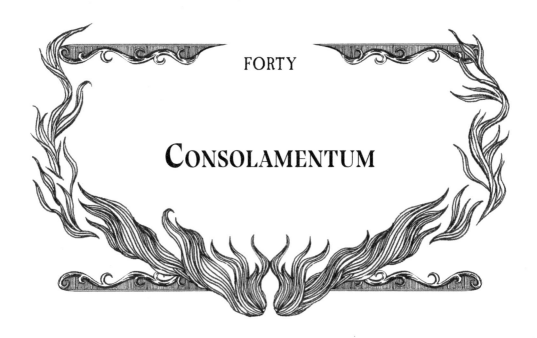

FORTY

CONSOLAMENTUM

The ritual of Consolamentum was central in *Église Gnostique* as it was a ritual that established the broken vinculum between humankind and the divine in the form of the Paraclete. The ritual was taken from the Cathar ritual with the same name and objective, namely to bring on the spiritual condition that was necessary to enable Gnostic communion with Wisdom. The Consolamentum aimed toward the first step in becoming perfect again or reintegrating into the perfect cosmic being. Consolamentum was considered to be a Baptism of Spirit or of Fire. For the purpose of this book, an adaption of Doinel's ritual for solitary use is presented as a way for solitary practitioners to dedicate themselves to seek communion with Wisdom, be it in the form of Heli, Seth, Sophia, or Norea.

As a preparation for the Baptism of Fire, it is necessary to undertake *Melhoramentum,* a ritual examination used in order to "be better" or "to be improved." This can be done three days prior to the ritual: dress in white, eat sparsely, avoid all forms of negative or intoxicating behaviour, and spend the first hour of the morning and the last hour before going to bed in prayer and contemplation. The deeper themes of Our Lord's Prayer can be used as a basis for this contemplation. The idea is to cast off the old skin and be ready to be vested in light.

The Lord's Prayer

Our Father, who art in heaven,
Hallowed be Thy name
Thy kingdom come
Thy will be done
On Earth as it is in Heaven.
Give us this day our daily bread
And forgive us our trespasses,
As we forgive those who trespass against us.
And lead us not into temptation
But deliver us from the evil one.
For Thine is the Kingdom,
The Power and the Glory,
Forever and ever. Amen.

On the day of the baptism, take a bath made from lavender and hyssop, and on a simple table, leave open the Bible to the Gospel of John. One or three white candles can be lit, and the fumigation might be done with ordinary church incense or a mix of benzoin, frankincense, and myrrh. Present wine and ordinary bread on the table.

Genuflect to the centre, left, and right, then lay down on the floor face down in the form of a cross, saying:

"I present myself to the eternal Aeon. I am Fallen, like Adam, like Sophia. Make me white in the blood of the Lamb. Make my soul to shine in the Empyrean fire. May the fire of Ennoia touch me. Release me from all mistakes of the past and allow me to rise from this floor and walk the path of the perfecti, the path toward the Paraclete."

Rise up and touch your head to the Gospel of John and read the first five verses in the first chapter:

"In the beginning was the Word, and the Word was with God, and the Word was God.
The same was in the beginning with God.
All things were made by him; and without him was not any thing made that was made.

In him was life; and the life was the light of men.
And the light shineth in darkness; and the darkness comprehended it not."[193]

Then the Valentinian Hymn is recited whilst a white cloth is draped around you:

"Beati vos Eones
Vera vita vividi;
Vos Emanationes
Pleromatis lucidi;
Adeste visiones
Stolis albis candidi."

You can then recite the Lord's Prayer in Greek or English:

"Pater hêmôn ho en tois ouranois:
Hagiasthêtô to onoma sou;
Elthetô hê basileia sou;
Genêthêtô to thelêma sou,
Hôs en ouranôi kai epi gês;
Ton arton hêmôn ton epiousion dos hêmin sêmeron;
Kai aphes hêmin ta opheilêmata hêmôn,
Hôs kai hêmeis aphêkamen tois opheiletais hêmôn;
Kai mê eisenenkêis hêmas eis peirasmon,
Alla hrusai hêmas apo tou ponêrou.
Hoti sou estin hê basileia,
Kai hê dynamis, kai hê doxa,
Eis tous aiônas. Amên."

Then, cross your arms on your chest and over the bread and wine, recite the Prayer of Transmutation of Bread and Wine:

"Eon Jesus, priusquam pateretur mystice, accepit panem et vinum in sanctas manus suas et, elevatis oculis ad coelum, fregit et dedis discipulis suis, dicens. Accipite et manducate et bibite omnes!"

---

193 John 1:5 (KJV).

Break and eat the bread and drink the wine. Then, say:

"Touto estin to soma pneumatikon tou Christou. Calix meus inebrians quam praeclarus est! Calicem Salutaris accipiam et nomen Domini invocabo, touto estin to aima pneumatikon tou Christou."

Then, recite:

"Consolemini!
Consolemini!
Popule meus
Consoletur me misericordia tua
Consoletur von Sanctissimum Pleroma
Eon Christos
Eon Sophia et
Eon Pneuma-Hagion
Amen."

Spend at least one hour in silent, receptive meditation.

BIBLIOGRAPHY

Agrippa, Henry Cornelius. *Three Books of Occult Philosophy*. Llewellyn, 1993.

Al-Arabi, Ibn. *The Bezels of Wisdom*. Paulist Press, 1980.

Alighieri, Dante and Charles Eliot Norton (trans.). *The Divine Comedy, Volume 1, Hell*. Project Gutenberg, 1999.

Apocalypse of Moses. Scriptural Research Institute, 2019.

Apocrypha Arabica. Alpha Editions, 2021.

Amadou, Robert. *Louis-Claude de Saint Martin et le Martinisme*. Éditions du Griffon D'or, 1946.

——. *Les leçons de Lyon aux Élus Coëns*. Dervy, 2011.

Attar, Farid Al-Din. *Conference of the Birds: A Seeker's Journey to God*. Red Wheel Weiser, 2001.

Baker, Oscar. *Axel, and Svea. Poems from the Swedish of Esaias Tegnér*. James Carpenter, Old Bond Street, 1840.

Bar Konai, Theodore and Addai Scher. *Liber scholiorum*. Impr. orientaliste L. Durbecq, 1954.

Baudelaire, Charles. *Les Fleurs du Mal: The Complete Text of The Flowers of Evil*. David R. Godine, 1982.

Betz, Hans Dieter. *The Greek Magical Papyri in Translation, Including the Demotic Spells, Volume 1*. University of Chicago Press, 2022.

Bialik, Hayyim Nahman (ed.). *The Book of Legends/Sefer Ha-Aggadah: Legends from the Talmud and Midrash*. Knopf Doubleday Publishing Group, 1992.

Blake, William. *Milton*. Shambhala, 1978.

——. *Auguries of Innocence*. Grossman Publishers, 1968.

——. *The Complete Poetry and Prose of William Blake*. University of California Press, 1982.

Borella, Jean. *Guénonian Esoterism and Christian Mystery*. Sophia Perennis, 2004.

Botterweck, G. Johannes, et al. (ed.). *Theological Dictionary of the Old Testament. XV Volumes.* Erdmans verlag, 1986.

Brann, Noel L. *The Abbot Trithemius.* Brill, 1981

Bruno, Giordano. *De Umbris Idearum and The Art of Memory.* Huginn, Munnin & Co., 1582/2013.

——. *Song of Circe and On the Composition of Images.* Huginn, Munnin & Co., 1591/2020.

——. *On Magic.* Huginn, Munnin & Co., 1592/2018.

——. *On the Infinite, the Universe and the Worlds: Five Cosmological Dialogues.* CreateSpace Independent Publishing Platform, 2014.

——. *De Magica Mathematica.* F. Frommann, 1962.

——. *Cantus Circaeus: Incantations of Circe.* Translated by Darius Klein. Ouroboros Press, 2009.

Budge, Ernest Alfred Wallis. *The Book of the Cave of Treasures.* Cosimo Classics, 2005.

Bullard, Roger A. and Martin Krause. *The Hypostasis of the Archons: The Coptic Text with Translation and Commentary.* De Gruyter, 2012.

Burckhardt, Titus. *Mirror of the Intellect.* Quinta Essentia, 1987.

Butler, Pierce. *Legenda Aurea—Légende Dorée—Golden Legend.* John Murphy Company, 1899.

Cause, Bruno. *Principle and Unity.* Cambridge University Press, 1998.

Chittick, William C. *The Self-Disclosure of God.* State University of New York Press, 1998.

Chodkiewicz, Michel, et al. *The Meccan Revelations.* Pir Press, 2001.

Christian, Paul. *The History and Practice of Magic.* The Citadel Press, 1963.

Conybeare, F. C. *The Testament of Solomon.* Gorgias Press, 2007.

Copenhaver, B.P. (trans.) *Corpus Hermeticum.* Cambridge University Press, 1992.

Corbin, Henry. *Temple and Contemplation.* KPI, 1986.

——. *The Man of Light.* Omega Publications, 1978.

——. *Swedenborg and Esoteric Islam.* Swedenborg Studies, 1995.

——. *Alone with the Alone.* Princeton University Press, 1969.

——. *Mundus Imaginalis or the Imaginary and the Imaginal.* University of Michigan, 1964.

Cotnoir, Brian. *Alchemy: The Poetry of Matter.* Khepri Press, 2017.

Crollius, Oswald. *Traité des signatures.* Durville, 1912.

Crowhurst, David. *Stellas Daemonum: The Orders of the Daemons.* Weiser Books, 2021.

D'Abano, Peter. *Heptameron.* Ouroboros Press, 2003.

Dan, Joseph (ed.). *The Early Kabbalah.* Paulist Press, 1986.

Doinel, Jules. *Église Gnostique.* Krystiania, 2017.

Eiseley, Loren. *Darwin, Coleridge, and the Theory of Unconscious Creation.* Daedalus, *Vol. 94, No. 3, Creativity and Learning* (Summer, 1965), pp. 588-602.

Evershead, M.A. *Dante and the Early Astronomers.* Gall and Inglis, 1913.

Evola, Julius. *Ride the Tiger.* Inner Traditions, 2003.

——. *Introduction to Magic. Volume II.* Inner Traditions, 2019.

Feldman, Daniel Hale. *Qabalah. The Mystical Heritage of the Children of Abraham.* Work of the Chariot, 2001.

Fine, Lawrence. *Safed Spirituality.* Paulist Press, 1984.

Ficino, Marcilio. *Platonic Theology, Book II.* Harvard University Press, 2001.

Flowers, Stephen (ed.). *Hermetic Magic.* Weiser, 1995.

Frisvold, Nicholaj de Mattos. *Arts of the Night.* Chadezoad, 2008.

Gagé, Jean. *Sur Les Origines du Culte de Janus in Revue de l'histoire des religions Vol. 195, No. 2* Association de la Revue de l'histoire des religions, 1979.

Gikatill, Rabbi Joseph. *Gates of Light: Sha'are Orah.* Harper Collins, 1994.

Green, Rosalie, et al. *Hortus Deliciarum: Commentary.* Warburg Institute, 1979.

Greer, John Michael. *The Complete Picatrix: The Occult Classic of Astrological Magic Liber Atratus Edition.* Adocentyn Press, 2011.

Guénon, René. *The Lord of the World.* Coombe Springs Press, 1927/1983.

——. *Spiritual Authority and Temporal Power.* Sophia Perennis, 1929/2001.

——. *The Reign of Quantity and the Signs of the Times.* Sophia Perennis, 1945/2001.

——. *Perspectives on Initiation.* Sophia Perennis, 1946/2004.

——. *Insights into Christian Esoterism.* Sophia Perennis, 1954/2001.

——. *Studies in Freemasonry and the Compagnonnage.* Sophia Perennis, 1964/2004.

——. *Symbols of Sacred Science.* Sophia Perennis, 1977/2004.

——. *Insights into Islamic Esoterism and Taoism.* Sophia Perennis, 1973/2003.

——. *L'Ésotérisme de Dante.* Gallimard, 1925/1957.

Ha-Kohen, Isaac. *Treatise on the Left Emanation.* Independently Published, 2023.

Hall, Manly, P. *Man, Grand Symbol of the Mysteries.* The Philosophical Research Society, 1972.

Heidegger, Martin. *The End of Philosophy.* Harper & Row, 1973.

Hesiod. *Theogony, Works and Days, Testimonia.* Harvard University Press, 2006.

Higgs, John. *William Blake vs. the World*. W&N, 2021.

Jackson, Nigel. *Celestial Magic*. Capall Bann, 2003.

——. *Guide to the Rumi Tarot*. Llewellyn Worldwide, 2009.

Josephus, Flavius and William Whiston. *The Genuine Works of Flavius Josephus, the Jewish Historian*. S. W. Bowyer and J. Whiston, 1737.

Julio, Abbé. *Le Livre secret des grands exorcismes et bénédictions*. Bussier, 1990.

Jumasi, Don. *Mystical Works of Meister Eckhart*. Crossroad Publishing Company, 2009.

Jung, Carl Gustav. *Aion: Researches into the Phenomenology of the Self*. Routledge, 1991.

Karr, Don. and Stephen Skinner. *Sepher Raziel: A Sixteenth Century English Grimoire*. Llewellyn Publications, 2018.

Karlsson, Thomas. *Adulrunan och den götiska kabbalan*. Ouroboros, 2005.

Kaplan, Aryeh. *The Living Torah*. Moznaim Publishing Corporation, 1981.

——. *Sefer Yetzirah*. Weiser Books, 1990.

——. *The Torah Anthology*. Moznaim Publishing Corporation, 1988.

Lacan, Jaques. *Ècrits*. W. W. Norton & Co., 2006.

La Mettrie, Julien Offray: *Machine Man and Other Writings*. Cambridge University Press, 1991.

Laurence, Richard (trans.). *The Book of Enoch the Prophet*. Wizards Bookshelf, 1995.

Lévi, Éliphas. *The History of Magic*. W. Rider & Son, 1859/1913.

Lilly, William. *Christian Astrology*. Astrology Classics, 1647/2004.

Lokeswarananda, Swami. *Chandogya Upanishad*. Ramakrishna Mission Institute of Culture, 2017.

Luck, Georg (trans.). *Arcana Mundi*. Johns Hopkins University Press, 2006.

Malan, Solomon Caesar. *The Book of Adam and Eve*. Creative Media Partners, LLC, 2019.

McIntosh, Christopher. *Eliphas Lévi and the French Occult Revival*. Rider & Co., 1972.

——. *Beyond the North Wind*. Weiser Books, 2019.

Milton, John. *Paradise Lost: A Poem in Twelve Books*. R. & A. Foulis, 1750.

Morgan, Michael A. (ed.). *Sepher Ha-Razim*. Society of Biblical Literature, 1983.

Moorjani, Angela. *Beckett and Buddhism*. Cambridge University Press, 2021.

Nachman, Rabbi. *R. Nachman's Teachings*. Breslov Research Institute, 1997.

Ovid. *Metamorphoses*. Penguin, 2002.

Pandit, M. P. *Kularnava Tantra*. Motilal Banarsidass, 2007.

"Pasqually, Martines de (ca. 1710-1774)." *Encyclopedia of Occultism and Parapsychology.* Encyclopedia.com. Accessed 8 Jan. 2024.

Pasqually, Martinez de. *Treatise Concerning the Reintegration of Beings.* The Johannine Press, 2001.

Pearson, B. *The Rediscovery of Gnosticism. Volume II.* Leiden University Press, 1981.

Pernety, Antoine-Joseph. *An Alchemical Treatise on The Great Art.* Samuel Weiser, 1973.

Peterson, Joseph, and Peter of Abano, *Elucidation of Necromancy Lucidarium Artis Nigromantice.* Ibis Press, 2021.

Pissier, Philippe (ed.). *Liturgie Eucharistique. 2 volumes.* Èditions Ramuel, 1996.

Plato. *Charmides.* Hackett, 1986.

Platt, Rutherford Hayes (ed.). *The Forgotten Books of Eden.* Alpha House, Inc, 1927.

Plotinus. *The Six Enneads.* William Benton Publisher, 1952.

Postel, Guillaume. *Cosmographicae disciplinae compendium.* Per J. Oporinum, 1561.

Pythagoras. *The Golden Verses of Pythagoras and other Pythagorean Fragments.* Forgotten Books, 2007.

Ravignat, Mathieu. *The French Gnostic Church.* Privately Published, 2019.

——. *The Original High Degree and Theurgical system of the Masonic Elect Cohen Knights of the Universe.* Privately Published, 2019.

Reuchlin, Johann. *De Arte Kabbalistica.* Abaris Books, 1983.

Riley, H. T. *The Pharsalia of Lucan.* George Bell & Sons, 1909.

Robinson, James M. *The Nag Hammadi Library.* Harper One, 1990.

Rustad, Mary S. *The Black Books of Elverum.* Galde Press, 1999.

Savedow, Steve (ed.). *The Book of the Angel Raziel.* Weiser, 2000.

Scholem, Gershom. *Kabbalah and Its Symbolism.* Schocken Books, 1988

Schopenhauer, Arthur. *The Essays of Arthur Schopenhauer; Studies in Pessimism.* Alpha Editions, 2021.

——. *The Wisdom of Life and Counsels and Maxims.* Prometheus Books, 1995.

Setbon, Jessica. *Sefer Zerubbabel: An Apocalypse of Two Messiahs and a Mother.* Tel Aviv University, 1999.

Skinner, Stephen and David Rankine. *The Veritable Key of Solomon.* Llewellyn Worldwide, 2009.

Smith, Wolfgang. *Christian Gnosis.* Angelico Press, 2008.

Stone, Michael E. (trans.). *The Penitence of Adam.* In Aedibus E. Peeters, 1981.

Stroumsa, G.A.G. *Another Seed. Studies in Gnostic Mythology.* Brill, 1984.

Sturluson, Snorri. *The Prose Edda.* Benediction Classics, 2015.

Suhrawardi. *The Shape of Light: Hayakal al-Nur.* Fons Vitae, 1998.

Swami, Bhaktivedanta A.C. *Sri Chaitanya-charitamrita, Madhya-lila.* The Bhaktivedanta Book Trust, 1974.

Taylor, Thomas. *Iamblichus' Life of Pythagoras.* Inner Traditions, 1986.

Tertullian. *The Prescription Against Heretics.* Blurb, Incorporated, 2020.

Thomas, and Reginaldus. *The "Summa Theologica" of St. Thomas Aquinas.* R. & T. Washbourne, 1922.

The Book of Jubilees: Or The Little Genesis. A. & C. Black, 1902.

The Book of Offices. The Church Pension Fund. 1949.

The Testaments of the Twelve Patriarchs. Society for Promoting Christian Knowledge, 1925.

Varāhamihira. *The Bṛihat Saṃhitâ of Varaha Mihira.* South Indian Press, 1884.

Vaughan, Thomas. *Magia Adamica.* T.W. for H. Blunden, 1650.

Wallis Budge, Sir E. A. *The Book of the Bee.* Clarendon Press: 1886.

——. *The Book of the Cave of Treasures.* Cosimo Classics, 2005.

Walker, D.P. *Spiritual and Demonic Magic.* Penn State Press, 1958/2000.

Williams, Michael Allen. *The Immovable Race.* Leiden/Brill, 1985.

Wilson, Peter Lamborn, et al. *Green Hermeticism: Alchemy and Ecology.* Lindisfarne Books, 2007.

Ya'qūbī. *Ta'rīkh.* Dār Ṣadir, 1960. From *UNC Charlotte,* pages.charlotte.edu/john-reeves/publications/unpublished-lectures-and-fragmenta/yaqubi-tarikh/. Accessed 9 Jan. 2024.

INDEX